Ilya Grigoryev

anylogic® 7

in three days

A quick course in simulation modeling

Third edition

2016

ISBN-13: 978-1508933748

ISBN-10: 150893374X

Preface

The first practical textbook on AnyLogic 7 from AnyLogic developers. AnyLogic is the unique simulation software tool that supports three simulation modeling methods: system dynamics, discrete event, and agent based modeling and allows you to create multi-method models.

The book is structured around four examples: a model of a consumer market, an epidemic model, a model of a small job shop, and an airport model. We also give some theory on different modeling methods.

You can consider this book as your first guide in studying AnyLogic 7. Having read this book and completed the exercises, you will be able to create discrete-event and pedestrian models using process flowcharts, to draw stock and flow diagrams, and to build simple agent based models.

About the third edition

If you are familiar with the first edition of *AnyLogic 7 in Three Days*, here are the main changes:

In the third edition:

- All the examples have been updated to conform to the latest version of the software, AnyLogic 7.3.1.

- Data import from an external Excel file into the built-in AnyLogic database is described in the last phase of the airport model.

In the second edition:

- A new discrete-event job shop model has been included in the book.

About the author

Ilya Grigoryev is Head of Training Services at The AnyLogic Company, a company specializing in simulation consulting and developing simulation software - AnyLogic.

Ilya Grigoryev is the author of AnyLogic documentation and AnyLogic training courses. He has presented numerous public trainings in U.S., Europe, Africa and Asia. Ilya Grigoryev has been a simulation consultant to several organizations. He has been working at The AnyLogic Company for more than ten years and knows almost everything about simulation and AnyLogic.

Acknowledgements

I would like to thank:

Edward Engel for his kind help in writing the book and Anna Klimont for taking screenshots.

All AnyLogic team leaders who made my time in AnyLogic development team really enjoyable: Alexei Filippov, Vasiliy Baranov, George Meringov, and Nikolay Churkov.

Timofey Popkov and George Gonzalez-Rivas for the idea to publish this book.

Andrei Borshchev for his contributions to the book.

My colleagues and good friends for their positive energy. Tatiana Gomzina, Alena Beloshapko, Evgeniy Zakrevsky (The AnyLogic Company), Vladimir Koltchanov (AnyLogic Europe), Clemens Dempers (Blue Stallion Technologies) and Derek Magilton (AnyLogic North America).

Vitaliy Sapounov for his advice and support.

Please let me know how I can improve the book.

Ilya V. Grigoryev
grigoryev@anylogic.com

Contents

Modeling and simulation modeling..7

Installing and activating AnyLogic...15

Agent-based modeling...21

    Market model..24

    Phase 1. Creating the agent population...24

    Phase 2. Defining a consumer behavior...43

    Phase 3. Adding a chart to visualize the model output..................................54

    Phase 4. Adding word of mouth effect..66

    Phase 5. Considering product discards..72

    Phase 6. Considering delivery time...75

    Phase 7. Simulating consumer impatience..81

    Phase 8. Comparing model runs with different parameter values.................93

System Dynamics modeling..101

    SEIR model..103

    Phase 1. Creating a stock and flow diagram..103

    Phase 2. Adding a plot to visualize dynamics...115

    Phase 3. Parameter variation experiment...120

    Phase 4. Calibration experiment..129

Discrete-event modeling with AnyLogic...135

    Job Shop model...137

    Phase 1. Creating a simple model...137

    Phase 2. Adding resources..151

    Phase 3. Creating 3D animation...159

    Phase 4. Modeling pallet delivery by trucks..170

Pedestrian modeling..191

    Airport model..192

Phase 1. Defining the simple pedestrian flow..193

Phase 2. Drawing 3D animation..203

Phase 3. Adding security checkpoints..208

Phase 4. Adding check-in facilities..215

Phase 5. Defining the boarding logic..225

Phase 6. Setting up flights from MS Excel spreadsheet 233

References..251

Index..253

Modeling and simulation modeling

Modeling is a way we can solve real-world problems. In many cases, we can't afford to experiment with real objects to find the right solutions: building, destroying, and making changes may be too expensive, dangerous, or just impossible. If that's the case, we can build a model that uses a modeling language to represent the real system. This process assumes abstraction: we include the details we believe are important and leave aside those we think aren't important. The model is always less complex than the original system.

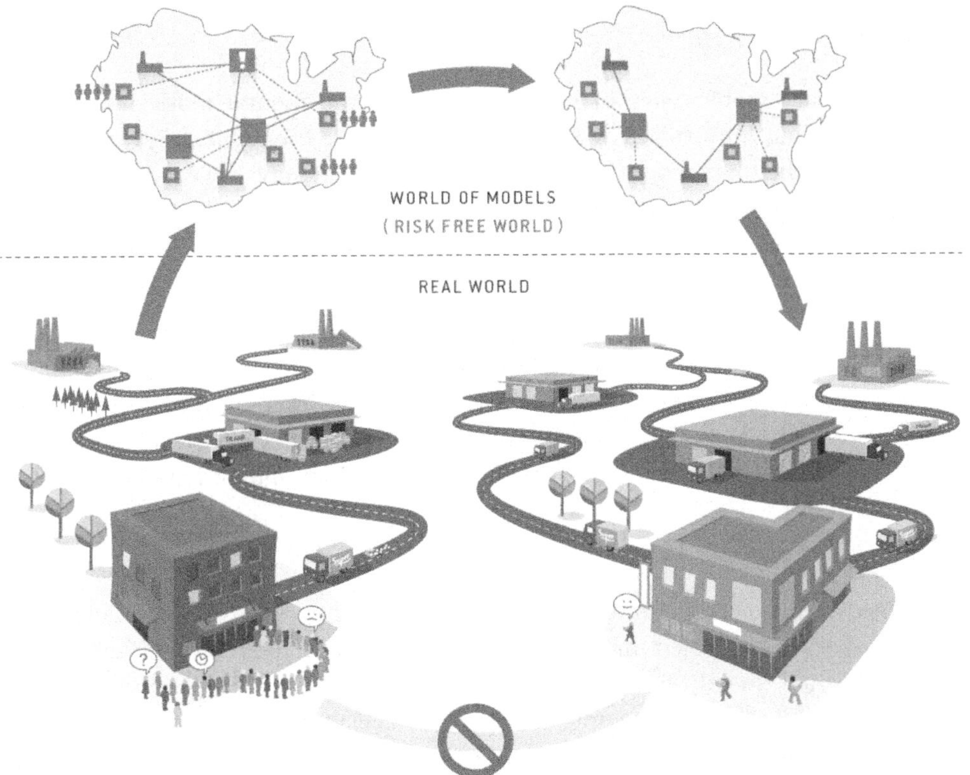

Modeling

- **The model-building phases - mapping the real world to the world of models, choosing the abstraction level, and choosing the modeling language - are all

less formal than the process of using models to solve problems. It's still more an art than a science.

After we've built the model – and sometimes even as we build it – we can start to explore and understand our system's structure and behavior, test how it will behave under a variety of conditions, play and compare scenarios, and optimize. After we find our solution, we can map it to the real world.

⬥ **Modeling is about finding the way from the problem to its solution through a risk-free world where we're allowed to make mistakes, undo things, go back in time, and start over again.**

Types of models

There are many types of models, including the mental models we all use to understand how things work in the real world: friends, family, colleagues, car drivers, the town where we live, the things that we buy, the economy, sports, and politics. All of our decisions - what we should say to our child, what we should eat for breakfast, who we should vote for, or where we should take our girlfriend to dinner - are all based on mental models.

Computers are powerful modeling tools, and they offer us a flexible virtual world where we can create nearly anything imaginable. Of course, there are many types of computer models, from basic spreadsheets that allow anyone to model expenses to complex simulation modeling tools that help experienced users explore dynamic systems such as consumer markets and battlefields.

Analytical vs. simulation modeling

Ask a major organization's strategic planning, sales forecasting, logistics, marketing, or project management teams to name their favorite modeling tool, and you'll quickly find Microsoft Excel is the most popular answer. Excel has several advantages: it's widely available, it's very easy to use, and it allows you to add scripts to your formulas as your spreadsheet's logic becomes increasingly sophisticated.

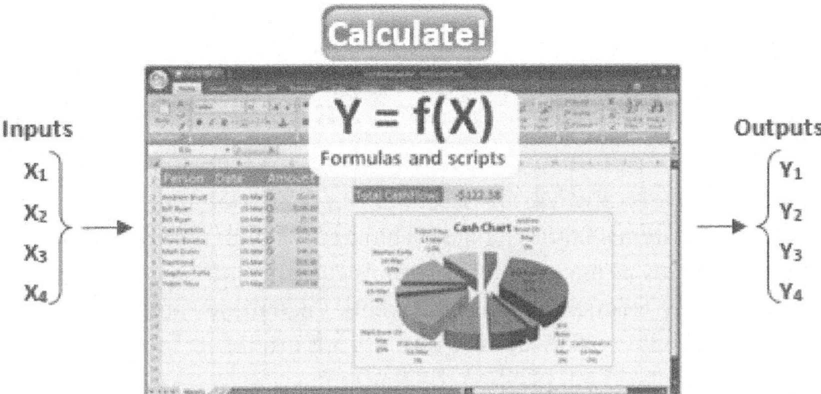

Analytical model (Excel spreadsheet)

The technology behind spreadsheet-based modeling is simple: you enter the data inputs in some cells and you view the data outputs in others. Formulas – and in more complex models, scripts – link the input and output values. Various add-ons allow you to perform parameter variation, Monte Carlo, or optimization experiments.

However, there's also a large class of problems where the analytic (formula-based) solution is either hard to find or simply doesn't exist. This class includes *dynamic systems* that feature:

- Non-linear behavior

- "Memory"

- Non-intuitive influences between variables

- Time and causal dependencies

- All above combined with uncertainty and a large number of parameters

In most cases, it's impossible to obtain the right formulas, much less put together a mental model of such a system.

Consider a problem that requires you to optimize a rail or truck fleet. It's difficult to use an Excel spreadsheet to manage factors such as travel schedules, loading and unloading times, delivery time restrictions, and terminal point capacities. A vehicle's availability at a given location, date, and time depends on a sequence of preceding events, and determining where to send the vehicle when it's idle requires us to analyze future event sequences.

> ◊ **Formulas that are good at expressing static dependencies between variables typically don't do well in describing systems with dynamic behavior. It's why we use another modeling technology - simulation modeling - to analyze dynamic systems.**

A *simulation model* is always an *executable model*: *running* it builds you a trajectory of the system's state changes. Think of a simulation model as a set of rules that tell you how to move from a system's current state to a future state. The rules can take many forms, including differential equations, statecharts, process flowcharts, and schedules. The model's outputs are produced and observed as the model runs.

Simulation modeling requires special software tools that use simulation-specific languages. While you'll need training to do simulation modeling well, your time and effort are rewarded when your model offers a high quality analysis of a dynamic system.

Many people - especially those who know Microsoft Excel well or who have programming experience - try to use a spreadsheet to model a dynamic system. As they try to capture more and more detail, they inevitably start reproducing the functionality of Excel's simulators. The resulting models are slow and unmanageable, and they're usually thrown away quickly.

It's virtually impossible to capture any of those details in an analytic solution. Even if there were formulas to guide your configuration, even a small process change could void them, and you'd need a professional mathematician to fix them.

Advantages of simulation modeling

Simulation modeling has six key advantages:

1. Simulation models allow you to analyze systems and find solutions where methods such as analytic calculations and linear programming fail.

2. Once you've chosen an abstraction level, it's easier to develop a simulation model than an analytical model. It typically requires less thought, and the development process is scalable, incremental, and modular.

3. A simulation model's structure naturally reflects the system's structure.

4. In a simulation model, you can measure values and track entities within the level of abstraction, and you can add measurements and statistical analysis at any time.

5. The ability to play and animate the system behavior in time is one of simulation's great advantages. You'll find animation useful for demonstrations, verification, and debugging.

6. Simulation models are far more convincing than Excel spreadsheets. If you use a simulation to support your proposal, you'll have a major advantage over those who only use numbers.

Applications of simulation modeling

Simulation modeling has accumulated a large number of success stories in a wide and diverse range of application areas. As new modeling methods and technologies emerge and computer power grows, you can expect simulation modeling to enter an ever-larger number of areas.

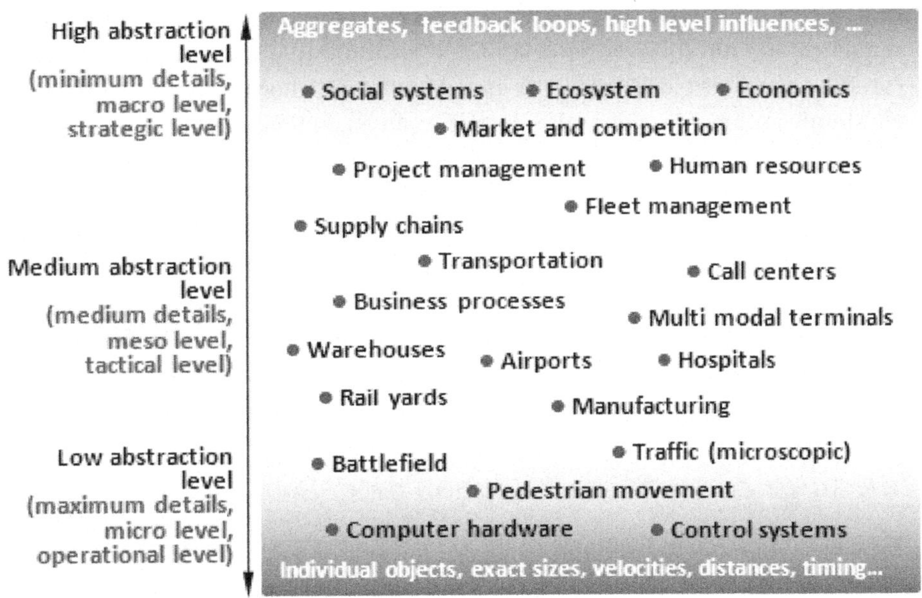

Applications of simulation

The figure above shows a number of simulation applications, all sorted by the abstraction level of the corresponding models.

At the bottom are the physical-level models that use highly-detailed representations of real-world objects. At this level, we care about physical interaction, dimensions, velocities, distances, and timings. An automobile's anti-lock brakes, the evacuation of football fans from a stadium, the traffic at an intersection controlled by a traffic light, and soldiers' actions on the battlefield are examples of problems that require low abstraction modeling.

The models at the top are highly abstract, and they typically use aggregates such as consumer populations and employment statistics rather than individual objects. Since their objects interact at a high level, they can help us understand relationships - such as how the money our company spends on advertising influences our sales - without requiring us to model intermediate steps.

Other models have an intermediate abstraction level. If we model a hospital's emergency department, we may care about physical space if we want to know how long it takes for someone to walk from the emergency room to an x-ray station, but the physical interaction among people in the building is irrelevant because we assume the building is uncongested.

In a model of a business process or a call center, we can model operations' sequence and duration rather than their location. In a transportation model, we carefully consider truck or rail car speed, but in a higher level supply chain model, we simply assume an order takes between seven and ten days to arrive.

⬥ **Choosing the right abstraction level is critical to your modeling project's success, but you'll find it's reasonably easy once you've decided what you want to include and what will remain below the level of abstraction.**

⬥ **In the model development process, it's normal - even desirable - to occasionally reconsider the model's abstraction level. In most cases, you'll start at a high abstraction level and add details as you need them.**

The three methods in simulation modeling

Modern simulation modeling uses three methods: discrete event, agent based, and system dynamics.

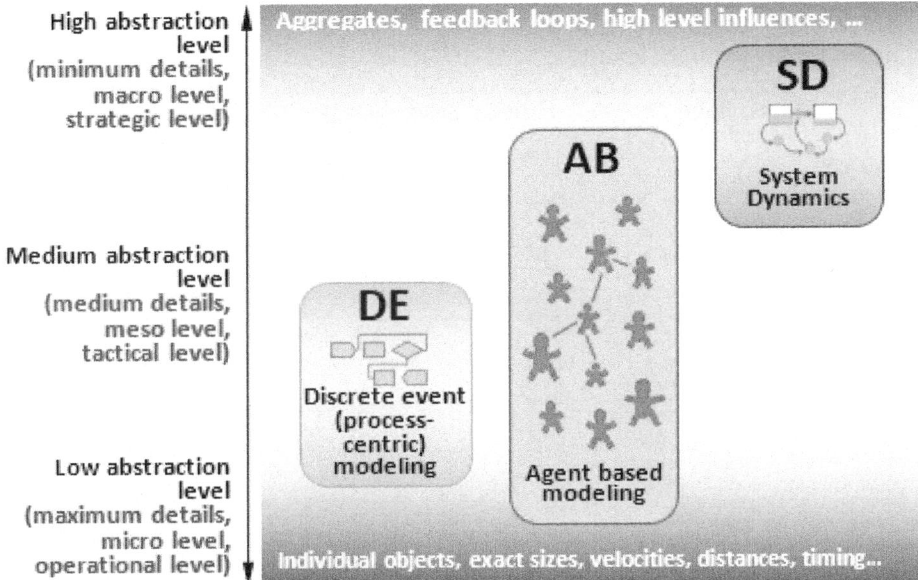

Methods in simulation modeling

In simulation modeling, a *method* is a framework we use to map a real world system to its model. You can think of a method as a type of language or a sort of "terms and conditions" for model building. There are three methods:

- *System Dynamics*

- *Discrete Event Modeling*

- *Agent Based Modeling*

Each method serves a specific range of abstraction levels. System dynamics assumes very high abstraction, and it's typically used for strategic modeling. Discrete event modeling supports medium and medium-low abstraction. In the middle are agent based models, which can vary from very detailed models where agents represent physical objects to the highly abstract models where agents represent competing companies or governments.

You should always select your method after you've carefully considered the system you want to model and your goals. In the figure below, the modeler's problem will largely determine how they model a supermarket. They could build a process flowchart where customers are entities and employees are resources, an agent based model where consumers are agents who are affected by advertising, communication, and their interactions with agents and employees, or a feedback structure where sales are in the loop with ads, quality of service, pricing, and customer loyalty.

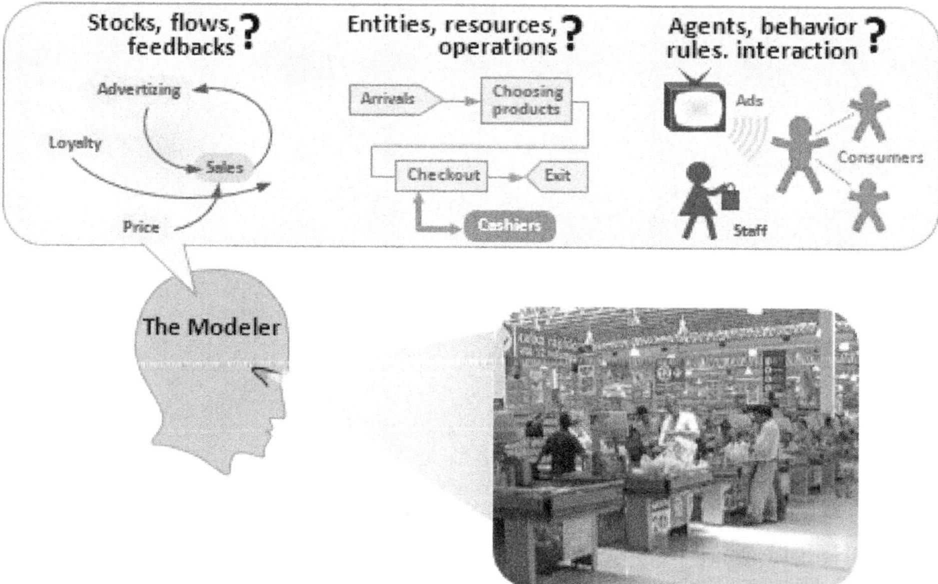

You may also find that the best way to model the different parts of a system is to use different methods, and in these situations a multi-method model will best meet your needs (Borshchev, 2013).

Installing and activating AnyLogic

AnyLogic 7 Professional's wizard-driven installation process is simple and straightforward. Download AnyLogic 7 from www.anylogic.com, and then use the following steps to install it:

1. Start AnyLogic. If it is not activated with a personal unlock key yet, the **AnyLogic Activation Wizard** will be displayed automatically.

2. On the **Activate AnyLogic** page, select **Request a time-limited Evaluation Key. The key will be sent to you by e-mail**, and then click **Next**.

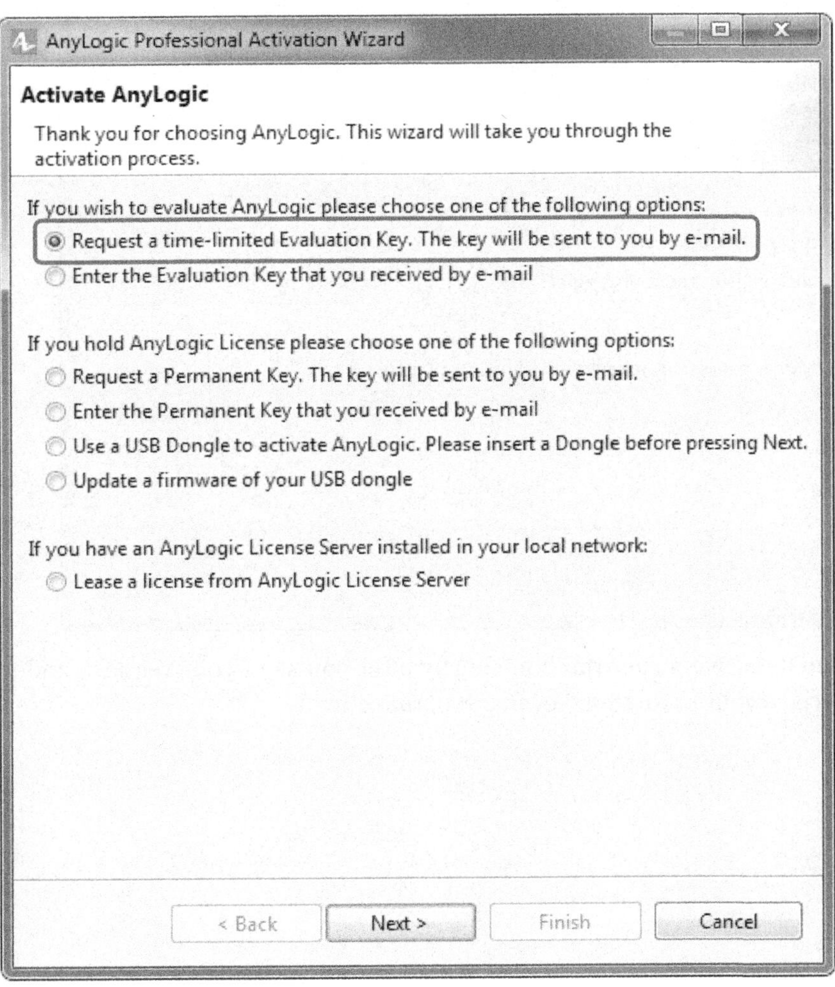

3. On the **AnyLogic License Request** page, provide your personal information and then click **Next**.

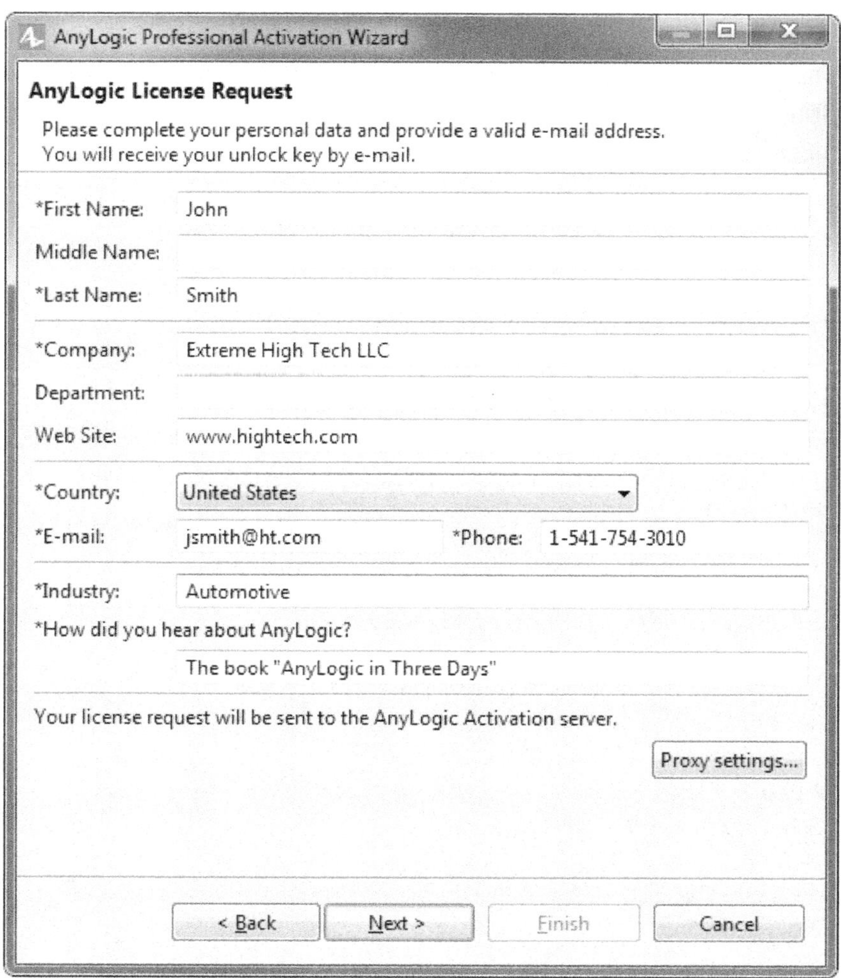

You'll receive a confirmation shortly after you send your request, and you'll receive your evaluation key in a separate e-mail.

4. After you receive your activation key, open the AnyLogic activation wizard, select **Enter the Evaluation Key that you received by email** on the first page, and then click **Next**.

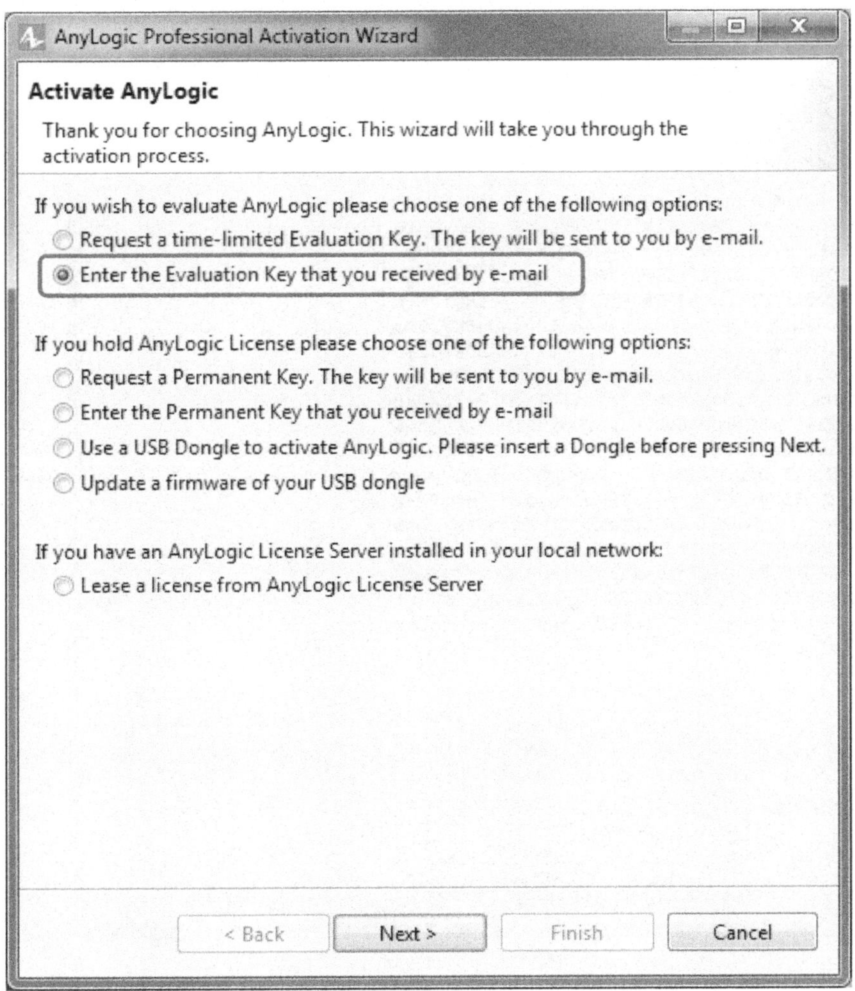

5. Copy the received activation key from the email message you received, paste it into the **Please paste the key here** field, and then click **Next**.

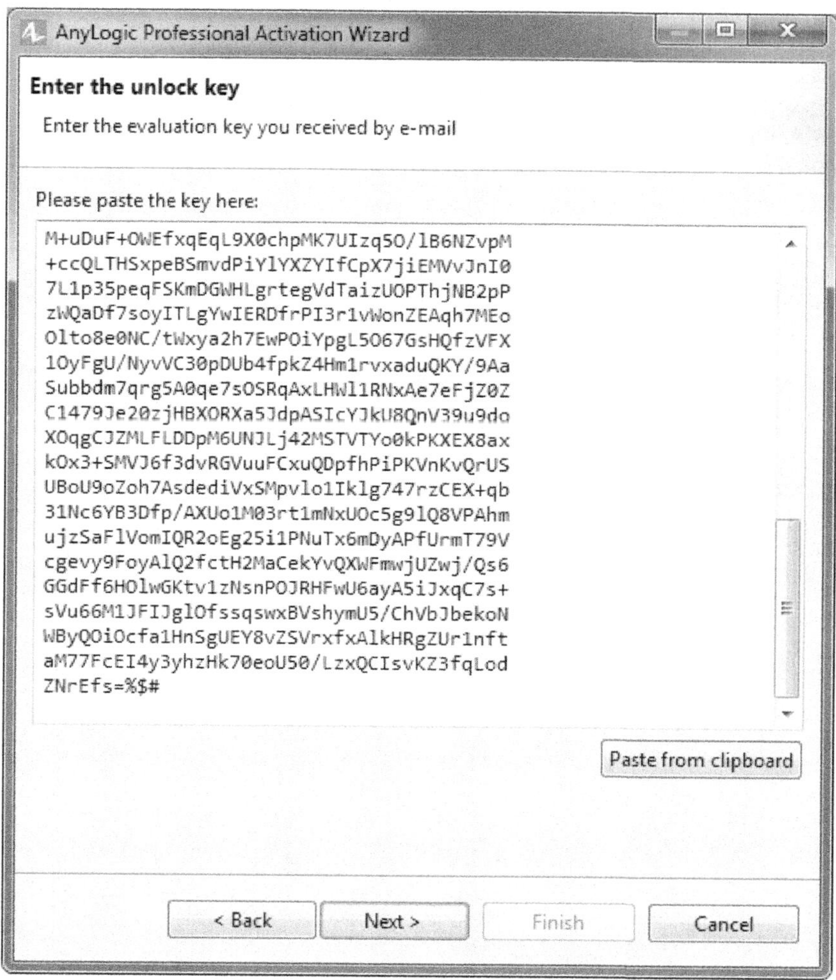

6. You should see a message that informs you the product has been activated successfully.

7. Click **Finish**.

You've completed AnyLogic's activation process, and you can start developing your first model.

Agent-based modeling

Agent based modeling is a relatively new method compared to system dynamics and discrete event modeling. In fact, agent based modeling was largely an academic topic until simulation practitioners began using it some 15 years ago.

It was triggered by:

- A desire to gain deeper insights into systems that traditional modeling approaches don't capture well

- Advances in modeling technology made possible by computer science, such as object oriented modeling, UML, and statecharts

- The rapid growth of CPU power and memory. Agent based models are more demanding than system dynamics and discrete event models.

Agent based modeling offers a modeler another way to look at the system:

◆ **You may not know how a system behaves, be able to identify its key variables and their dependencies, or recognize a process flow, but you may have insights into how the system's objects behave. If that's the case, you can start building your model by identifying the objects (agents) and defining their behaviors. Afterward, you may connect the agents you've created and allow them to interact or put them in an environment which has its own dynamics. The system's global behavior emerges from many (tens, hundreds, thousands, millions) concurrent individual behaviors.**

There's no standard language for agent based modeling, and an agent based model's structure comes from graphical editors or scripts. There are many ways to specify an agent's behavior. Frequently agent has a notion of state and its actions and reactions depend on the state; then behavior is best defined with statecharts. Sometimes behavior is defined in rules executed upon special events.

In many cases, the best way to capture the agent's internal dynamics is to use system dynamics or a discrete event approach, and then place a stock and flow diagram or a process flowchart inside an agent. Similarly, outside agents the dynamics of the environment where they live is often naturally modeled using traditional methods. It's why many agent based models are multi-method models.

Agents in an agent based model may represent very diverse things: vehicles, units of equipment, projects, products, ideas, organizations, investments, pieces of land, people in different roles, etc.

People in different roles:
consumers, citizens, employees,
patients, doctors, clients, soldiers, ...

Equipment, vehicles:
trucks, cars, cranes, aircrafts,
rail cars, machines, ...

Non-material things:
projects, products, innovations,
ideas, investments ...

Organizations:
companies, political parties, countries, ...

Academics still debate which properties an object should have to be an "agent": proactive and reactive qualities, a spatial awareness, an ability to learn, social ability, "intellect", etc. In applied agent based modeling, however, you'll find all kinds of agents: some communicate while others live in total isolation, some live in a space while others live without a space, and some learn and adapt while others never change their behavior patterns.

Here are some useful facts to ensure you aren't misguided by academic literature or the various theories of agent based modeling:

- **Agents aren't cellular automata.** Agents don't have to live in discrete space (like the grid in The Game of Life, ("The Game of Life", n.d.)), and space isn't part of many agent based models. When you need to represent space, it's typically continuous such as a geographical map or a facility floor plan.

- **Agents aren't necessarily people.** Anything can be an agent: a vehicle, a piece of equipment, a project, an idea, an organization, or even an investment. A model of a steel converter plant where each machine is modeled as an agent and their interactions produce steel is an agent based model.

- **An object that seems to be absolutely passive can be an agent.** You could model a single pipe segment in a larger water supply network as an agent and then associate maintenance and replacement schedules, costs, and breakdown events with it.

- **An agent based model can have many or few agents**. The model can also have one or many types of agents.

- **There are agent based models where agents don't interact.**
  Health economics, as an example, uses alcohol use, obesity, and chronic disease models where individual dynamics depend only on personal parameters and, sometimes, on the environment.

Market model

We'll build an agent-based model of a consumer market – one where each consumer will be an agent – to help us understand how a product enters the market. Since human decisions always include stochastics, agent based modeling is ideal for modeling market simulations.

Let's assume the following:

- The model includes 5000 people who don't use the product, but a combination of advertising and word of mouth will eventually lead them to purchase it.

Phase 1. Creating the agent population

We'll start by creating a simple model that depicts how advertising leads consumers to purchase our product.

Our model's consumers won't use the product at first, but they are all potentially interested in using it. We'll also represent advertising's influence on consumer demand by allowing a specific percentage of them to become interested in purchasing the product during a given day. For our purposes, *Advertising effectiveness = 0.1* determines the percentage of potential users that become ready to buy the product during a given day.

Start AnyLogic and the *Welcome* page displays.

The *Welcome page* introduces you to AnyLogic, offers a helpful overview of the program and its features, and allows you to open the example models.

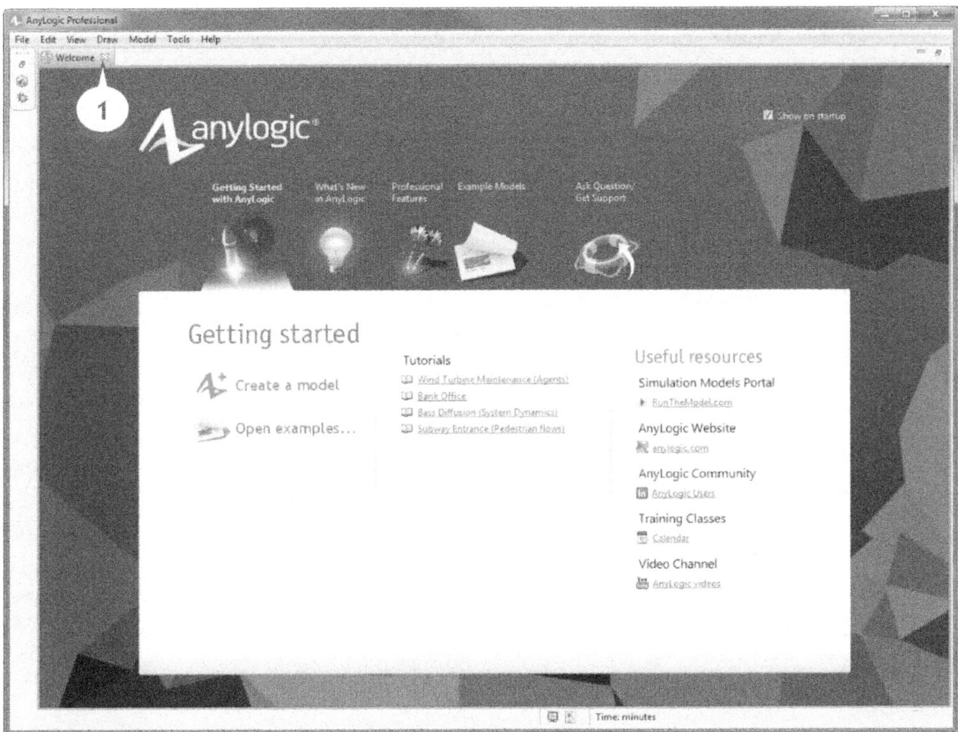

Welcome page

1. Close the Welcome page, and create a new model by selecting **File** > **New** > **Model** from AnyLogic's main menu. The **New Model** wizard will open.

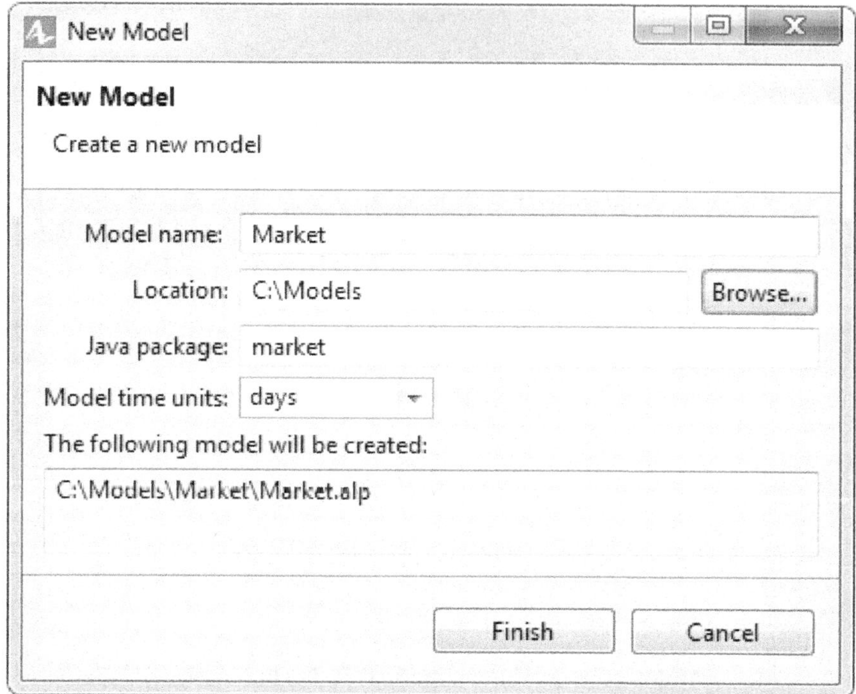

2. In the **Model name** box, enter the new model's name: *Market*.

3. In the **Location** box, select the folder where you want to create the model. You can browse for a folder by clicking **Browse** or type the name of the folder you want to create in the **Location** box.

4. Click **Finish**.

Now, let's briefly review AnyLogic's interface.

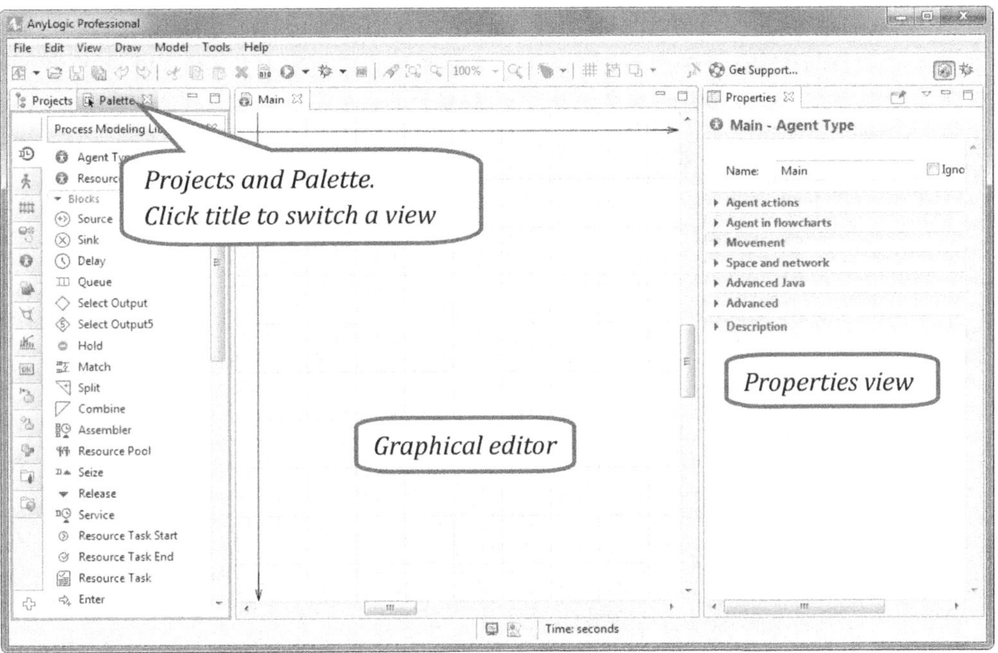

AnyLogic workspace

- The graphical editor allows you to edit the agent type's diagram, and you can add model elements by dragging them from the **Palette** on to the diagram and placing them on the editor's canvas. The elements you place inside the blue frame will appear inside the model window when you run it.

- The **Projects** view allows you to access the AnyLogic models you have open in the workspace, and the workspace tree helps you easily navigate them.

- The **Palette** view lists the objects grouped in palettes. To add an element to your model, drag the element from the palette on to the graphical editor.

- The **Properties** view allows you to view and modify the selected item's properties.

- To open/close a view, choose the corresponding item from the **View** menu. If the item is selected, the corresponding view will be visible.

- To resize a view, use your mouse to drag the view's edge.

- You can always use the option **Reset perspective** in the **Tools** menu to return the views to their default positions.

5. Let's open the **Projects** view to examine the model's structure. You'll find the **Palette** and **Projects** views in the workspace's left section, and you can switch from the **Palette** view to the **Projects** view by clicking the **Projects** tab.

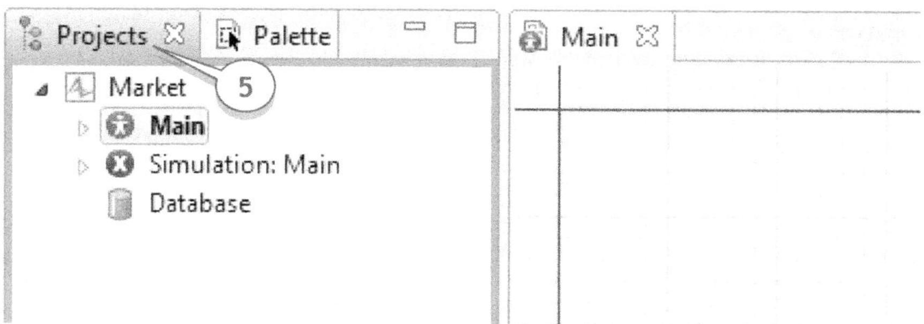

Navigating through the model in the Projects view

- The **Projects** view allows you to access the AnyLogic projects you have open in the workspace, and you can use the workspace tree to quickly and easily navigate them.

- AnyLogic uses a tree structure to display your model. The top level displays the model, the level below displays agent types and experiments, and the lower-level branches organize the elements that make up the agent structure.

- By default, a model has one agent type - **Main**, one experiment **Simulation** and built-in database to read input data and write simulation output **Database** (empty by default).

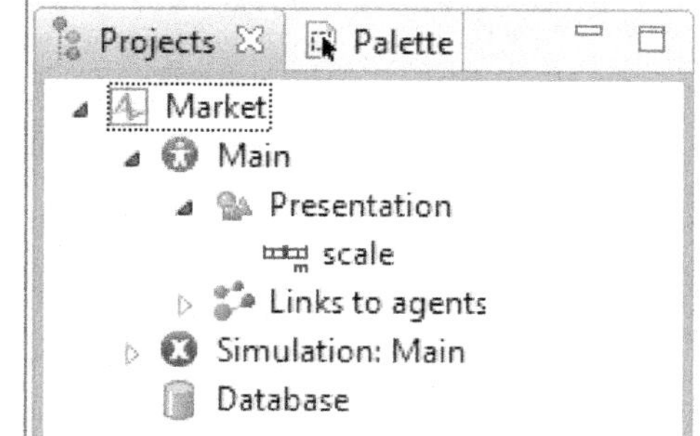

- Double-clicking the agent type or the experiment opens its diagram in the graphical editor.

- Clicking the model element in the tree selects the element and centers it in the graphical editor. This may be helpful when you can't find an element on the graphical diagram.

In the graphical editor, you'll see the empty diagram of the model's *Main* agent type.

Agents

- Agents are a model's building blocks, and you can use them to model all kinds of real-world objects, including organizations, companies, trucks, processing stations, resources, cities, retailers, physical objects, controllers, and so on.

- Each agent typically represents one of the model's logical sections. This allows you to decompose a model into many levels of detail.

  Our model has one agent type, *Main*. To add consumers, we'll need to create an agent type to represent consumers, and then create an agent population made up of instances of this consumer agent type. In AnyLogic 7, you can use the helpful **New agent** wizard to create agents.

6. We want to add a new model element, but we first need to switch to the **Palette** view by clicking the **Palette**  tab.

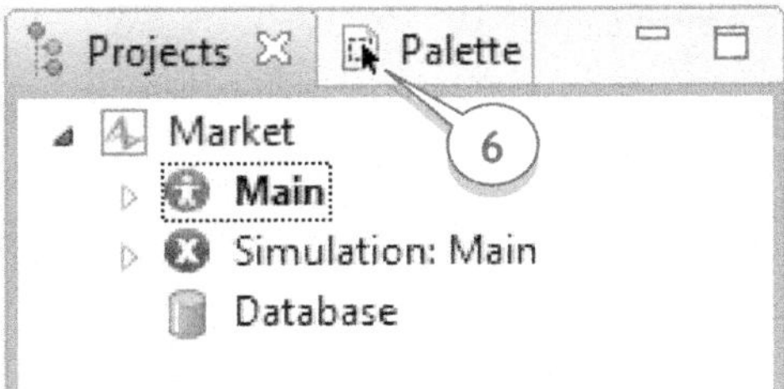

7. Open the **Agent** palette. To open a specific palette, go to the **Palette** view and hover your mouse over the view's vertical navigation panel.

8. It will expand to show the names of all palettes so you can select the one you need. Click the **Agent** palette in the list to select it.

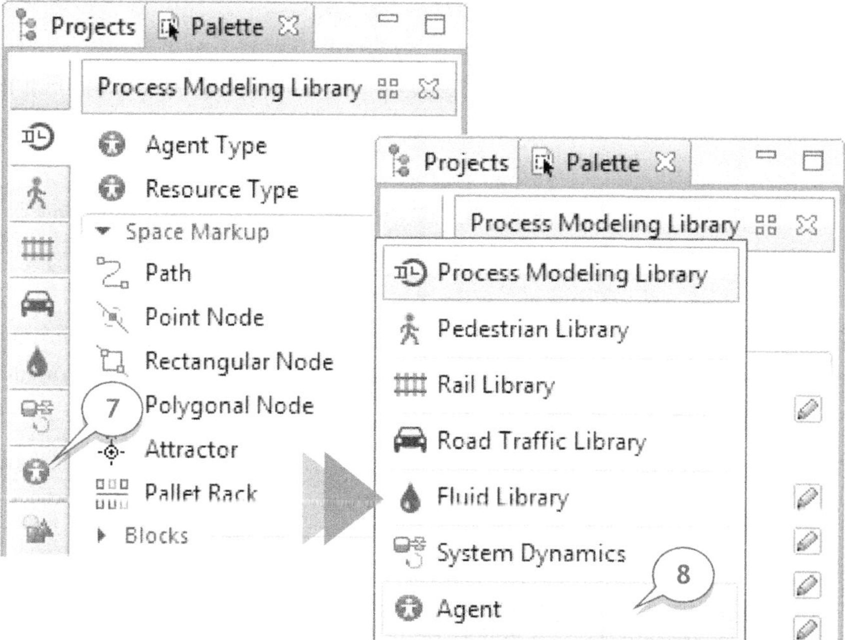

Once you're familiar with the icons, you can click the palette icon you want in the navigation bar.

9. Drag the **Agent** ⊕ from the **Agent** palette on to the *Main* diagram, and the **New agent** wizard will open.

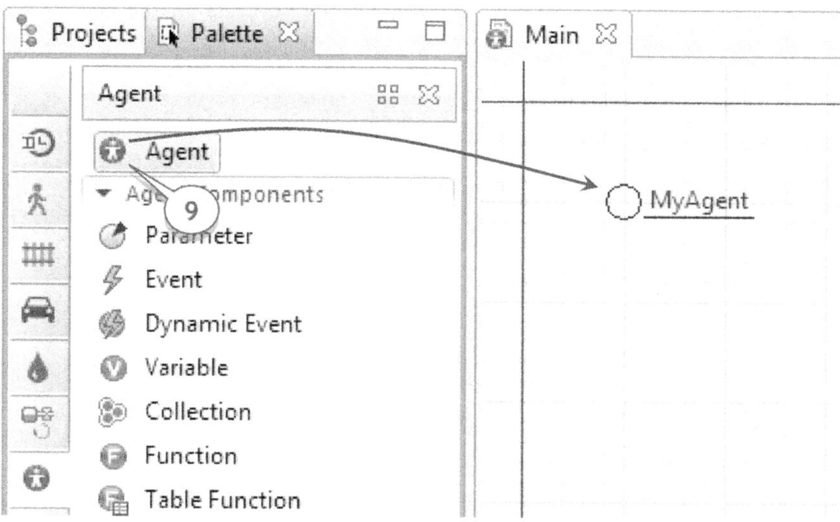

10. On the **Step 1. Choose what you want to create** page, select the option that best meets your needs. Since we want to create multiple agents of the same type, select **Population of agents** and click **Next**.

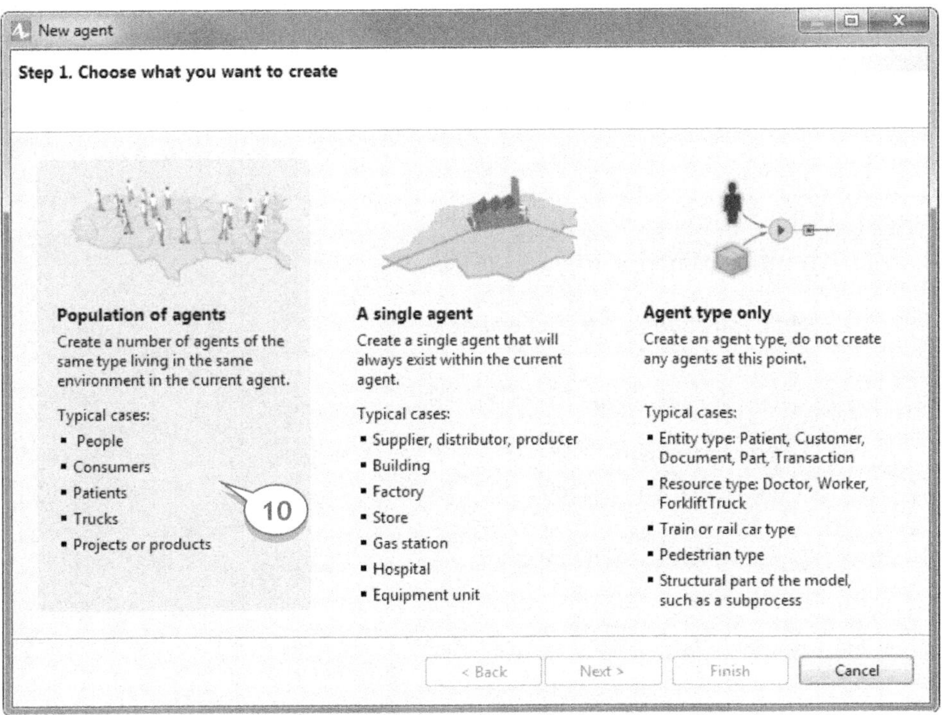

11. On the **Step 2. Creating new agent type** page, in **Agent type name** box, type *Consumer*. The information in the **Agent population name** box will automatically change to *consumers*.

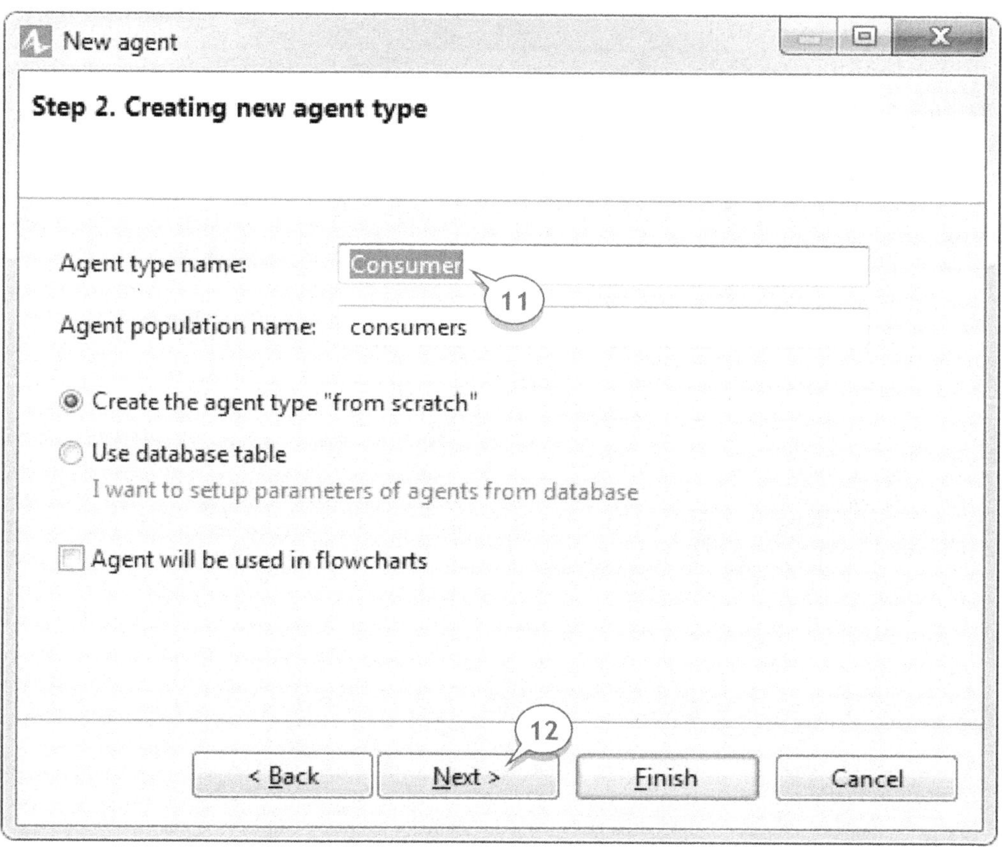

12. Click **Next**.

13. On the **Agent animation** page, choose the agent's animation shape. Since we're creating a simple model that uses 2D animation, choose **2D**, select the **General** list's first item: **Person**, and click **Next**.

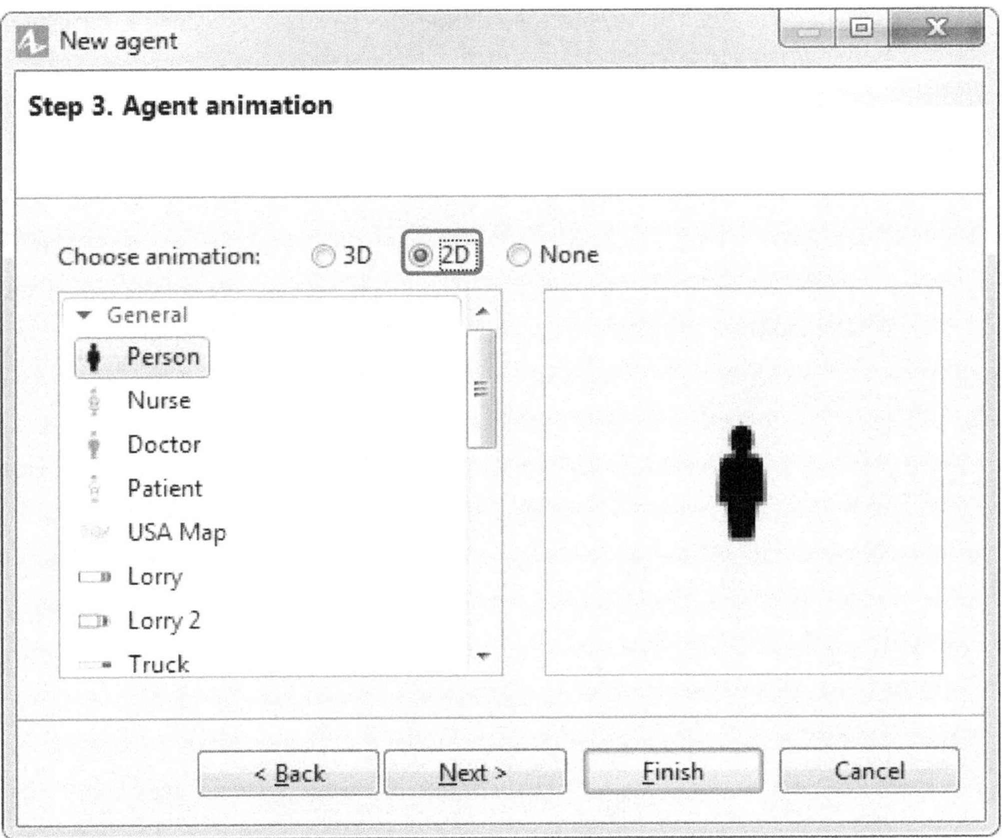

14. On the **Agent Parameters** page, define the agent's parameters or characteristics.

Since our model only considers advertising-related product purchases, we'll add a parameter – *AdEffectiveness* – to define the percentage of potential users who become ready to buy the product during a given day.

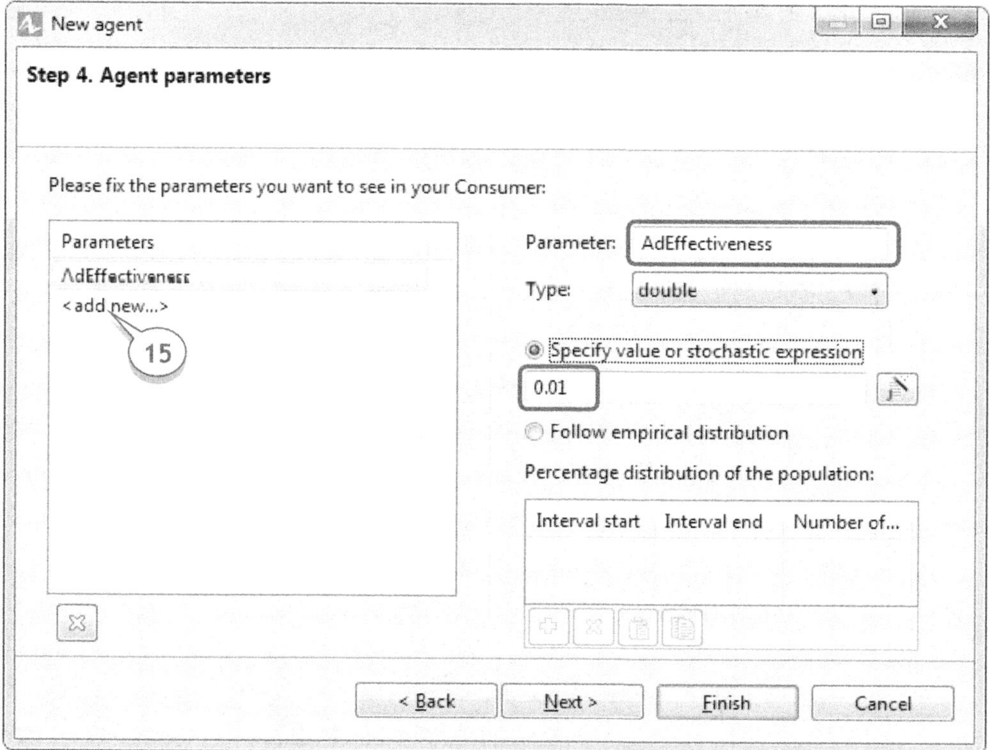

15. On the left section, in the **Parameters** table, click **<add new...>** to create a parameter.

16. In the **Parameter** box, change the default parameter's name to *AdEffectiveness*, and choose **double** as the parameter **Type**. We'll assume an average of 1% of our model's potential users will want to buy the product during a given day, so specify *0.01* as the parameter's value.

17. Click **Next**.

18. On the **Population size** page, type 5000 in the **Create population with ... agents** box to create 5000 instances of the *Consumer* type. Each instance in the population will model a specific agent-consumer.

    While we've created our agent population, we won't see 5,000 *Person* animation figures on *Main* diagram. Instead, AnyLogic will use the 5000 agents in the population we've called *consumers* to simulate the market when we run our model.

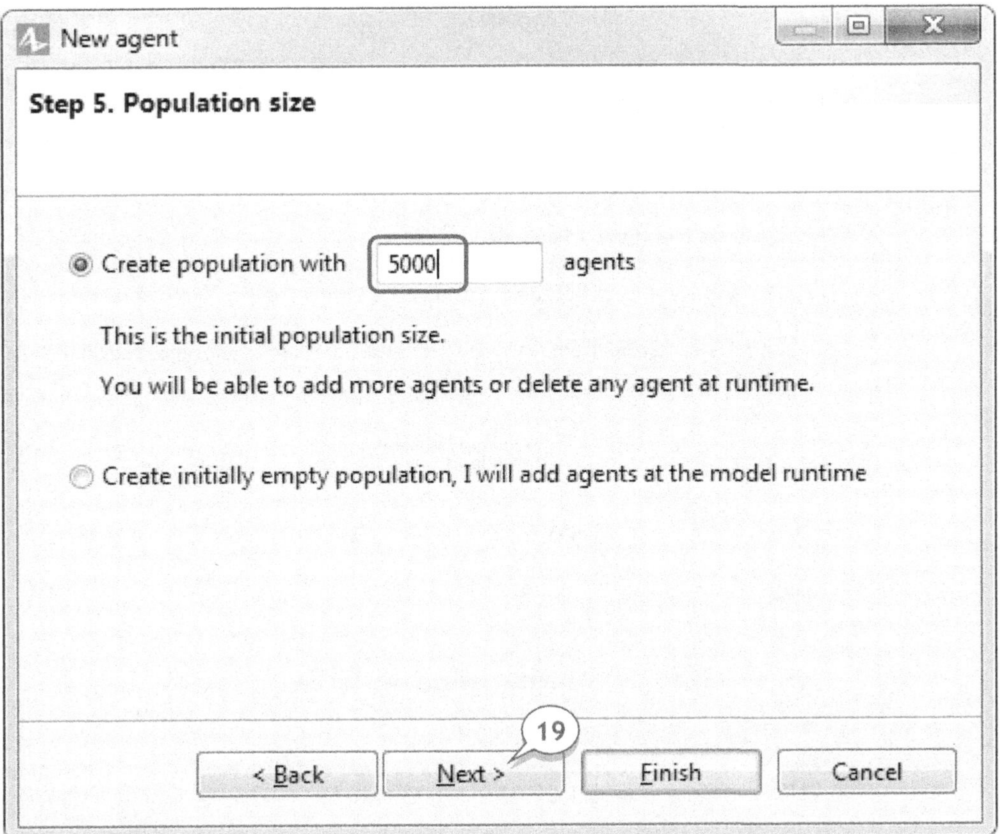

19. Click **Next**.

20. On the **Configure new environment** page, accept the default values for the environment's space type (**Continuous**) and both its **Width** and **Height** values (500). AnyLogic will display the agents in a 500x500 pixel rectangle.

21. Select the **Apply random layout** box to randomly distribute the agents across the 500 pixel width and height we've defined. Since we don't want to create an agent network, we'll accept the default **No network/User-defined** network type.

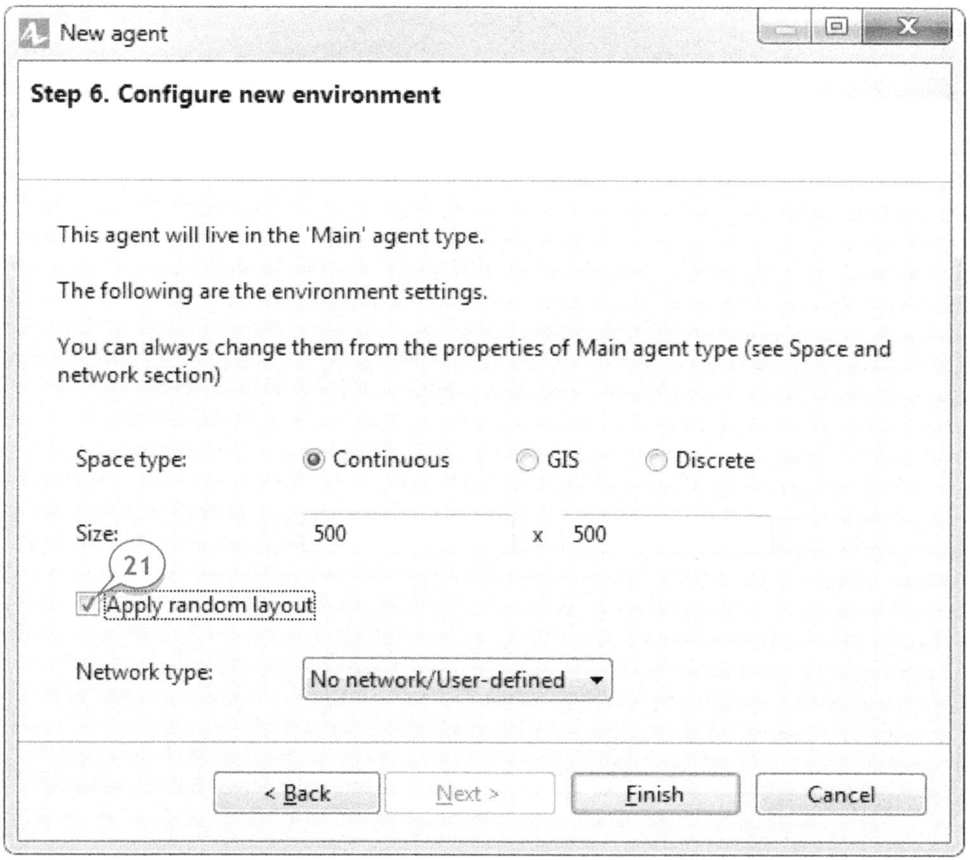

22. Click **Finish**.

23. Let's use the **Projects** view to see the new elements that the wizard created. Expand the model tree branches to see the internals.

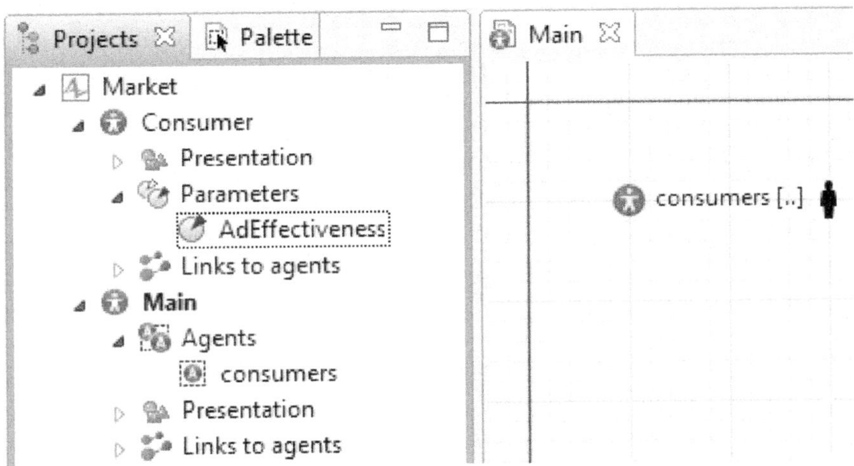

Our model now has two agent types: *Main* and *Consumer*.

- The *Consumer* agent type has the agent's animation shape (*person*, in the **Presentation** branch) and the parameter *AdEffectiveness*.

- The *Main* agent type contains the agent population *consumers* (a set of 5000 agents of type *Consumer*).

Agent's environment

The *Main* agent acts as the *environment* for the *consumers* population. Since the environment defines the space, layout, network, and communication that our agents use, we'll need an environment to arrange our agent presentations and model the "word of mouth" advertising that occurs when our agents interact.

24. Click **Main** in the **Projects** to open its properties in the **Properties** view (you'll find **Properties** in the AnyLogic window's right half).

In the **Space and network** section of *Main* properties, you can adjust the environment settings for the *consumers* agent population.

The Properties view

- The **Properties** view is a context-sensitive view of the element's properties.

- To modify an element's properties, select the element by clicking it in the graphical editor or in the **Projects** view, and then use the **Properties** view to modify the properties.

- The **Properties** view has several sections. To expand or collapse a section, click its title.

- The selected element's name and type display at the top of the view.

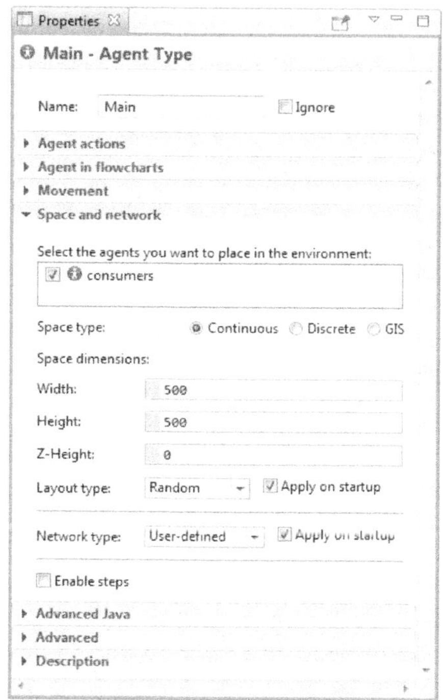

25. On *Main* diagram, select the agent population's non-editable embedded animation shape, open the **Advanced** properties section, and select the **Draw agent with offset to this position** option.

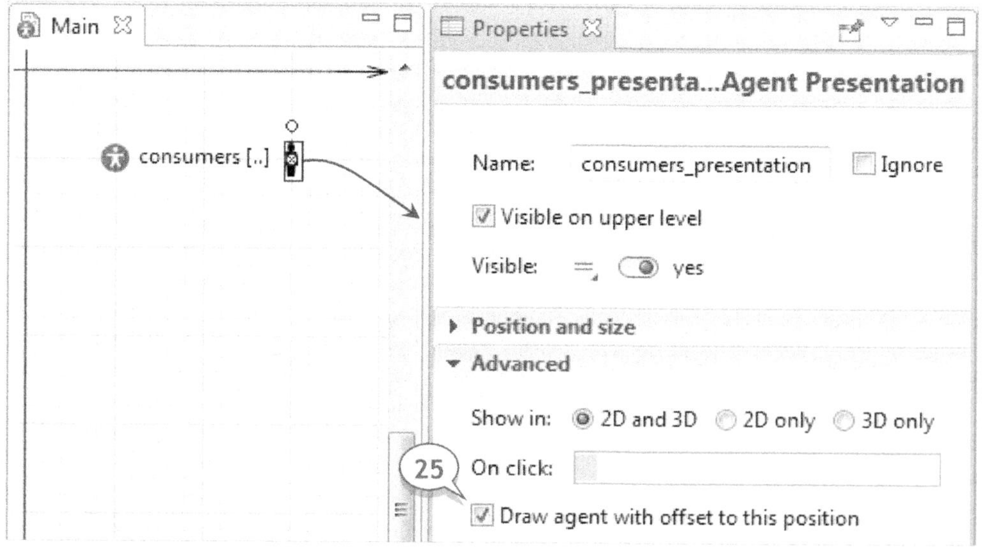

As you can see in the following figure, the animation shape defines the upper-left corner of the 500x500 pixel space where the individual agents will reside when we run the model.

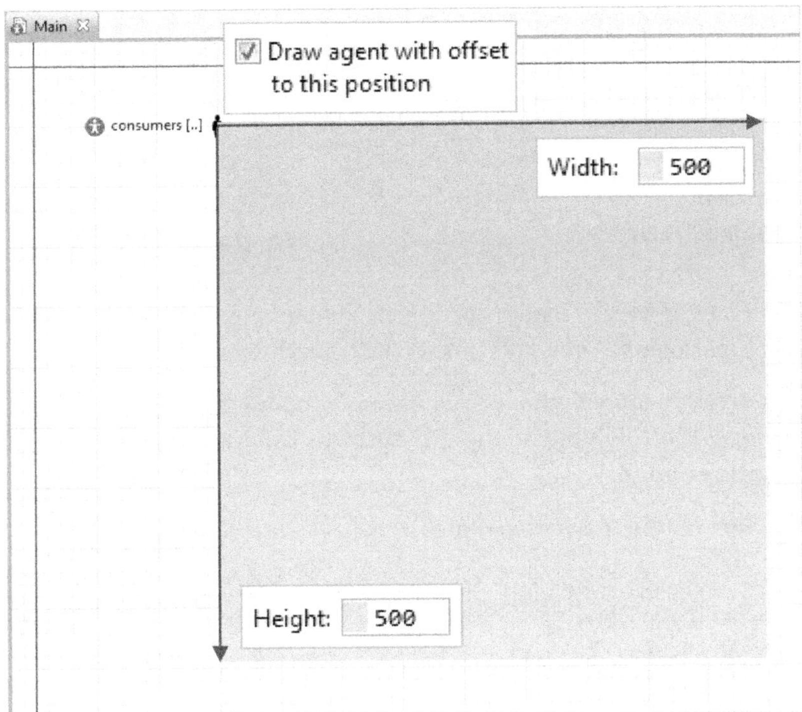

We've finished building this very simple model, and you can now run it and observe its behavior.

26. On the toolbar, click the **Build** button to build the model and check it for errors.

27. Locate the **Run** button, and click the small triangle to the right. Select the experiment you want to run. Choose **Market / Simulation** from the list.

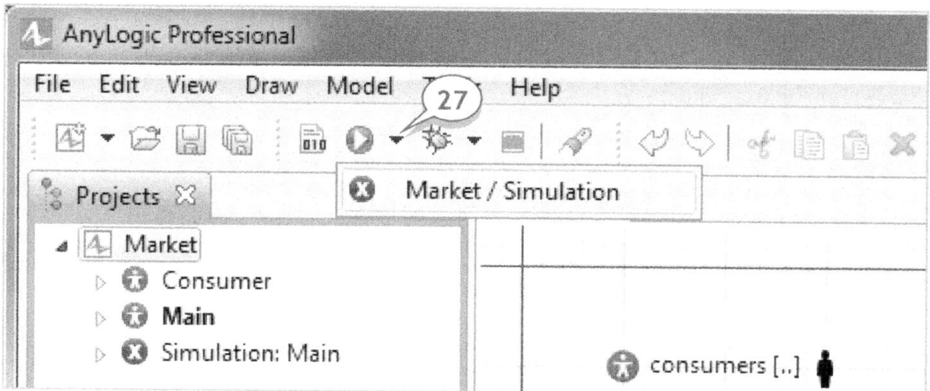

Since you can have several models open at the same time - and each model may have several experiments – you must select the correct experiment.

After you start the model, the presentation window displays the launched experiment *Simulation*. By default, the presentation window displays the model's name and the **Run** button.

28. Click the **Run** button to run the model.

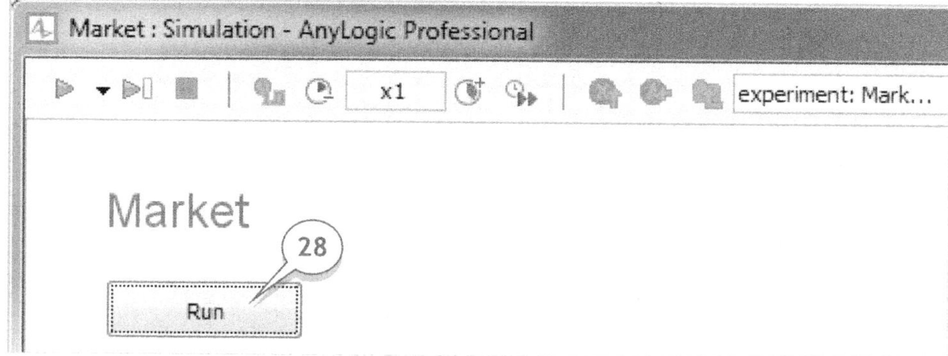

You'll see the model's presentation (the presentation you created for *Main* agent) that shows 5000 animations for the agents that comprise the *consumers* population. Since we didn't create any behavior for our agents, the animation appears still.

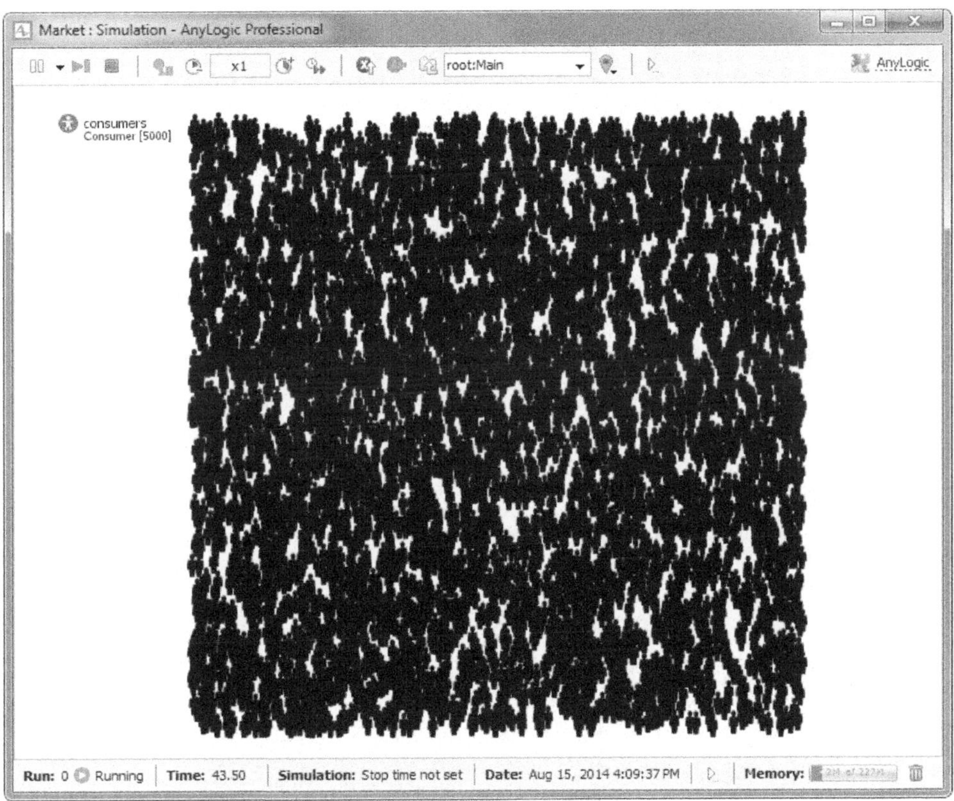

Model window's status bar

- To ensure the model is running, look at the status bar at the bottom of the model window:

- The status bar displays the model's simulation status (Running, Paused, Idle, or Finished), current model time, model date, etc.

- You can customize the status bar by clicking the button ▷.., and choosing the required sections from the pop-up list.

You can use the toolbar at the top of AnyLogic's presentation window to control the model's execution.

Controlling the model execution

Run from the current state

[Visible when the model is not running] Starts the simulation or, if the simulation was paused, resumes it.

Step

Executes one model event and then pauses the model execution.

Pause

[Visible when the model is running] Pauses the simulation. You can resume a paused simulation at any time.

Terminate execution

Terminates the current model execution.

29. We're ready to define the consumer's logic. To continue developing our model, close the presentation window.

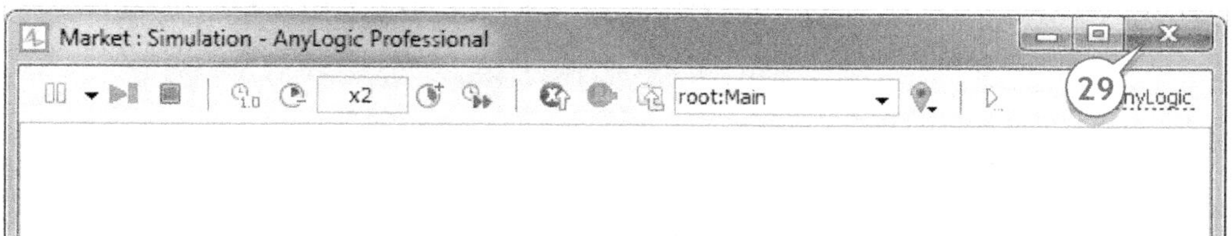

Phase 2. Defining a consumer behavior

We'll continue developing our model by defining consumer characteristics and behavior. The best way to define a behavior is to use a statechart.

Statecharts

- *Statecharts* are the most advanced construct for describing event- and time-driven behavior. For some objects, this event- and time-ordering of operations is so pervasive that you can best characterize their behavior using a state transition diagram – a statechart.

- Statecharts have *states* and *transitions*. The statechart's states are alternative, which means the object can only be in one state at a time. A transition execution may lead to a state change that makes a new set of transitions active. The statechart's states may be hierarchical – they may contain still other states and transitions.

- One agent may have several statecharts that describe independent parts of the agent's behavior.

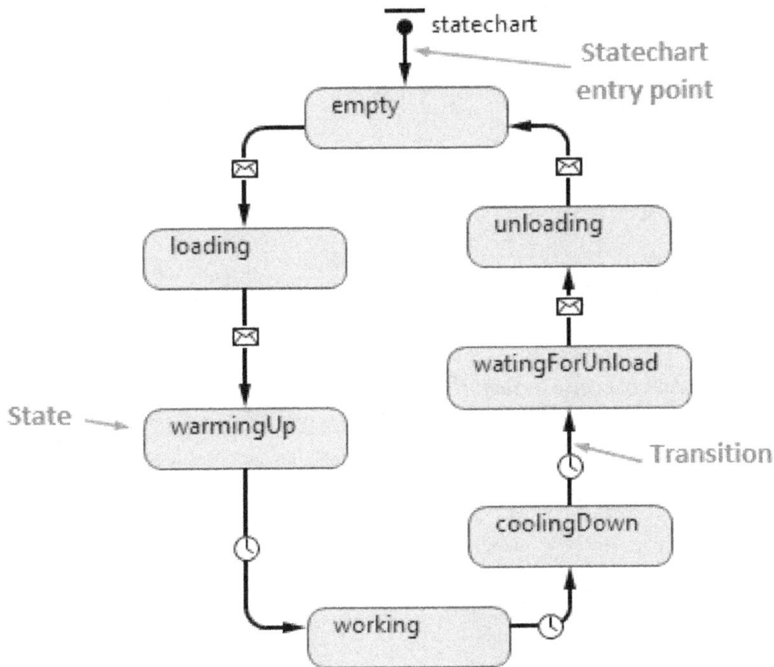

We'll define a consumer's behavior as a two state sequence:

- A consumer in the *PotentialUser* state is only potentially interested in buying the product.

- A consumer in the *User* state has purchased the product.

1. In the **Projects** view, open the *Consumer* diagram by double-clicking it. You'll see the agent's graphical diagram with the animation figure in the axis origin and the parameter.

How do you know what agent type you're editing?

Since our model has two agent types, you may wonder which agent type you're editing in the graphical editor.

- AnyLogic selects the tab of the agent type you have open in the graphical editor and emphasizes its item in the **Projects** tree (see the figure below).

- You can navigate between open graphical diagrams of different agent types by clicking the tab names (for example, *Main* and *Consumer* in the example below):

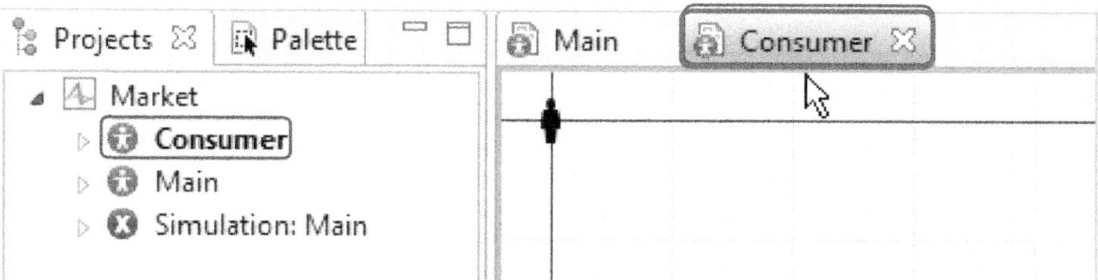

2. Start drawing a statechart by drawing two states. Open the **Statechart** palette.

3. Drag the **Statechart Entry Point** from the **Statechart** palette on to the *Consumer* diagram. You start drawing a statechart by adding a *statechart entry point*. The entry point defines the start of the statechart control flow and the statechart's name.

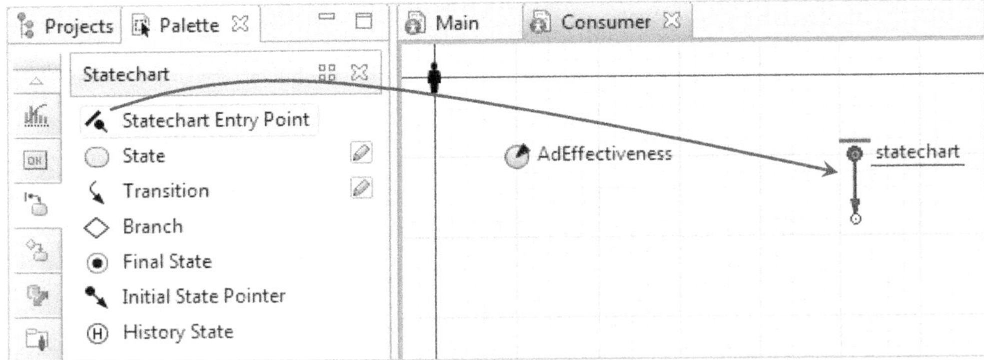

● **Please be careful – it's easy to confuse the Statechart entry point with the Initial state pointer , or Transition since they look alike.**

You can see how AnyLogic has highlighted the statechart entry point in red. It means the entry point isn't connected to any state, and the current statechart is invalid.

Let's add the first state in the consumer's statechart.

4. Drag the **State** from the **Statechart** palette on to the graphical diagram, and connect it to the statechart entry point.

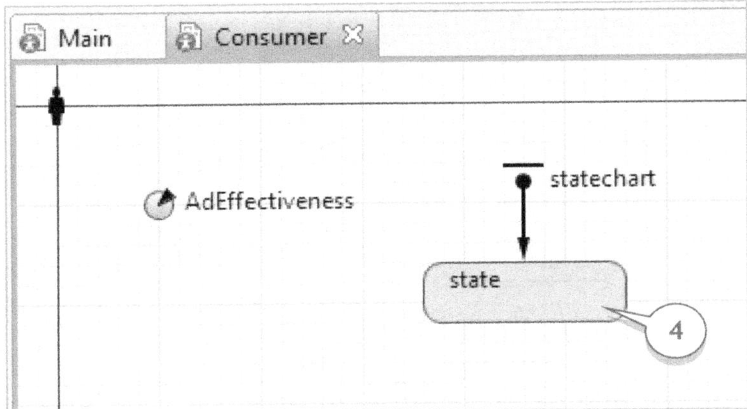

● **Make sure you're drawing the statechart on the Consumer diagram rather than on Main.**

5. Select the state in the graphical editor, and modify its properties. Name the state *PotentialUser*.

6. Use the **Fill color** control to change the state's color to *lavender*.

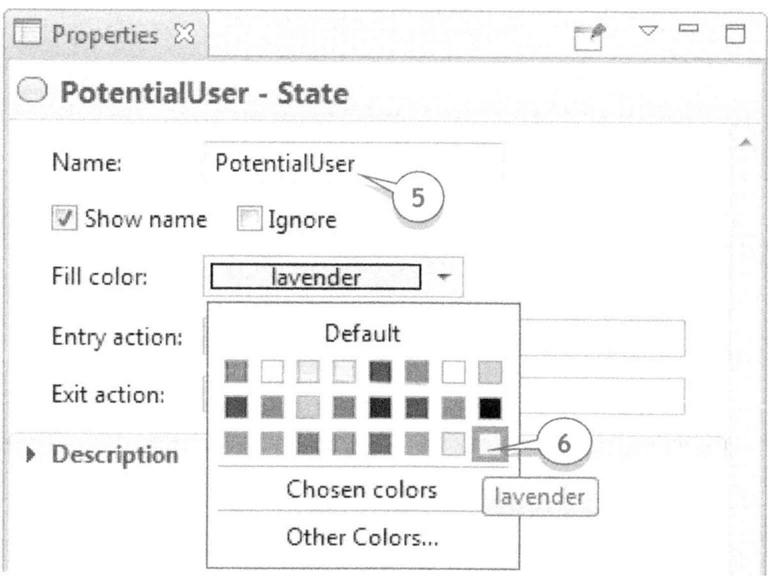

7. Type the following Java code in the state's **Entry action** field: *shapeBody.setFillColor(lavender)*

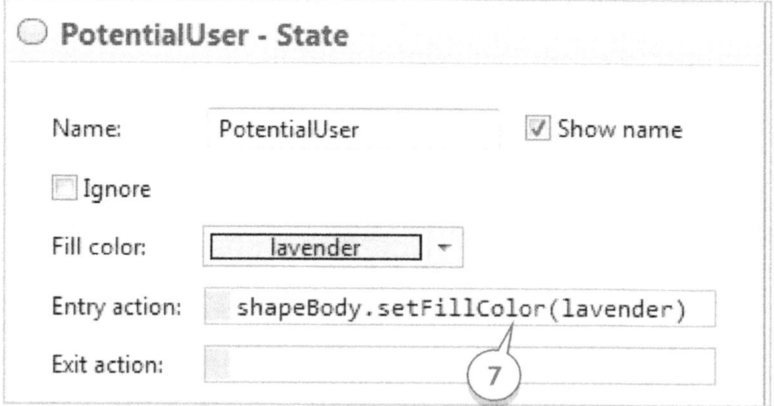

Code completion assistant

- You can use the code completion assistant to avoid typing the full names of elements and functions. To open the assistant, click the desired position in the edit box and press Ctrl+space (Alt+space on Mac OS). The popup window lists the model elements that are available in the given context, such as model variables, parameters, or functions.

- Scroll to the name of the element you want to add or type the element's first letters until it appears in the list, and press Enter to insert the element's name in the edit box.

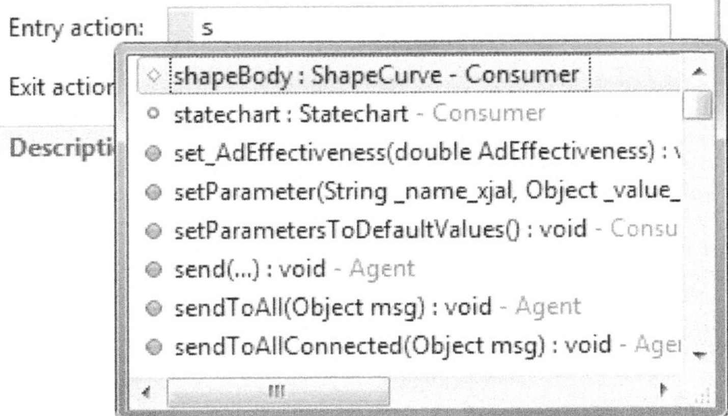

Entry **action** is executed when consumer switches to another state. This code displays the state change by changing the consumer animation color.

Here, *shapeBody* is the name of consumer's animation shape that the new agent wizard created. (If you expand the *Consumer's* **Presentation** branch in the **Projects** tree, you'll see the *shapeBody* shape inside the *person* group).

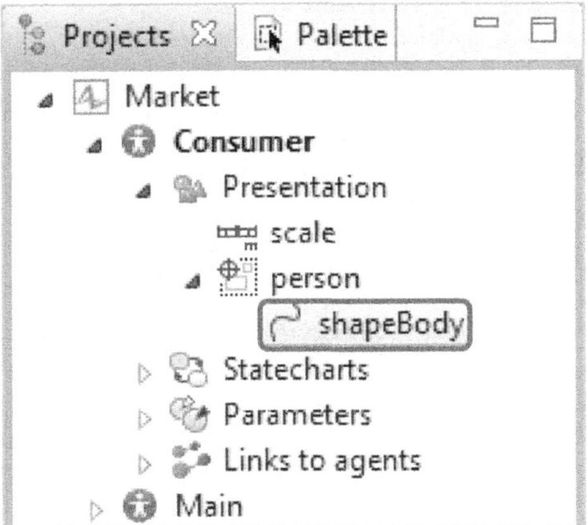

Here we call the function of *shapeBody*. To access the element's function, type the element name (*shapeBody*), type a dot, and then use the code completion feature to list the element's functions or select the function name from the list.

setFillColor() is one of the standard shape's functions that allows you to dynamically change the shape's fill color. It takes just one argument - a new color.

8. Add another state in the consumer's statechart:

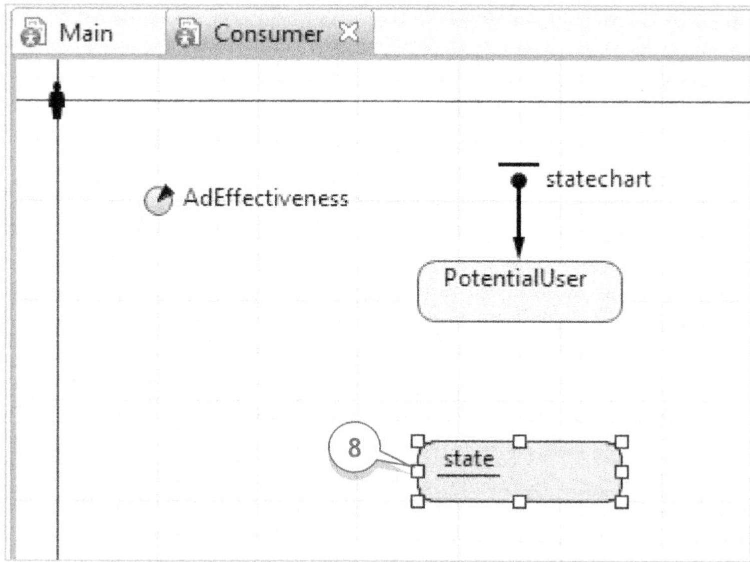

9. Modify the state's properties like you did earlier:

Name: *User*

Fill color: *yellowGreen*

Entry action: *shapeBody.setFillColor(yellowGreen);*

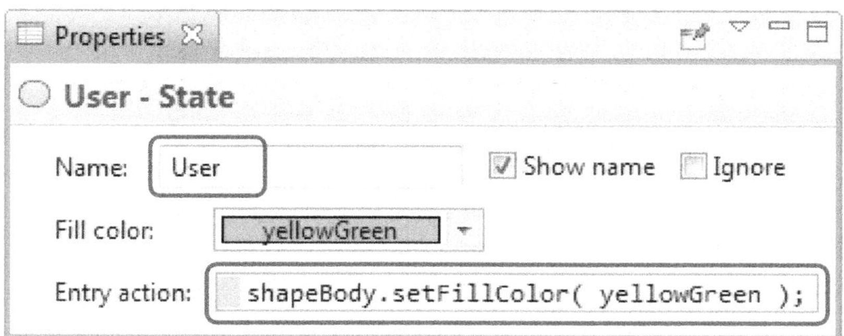

10. Draw a transition from *PotentialUser* to *User* state to model how persons purchase the product and become product users. To do so, double-click the

Statechart palette's **Transition** element (the element's palette icon should change to), click *PotentialUser* state, and click *User*.

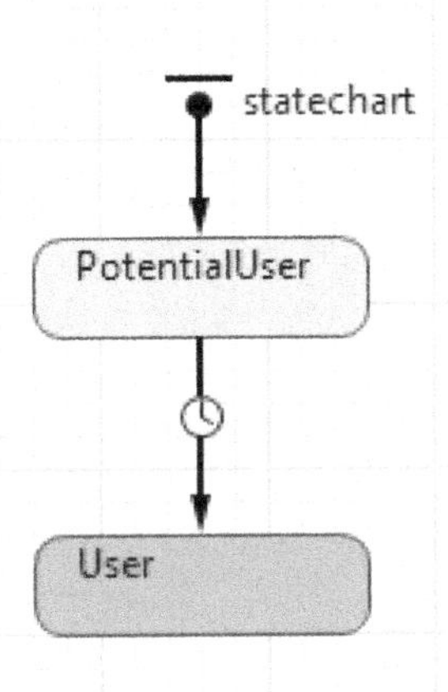

- **Make sure that the transition connects the states. If the transition is not connected, AnyLogic highlights it in red.**

11. Name the transition *Ad* to represent "advertising".

12. Select the **Show name** checkbox to display the transition's name on the graphical diagram.

13. The transition from *PotentialUser* to *User* state will model how advertising leads the person to buy the product. In the **Triggered by** list, click **Rate**. In the **Rate** field, type *AdEffectiveness*, and then click **per day**.

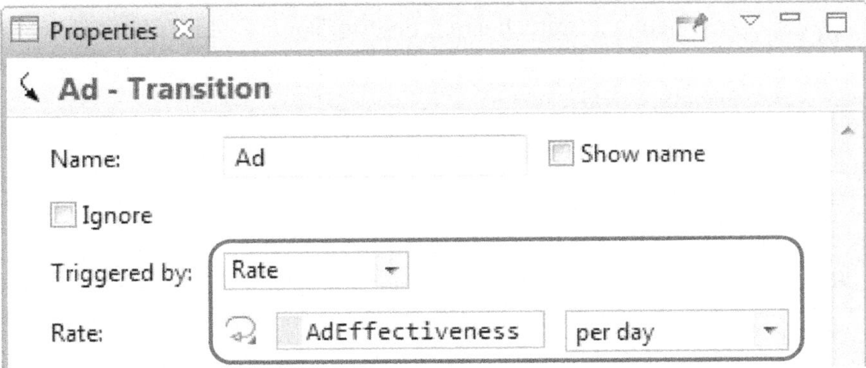

You can see that the icon drawn over the transition has changed from ⊙ to ⬓. This sign shows the transition's *trigger type*.

To move the transition's name or icon, select the transition, and use your mouse to drag the corresponding element to a new location.

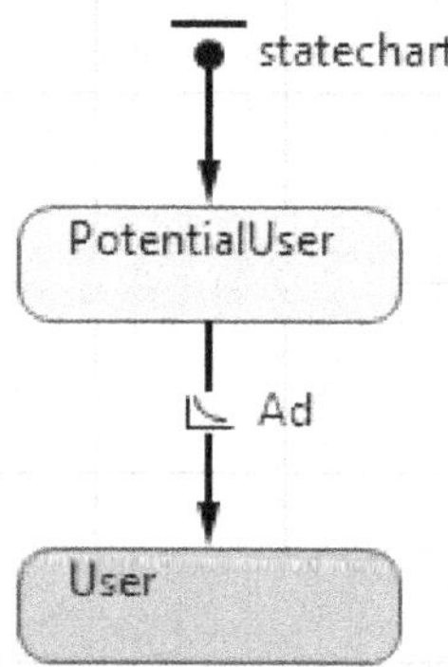

Transition trigger types

Many types of events can trigger a transition. The following table lists the transition trigger types as well as the icons that are drawn over the transitions to help you understand their trigger type.

Transition trigger	Description
Timeout ⊙	Transition occurs after a specified time interval counted from the moment the statechart enters the "source" state of the transition. The timeout expression can be stochastic or deterministic. Primary uses: **Delay**: stay in a state for a given time, then leave. **Timeout**: change state if other awaited events don't occur within the specified time interval.
Rate ⬓	Used to implement a sporadic state change with a known mean time. Acts in the same way as a timeout triggered transition, but the time interval is drawn from an exponential distribution parameterized with the given rate. For example, if the rate is 0.2 the timeouts will have mean values of $1/0.2 = 5$ time units.

Condition ⑦	Transition monitors a specified Boolean condition and reacts when it becomes true. The condition is an arbitrary boolean expression and may depend on the states of any objects in the whole model with continuous as well as discrete dynamics. *Please note that the condition is checked only when some events occur in the model. To ensure you do not miss the state switch moment, we recommend you add a cyclic event inside the agent and make it occur often enough not to miss the moment when the transition's condition becomes true.*
Message ✉	Reacts to messages from other agents. The messages can model communication between people, commands given to a machine, etc. You can define the message template in the transition properties, but only the messages that match this template will trigger the transition.
Arrival 🏁	Reacts to arrival of this agent to its destination. *Please note that the transition reacts only if the movement was initiated by calling the agent's function moveTo().*

Our transition is triggered with the specified rate. In our case, when the statechart enters the state *PotentialUser*, a draw from the exponential distribution is made and the timeout is set up. Each consumer's adoption time will differ, though an average 1% of potential users will buy the product on a given day.

14. Now, let's set up the model's time units. To tune the model setting, switch from **Palette** to **Projects**, and then click the model item in the tree (the tree's top object, *Market* 📐). In the **Properties** view, choose **days** as the **Model time units**.

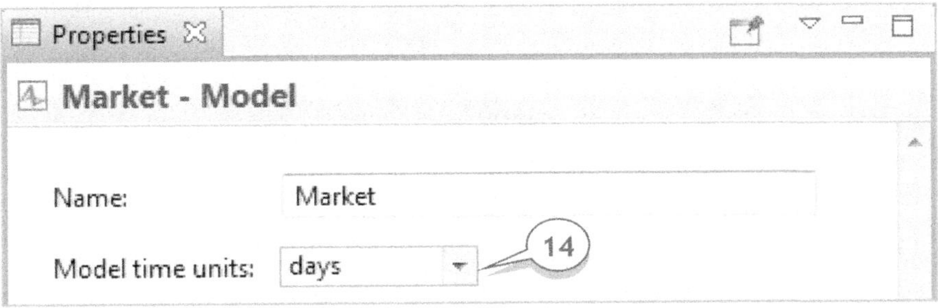

Model time. Model time units

- *Model time* is the virtual (simulated) time that the AnyLogic simulation engine maintains. The model time isn't related to the real time or the computer clock, though you can run the model in a scale to real time.

- To set the relationship between the model time and real world time where the system being modeled lives, you'll need to define the *time units*. You should choose the most suitable model time unit for your model, close to your model's typical operation durations.

  For example, pedestrian flow models typically use seconds and manufacturing service systems typically use minutes, but some global economics, social and ecological models defined in system dynamics style may use months or even years.

15. Run the model. The population should gradually turn green – a change that represents the effect of advertising - until every consumer buys the product.

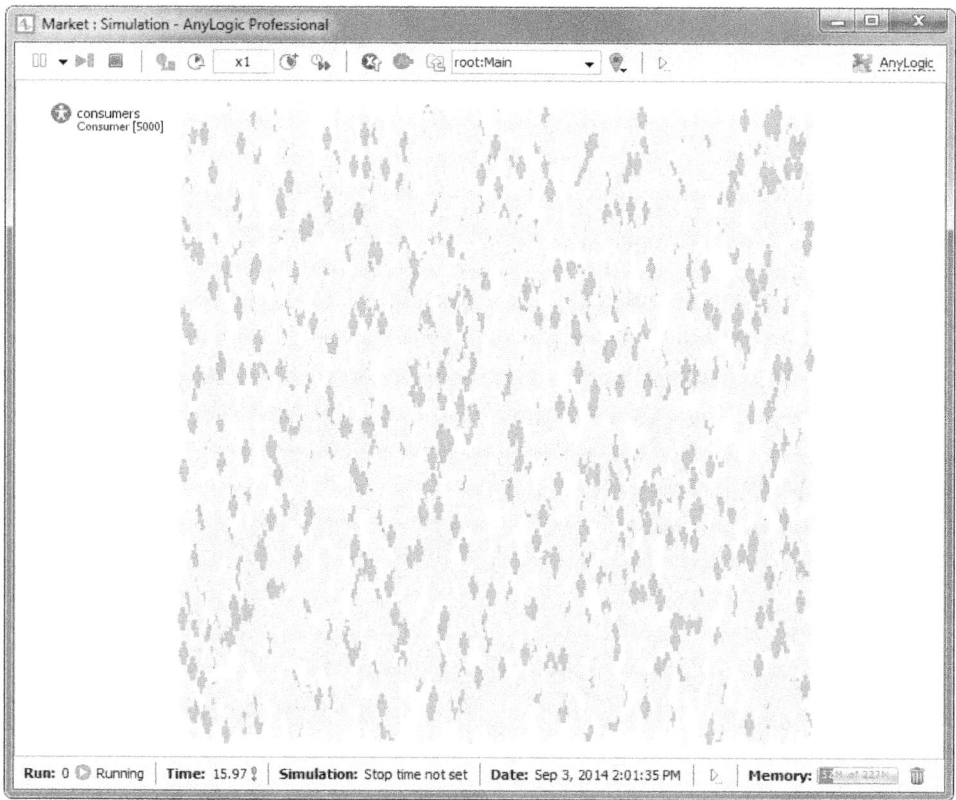

When advertising's effects cause an agent to purchase the product, the agent's state *User* becomes active, the state's **Entry action** is executed, and the agent animation shape's color changes to *yellowGreen*. As more people purchase the product, you'll see your model's agent animations gradually turn green.

Model execution modes

You can run an AnyLogic model in *real time* or *virtual time mode*.

- In *real time mode*, you set the relationship between your model's time and real time by selecting how many model time units are equal to one second of actual time. You'll typically use real time mode when you want your animation to appear lifelike.

- In *virtual time mode*, the model runs at its maximum speed. Virtual time mode is useful when you need to simulate your model for an extended period, and the model does not require you to define the relationship between model time units and seconds of astronomical time.

In *real time mode*, you can increase or decrease your model's execution speed by changing the model's *simulation speed scale*. For example, **x2** means the model runs twice as fast as the specified model speed.

The **Time scale** toolbar allows you to adjust the model's execution speed:

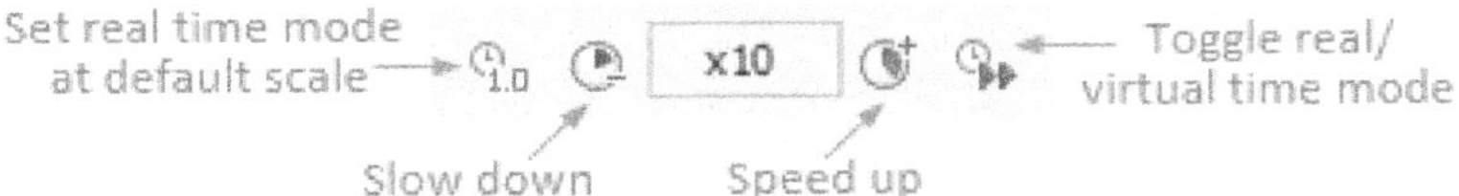

16. To adjust the model's execution speed, click the toolbar's **Slow down** or **Speed up** buttons. If you increase the speed to *10x* – you'll see the speed at which the population turns green also increase.

Phase 3. Adding a chart to visualize the model output

We want to know how many people have purchased our product at a given moment. With that in mind, we'll define functions that count our product's users and potential users, and then add a chart to show the dynamics.

1. First, define a function to count potential users. To add a new function that collects statistics for agents, open the diagram of the agent type *Main*, select the agent population *consumers*, and go to the **Statistics** properties section.

2. Click the ⊕ **Add statistics** button.

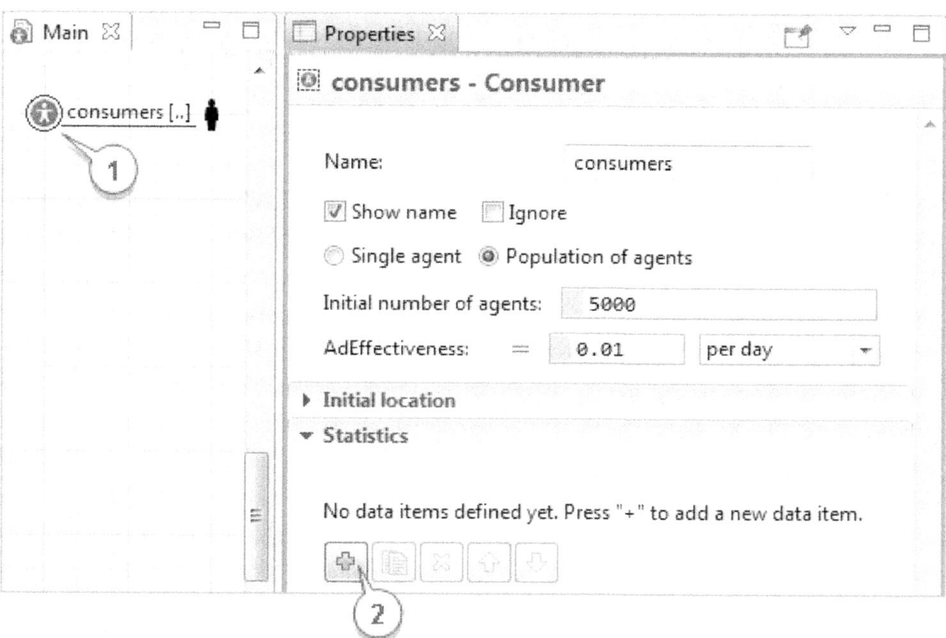

We need to determine how many agents are in the *PotentialUser* state.

3. Define the function of type **Count** with the **Name** *NPotential*. The statistics of type **count** iterates through a given population – in our case, the number of agents – to count those that meet the selected condition.

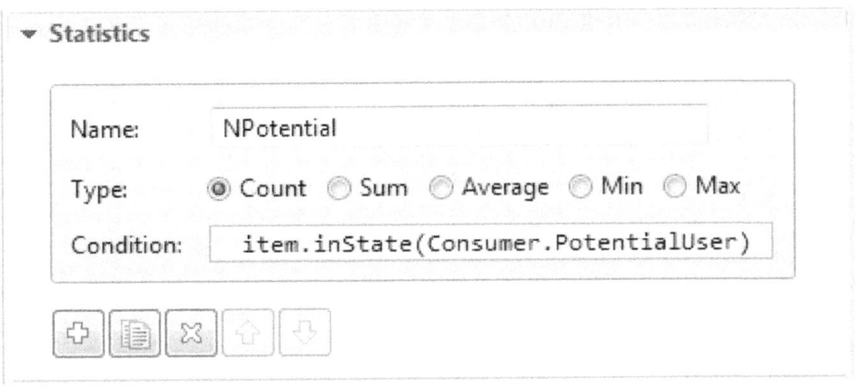

4. Enter *item.inState(Consumer.PotentialUser)* as the function **Condition**.

- *item* represents the agent being currently checked in the iteration.

- *inState()* is a function that checks whether the specified state of the statechart is active.

- *PotentialUser* is the name of the agent-defined state, which is why it needs the agent type prefix *Consumer*.

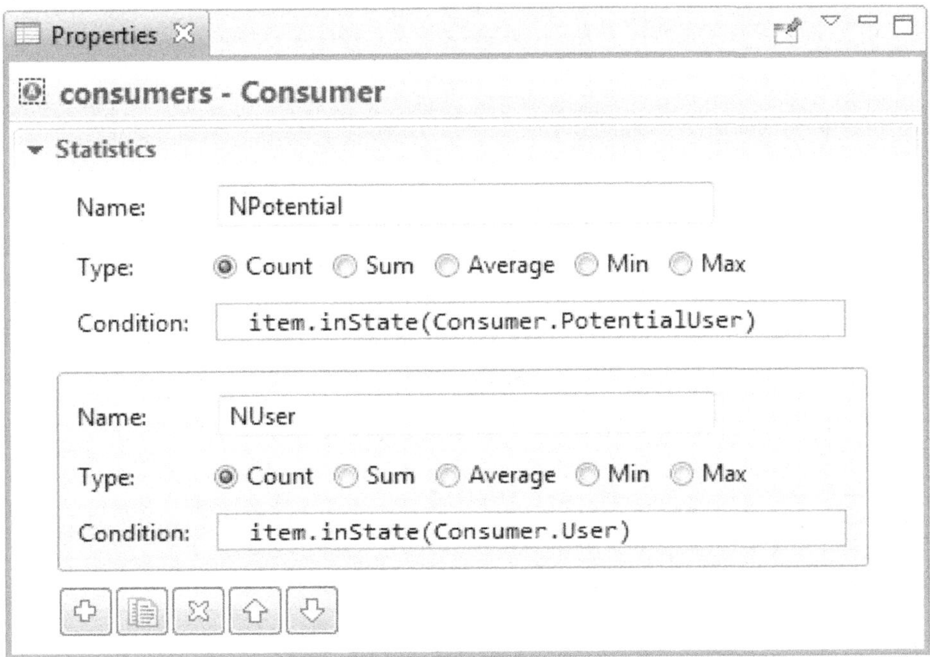

5. Define a second statistics function to calculate the number of product users. Name it *NUser* and let it count the number of agents, conforming the **Condition** *item.inState(Consumer.User)*. You can duplicate the other statistics function by clicking the 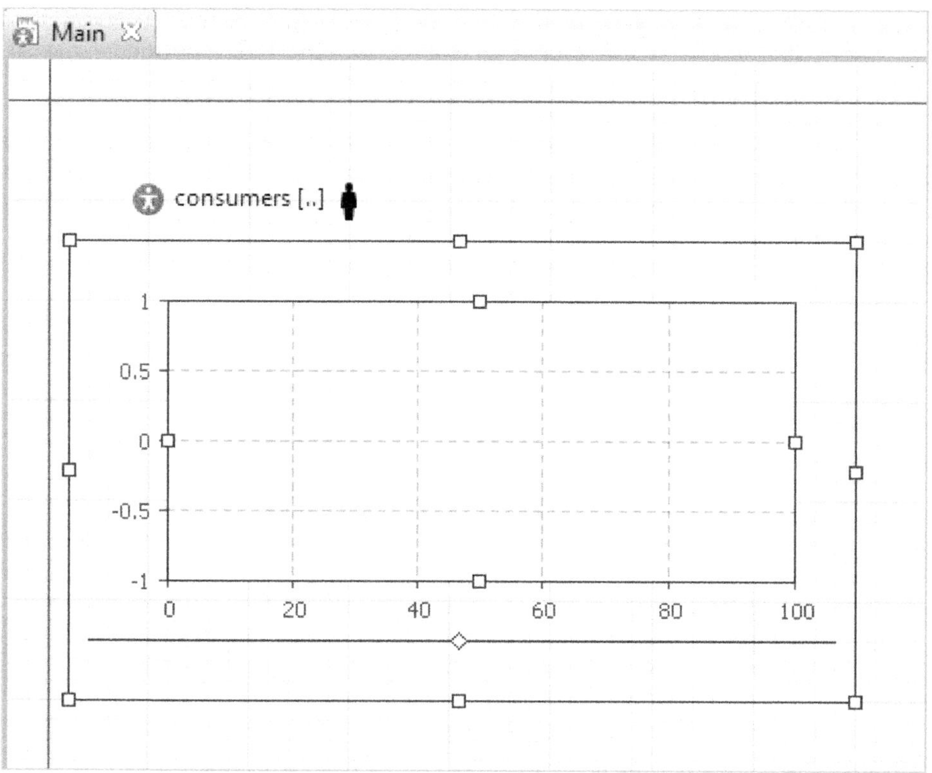 **Duplicate** button and changing its **Name** and the **Condition**.

Now, let's add a chart to show the statistics these functions collect and display the adoption process dynamics.

6. Open the **Analysis** palette, and drag the **Time Stack Chart** from the **Analysis** palette on to the *Main* diagram to create a chart that will display the dynamics of users and potential users. Increase the time stack chart as shown in the figure below:

Charts

AnyLogic provides several *charts* that you can use to visualize the data your model creates. You can find them on the **Analysis** palette in the **Charts** section.

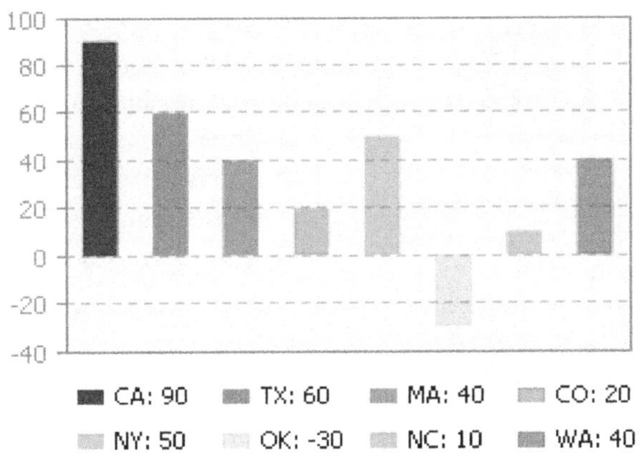

Bar Chart

Displays data items as bars aligned at one end. The bar sizes are proportional to the corresponding data item values.

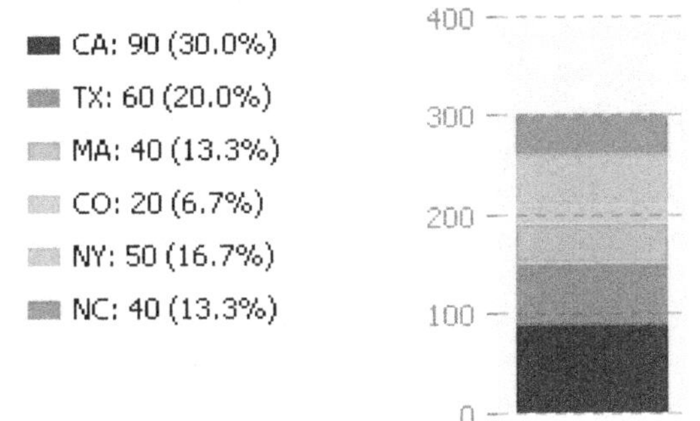

Stack Chart

Displays the contribution of several data items into a total as stacked bars. The bar sizes are proportional to the corresponding data item values.

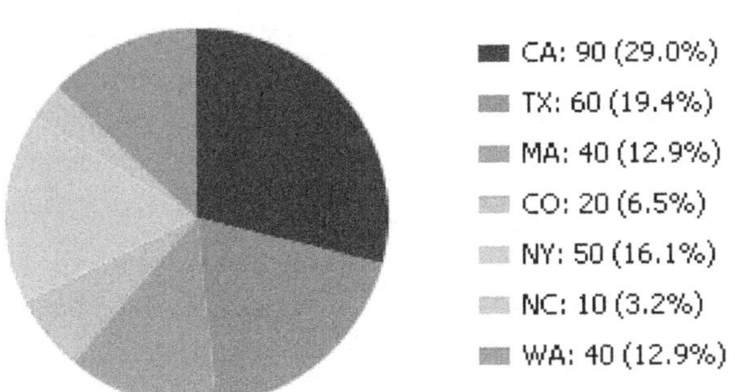

Pie Chart

Displays the contribution of several data items into a total as sectors of a circle. The sector arcs are proportional to the corresponding data item values.

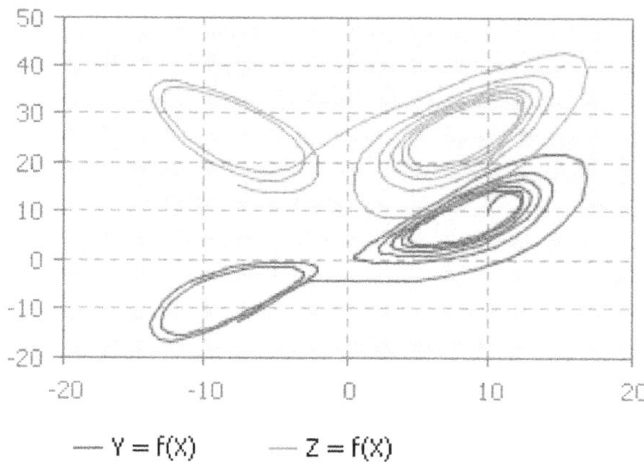

Plot

Plot plays a role of phase diagram. Each data set is a set of value pairs <x,y>. Plot displays Y-values of a data set plotted against corresponding X-values. X-values are mapped to X-axis, Y-values - to the Y-axis. Plot can display several data sets at the same time.

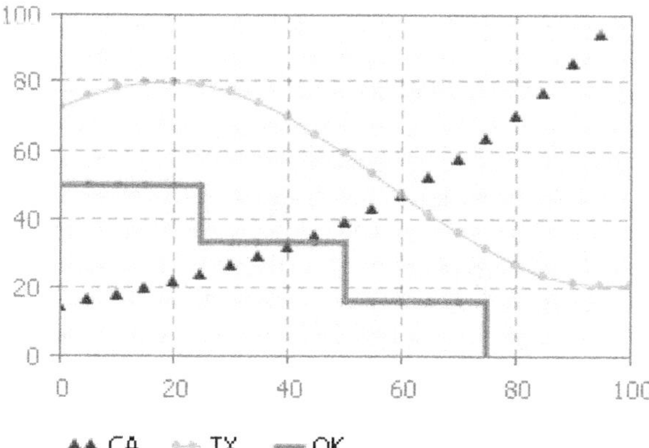

Time Plot

Displays the history of several data items during the latest time horizon. Depending on the interpolation type, the line between two data samples is interpolated linearly or keeps the previous value until the next one.

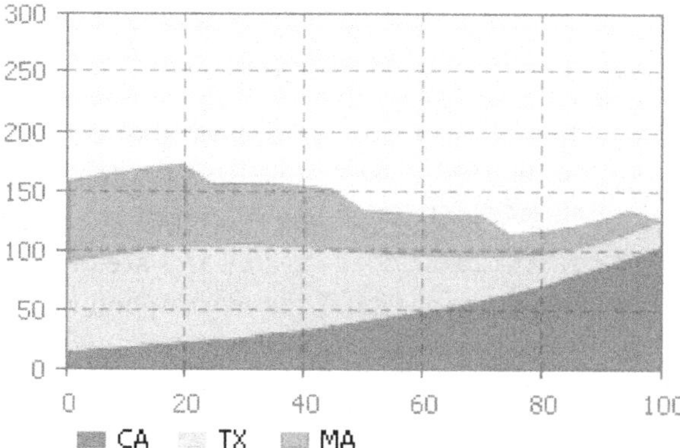

Time Stack Chart

Displays the history of contribution of a number of data items into a total during the latest time horizon as stacked areas. The values are continually stacked one on top of the next with the first added data item at the bottom.

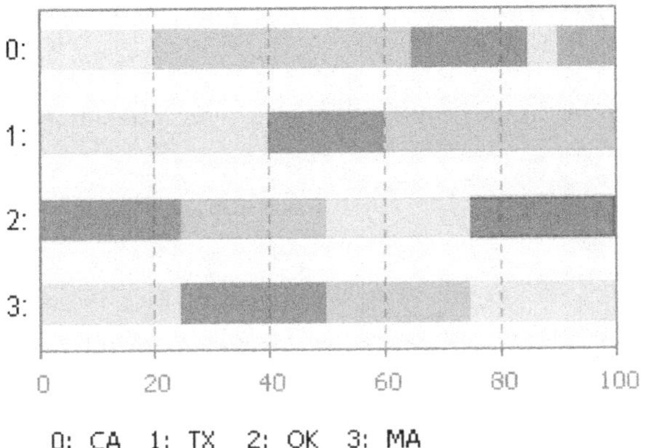

Time Color Chart

Displays the trend of a number of data sets during the latest time as bars of horizontal stripes of different colors (color depends on the data value). If a condition evaluates to true, the bar stripe's color will match the color you defined for this condition. Use the chart to visualize the change of agent state over time, e.g. busy / idle.

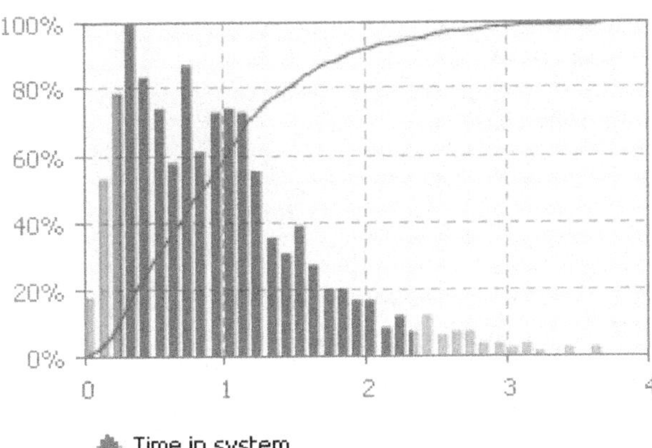

Histogram

Displays statistics collected by Histogram Data objects. The histograms are also scaled along the Y axis so the histogram's highest bar occupies the picture's full height. You can also opt to show the PDF bars, CDF line, and mean location.

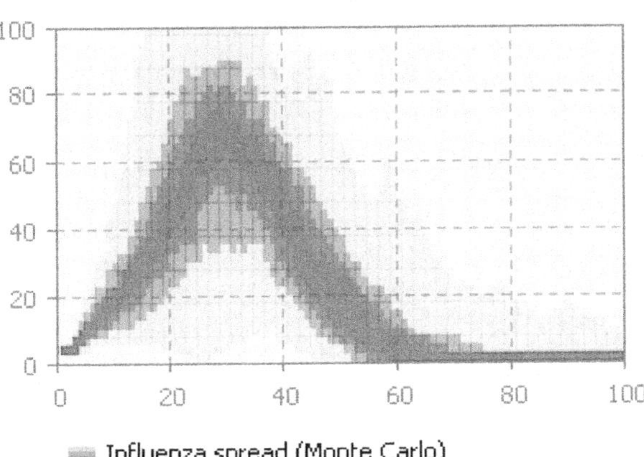

Histogram2D

Displays a collection of two-dimensional histograms. Each histogram is drawn as a number of rectangular color spots reflecting the PDF value or envelope at the corresponding (X,Y). The chart's X and Y axes are always scaled to fit all histograms.

Add two data items for the chart to display. Here we'll call our statistics functions *NUser* and *NPotential* we have defined for *consumers* population on the previous step.

7. Click **Add data item** to add the statistics you want to draw on the chart.

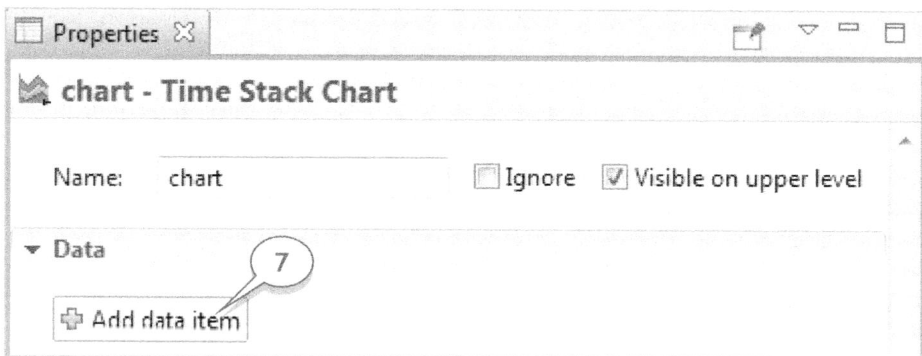

8. Modify the data item's properties:

   - **Title**: *Users* – the data item's title.

   - **Color**: *yellowGreen*

   - **Value**: *consumers.NUser()*

     Our agent population name is *consumers*, and *NUser()* is the statistics function that we defined for this population.

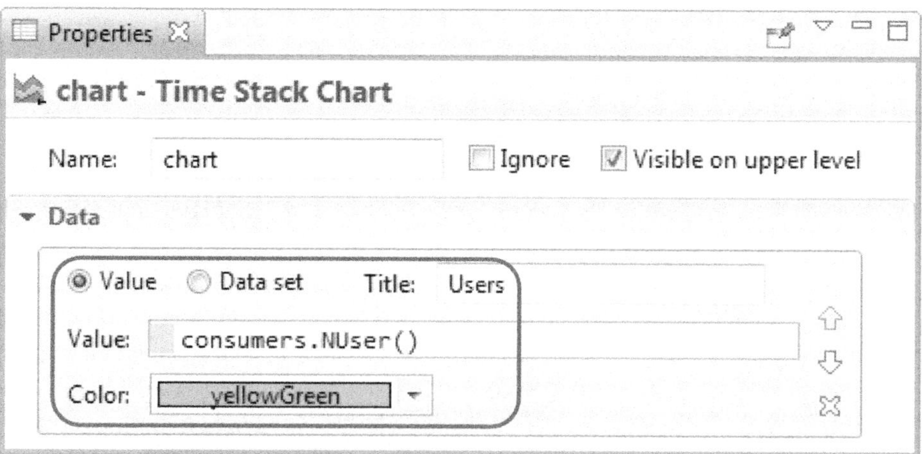

9. Add one more data item:

   - **Title**: *Potential users*

- **Color**: *lavender*

- **Value**: *consumers.NPotential()*

Tuning the chart's time scale

- Charts with history (time plot, time stack chart, time color chart) allow you to adjust the time scale.

- You configure the time chart's time range with the property **Time window**. Since time charts display only a limited number of data samples at a given moment, make sure you have an adequate number of samples for the selected time window.

- If you run your model and your chart resembles the figure below, you should increase the number of data samples the chart displays or decrease the chart's *time window*.

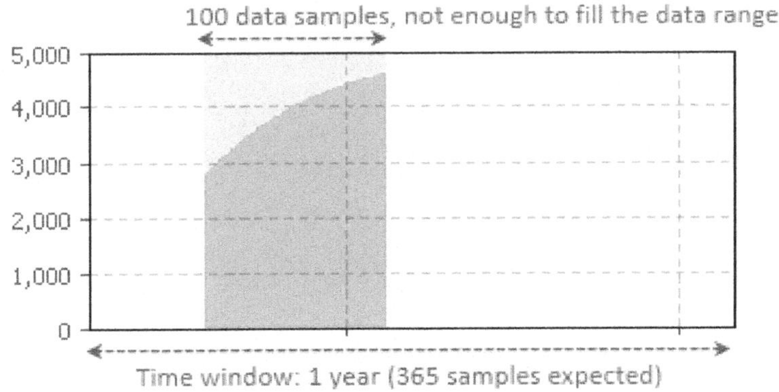

Since we want to show a one year range, we need to adjust the chart's settings.

10. Go to the **Scale** section and set **Time window** equal to *1 year*.

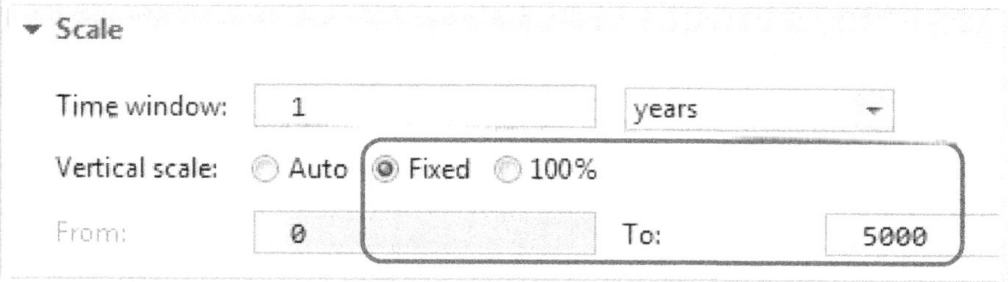

11. Since our chart will show statistics for *consumers* population and our model has 5,000 consumers, set the chart's **Vertical scale** to **Fixed**, and enter *5000* in the **To:** box.

12. Now that we've set the time window, change the maximum number of data samples that the chart displays by navigating to the section **Data update** and setting **Display up to** *365* **latest samples**. Since we'll add one data sample each day, 365 data samples is an ideal amount for a one year range.

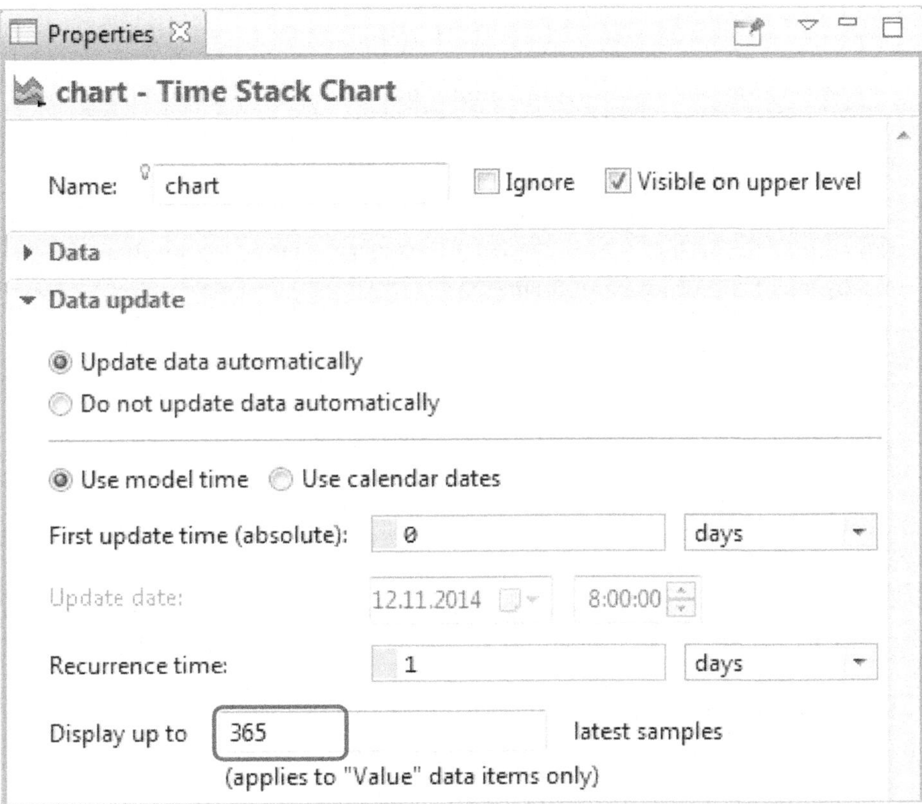

13. Go to the time stack chart's **Appearance** properties and set it to display **Model date (date only)** near the time axis.

Formatting timestamps in time chart labels

Charts with history can display model dates in time (x-) axis labels, and you can format the timestamps by choosing one of the suggested formats or using the custom format that best meets your needs.

Customize the timestamp format in the **Time axis format** property (located in the chart properties' **Appearance** section). The section below displays several examples of the timestamp formats:

Model date (date only)

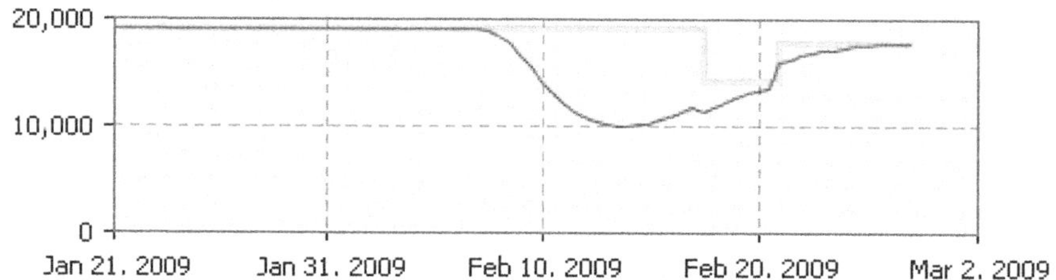

Model date (time only)

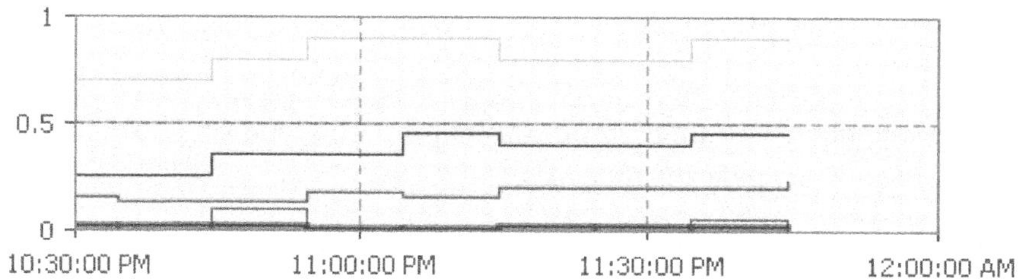

***Custom (HH:mm)* - Only hours and minutes are displayed**

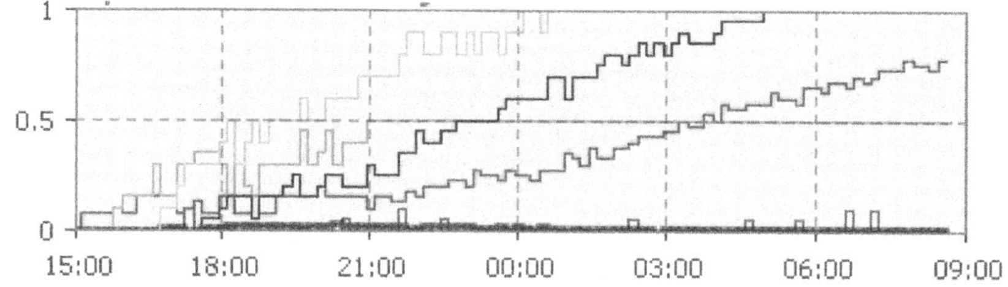

14. On the *Main* diagram, move the presentation of the *consumers* agent population to the right.

15. Run the model and use the time stack chart to review the process.

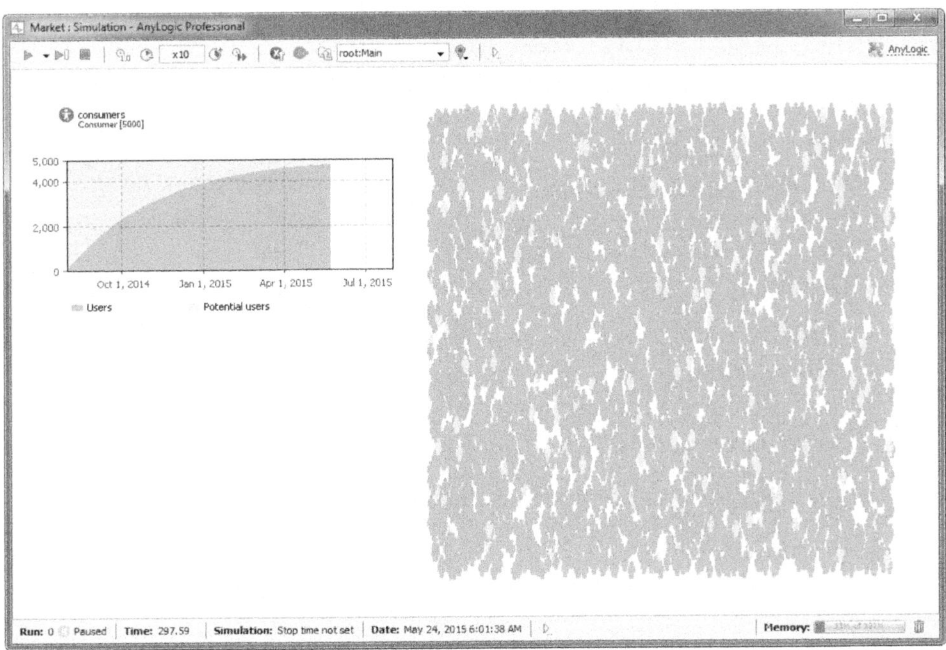

Phase 4. Adding word of mouth effect

In this phase, we'll model what's often called the word of mouth effect – the way people persuade others to purchase our product.

- Allow people to contact one another. In our model, a consumer contacts an average of one other person each day.

- Our product's current users may influence potential users during these meetings. We'll define the probability of a potential user buying the product as *AdoptionFraction=0.01*.

Let's develop the model's logic by adding two consumer parameters: *ContactRate* and *AdoptionFraction*.

1. In the **Projects** tree, open *Consumer* diagram by double-clicking *Consumer*.

2. Add a parameter to define a consumer's average daily contacts. Drag the **Parameter** ⟳ from the **Agent** ✪ palette on to the diagram.

3. Name the parameter *ContactRate*.

4. The rate is 1 contact per day, so type 1 as the parameter's **Default value**.

5. Add another parameter - *AdoptionFraction* - to define a person's influence on others, a number that we'll express as the percentage of people who will use the product after they come into contact with the consumer. Leave the default parameter's **Type:** *double*, and set the **Default value:** *0.01*.

The *Consumer* diagram should look like this:

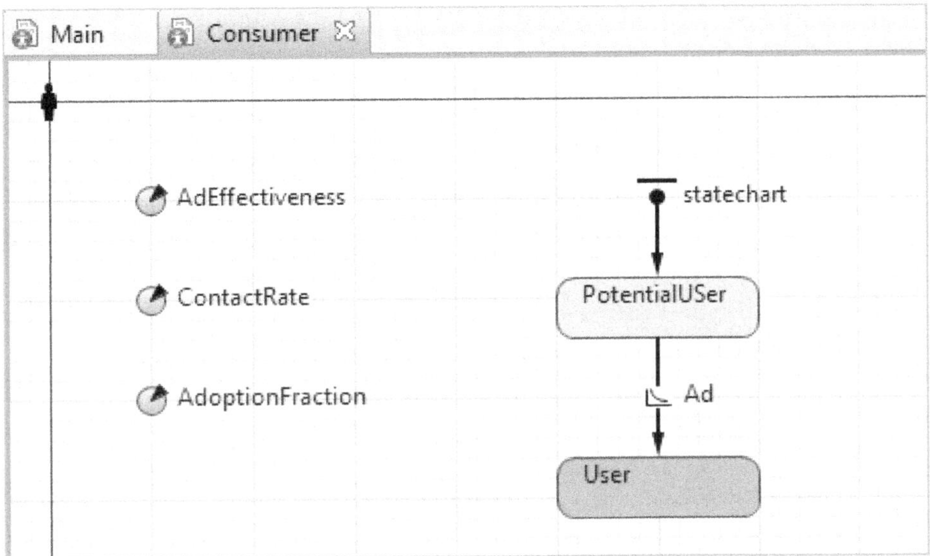

Now, we'll allow our agents to interact. This represents the word of mouth discussions that will convince a percentage of consumers to buy the product.

Agent interaction

AnyLogic supports a communication mechanism unique to agent based modeling: *message passing*.

- An agent can send a message to an individual agent or a group of agents.

- A message can be an object of any type or complexity, including a text string, an integer, a reference to an object, or a structure with multiple fields.

- To send the message to other agent, you use specific agent's function. The information below lists the most frequently used functions for sending messages from one agent to other(s):

  sendToAll(msg) – sends the message to all agents of the same population.

  sendToRandom(msg) – sends the message to one randomly chosen agent from the same population.

  send(msg, agent) – sends the message the given *agent* (you pass the reference to the agent-recipient as the function's second argument)

In our model, only users who are in the *User* state will send messages. The best way to define an activity that an agent performs while in a state – in other words, an activity they perform without exiting their current state – is to use an *internal transition*.

6. Open the *Consumer* diagram, and increase the *User* state to fit the internal transition we'll draw inside the state on the next step.

7. Draw an internal transition inside the *User* state. To draw a transition like the one shown below, drag the **Transition** ⟨ from the **Statechart** palette inside the state so the transition's start point lies on the state border. Afterward, you can move the transition end point to another point on the state border. To add a salient point, double-click the transition.

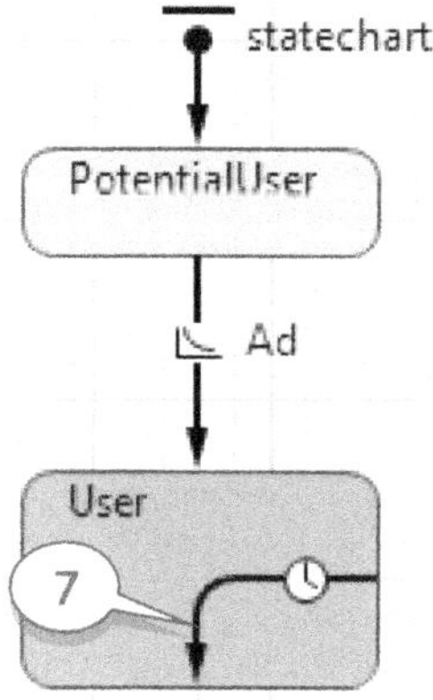

♦ **Internal and external transitions behave differently, so you must ensure your newly-created transition lies completely *inside* the state.**

Internal transitions

- An internal transition is a cyclic transition that lies inside a state. The transition's start and end points both lie on the state's border.

- Since an internal transition does not exit the enclosing state, it does not take the statechart out of this state. Neither the exit nor entry actions are executed when the transition occurs, and the current simple state in the state is not exited.

8. Modify the transition properties. This transition will occur with the specified **Rate** *ContactRate* (use code completion rather than typing the parameter's full name). Name the transition *Contact* and set it to show its name.

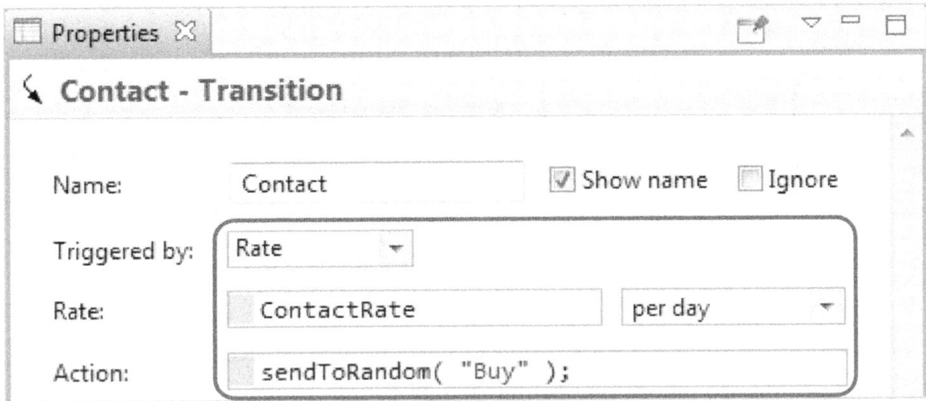

9. Specify the **Action** that will be executed on triggering this transition (use the code completion to write the code):

```
sendToRandom("Buy");
```

Since we want our product's users to speak to potential users, we'll set up a cyclic transition in the state *User.* Each time the transition takes place, the code `sendToRandom("Buy");` causes the consumer to randomly choose another agent and send them a *"Buy"* text message. If the agent who receives the message is a potential user (in other words, if the receiving agent is in the state *PotentialUser*), the receiving agent's state will change to *User.*

Let's add this transition now:

10. Draw another transition from *PotentialUser* to *User* state, and name it *WOM.* This transition will model purchases caused by word of mouth.

11. Modify the transition properties:

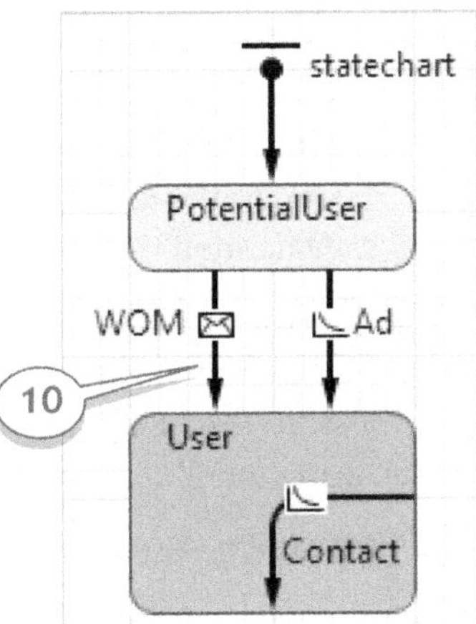

- In the **Triggered by** list, click **Message.**

- In the **Fire transition** area, select **On particular message.**

- In the **Message** field, type "Buy"

- Since we know not every contact is successful – in other words, a contact may not convince the potential user to buy our product – we'll use *AdoptionFraction* to make successful contacts less common. Specify the transition's **Guard:** `randomTrue(AdoptionFraction)`

Properties ⊠

↖ WOM - Transition

| Name: | WOM | ☑ Show name | ☐ Ignore |

Triggered by: Message ▾

Message type: String ▾

Fire transition: ○ Unconditionally
● On particular message
○ If expression is true

Message   `"Buy"`

Action:

Guard: `randomTrue(AdoptionFraction)`

Guards in transitions

- When a statechart enters a simple state, the triggers of all outgoing transitions are collected and the statechart begins to wait for any of them to occur.

- When a trigger event occurs, the guard of the corresponding transition is evaluated. If the guard is *true*, the transition may be taken (though alternative simultaneous events could reset the trigger). This algorithm of guard evaluation is called *"guards-after-triggers"*.

This is the last step in modeling word of mouth marketing. AnyLogic forwards the message from another agent to the statechart, and, if the statechart is in the state *PotentialUser*, it causes an immediate transition to the *User* state. If the statechart is in any other state, it will ignore the message.

12. In the **Projects** view, you may see an asterisk near the model item that shows your model has unsaved changes. On the toolbar, click 🖬 **Save** to save your model.

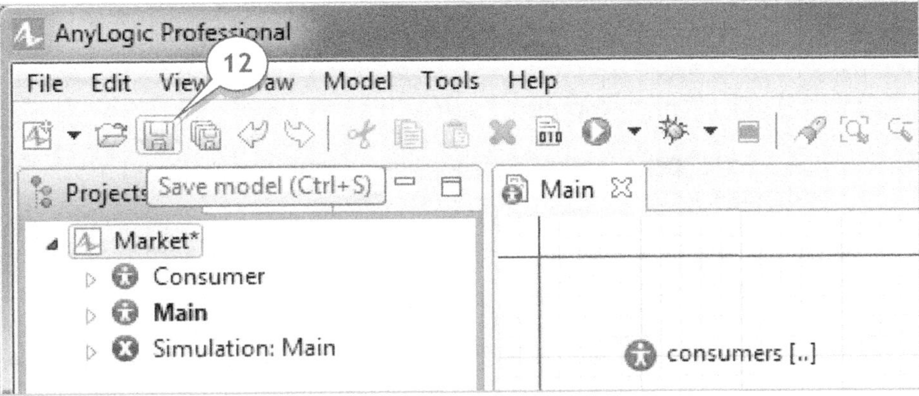

13. Run the model.

The market saturation should occur more quickly, and the chart shows the well-known S-shaped product adoption curve.

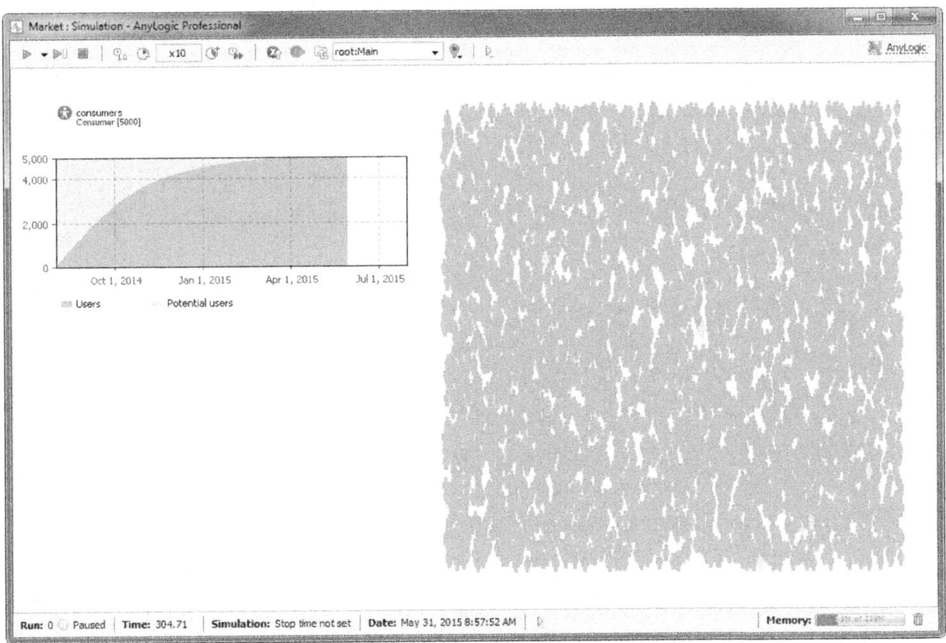

Phase 5. Considering product discards

In this phase, we'll model product discards.

- Let's assume the average duration of our product's active use is six months.

- Once a user discards or consumes the product, they'll need a replacement. We'll model repeat purchase behavior by assuming adopters become potential adopters when they discard or consume their first units (in other words, when the *User* reverts to the *PotentialUser* state).

1. Open the *Consumer* diagram and add a *DiscardTime* parameter.

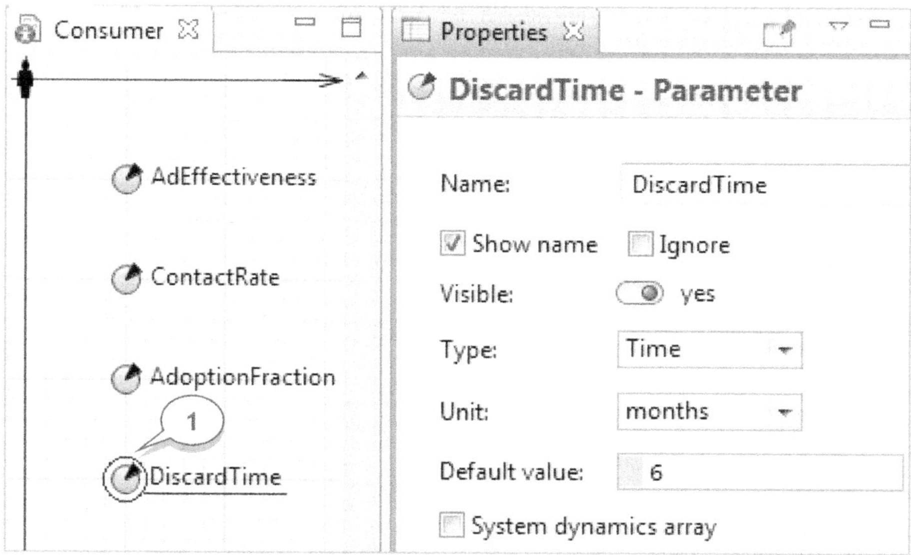

2. This parameter will define our product's lifespan. Choose **Time** as the parameter's **Type**, click **months** in the **Unit** list, and type *6* as the **Default value**.

3. Draw a transition from *User* to *PotentialUser* state to model product discards. To draw a transition with salient points like those shown in the figure, double-click the ↖ **Transition** element in the **Statechart** palette (this should change the element's icon in the palette to 🖉), click the transition's source state *User*, click at the salient point places, and click the target state *PotentialUser*.

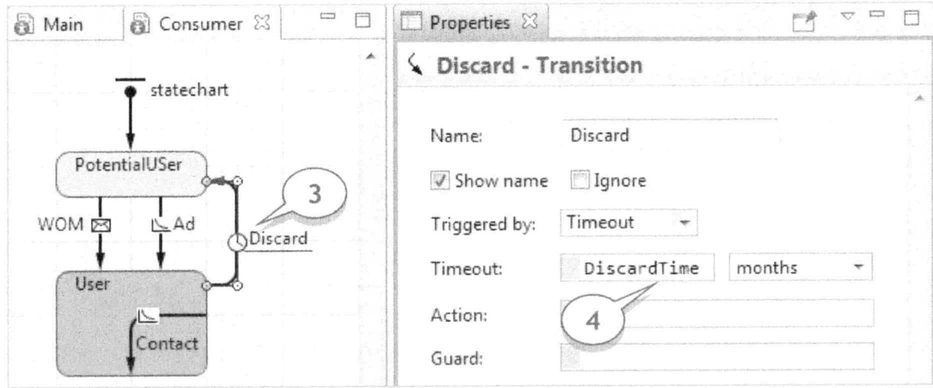

4. Name the transition *Discard* and set it to be triggered by a constant timeout *DiscardTime*. In the list to the right, click **months**.

♦ **AnyLogic uses red highlights to draw your attention to transitions (as in the lower left figure) where the end point is not connected to the state. To locate the error, select the transition and the connected points will be highlighted in cyan (see the right figure, connection to *PotentialAdopter*). If AnyLogic does not highlight the transition's start point at *User*, you should manually move this point on to the state to establish the connection and fix the error.**

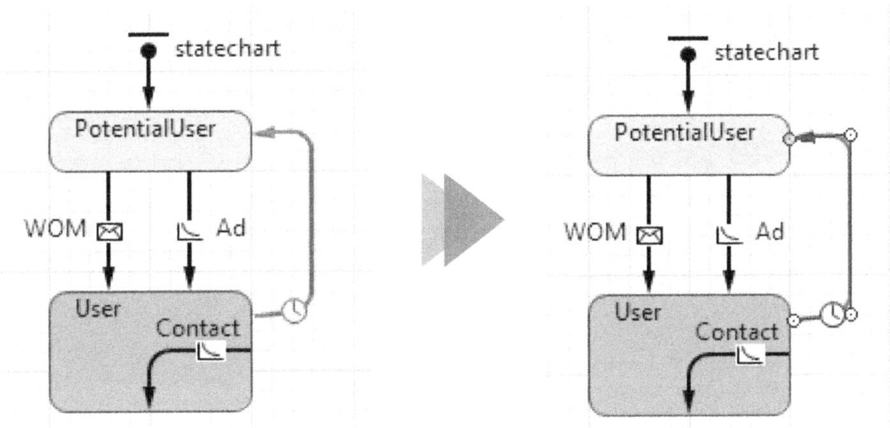

Fixing mistyping errors

A misnamed model element is a common error. AnyLogic's names are case-sensitive, which means typing *Discardtime* (instead of *DiscardTime*) in a model element's property will cause the following error:

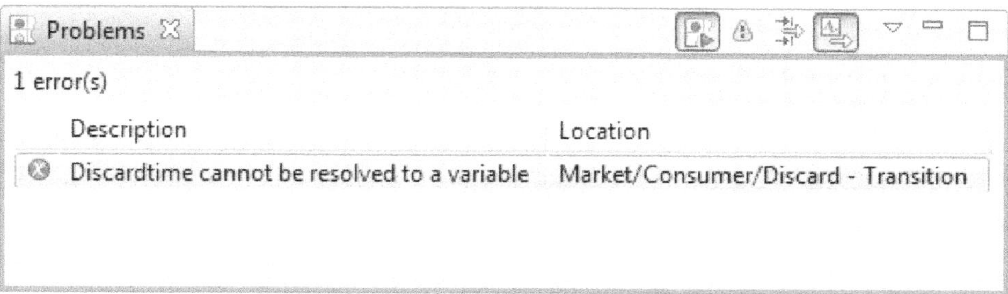

To fix the error, double-click it in the **Problems** view. If the error is graphical, AnyLogic will highlight the element that caused the error in the graphical editor. If the error is in an element's property, AnyLogic will open the element's properties and display the field where the problem occurred.

Our work to model product discards is complete, and any discards will generate an immediate need to purchase a replacement.

5. Run the model and watch how discards affect adoption dynamics. Even after our product saturates the market, you'll notice occasional product discards.

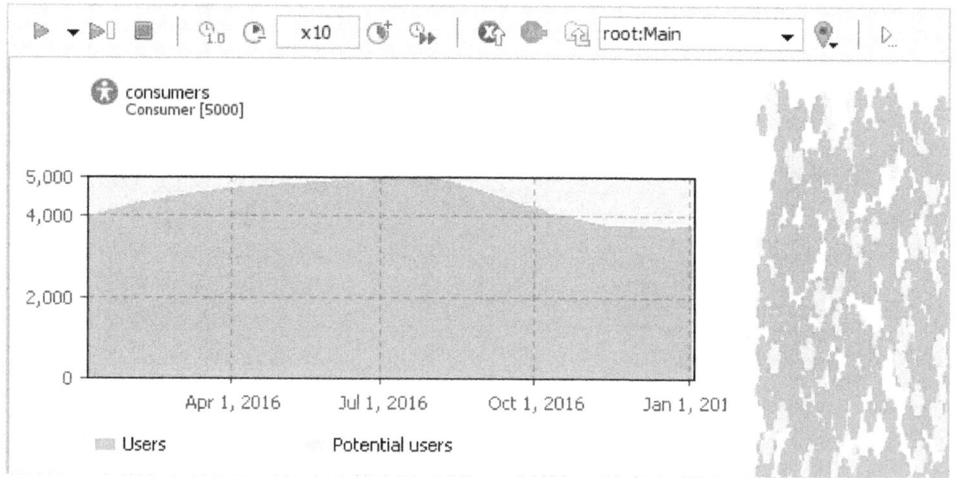

Phase 6. Considering delivery time

Our model assumes the product is always available and the transition from *PotentialUser* to *User* is unconditional and immediate. Now, we'll improve the model by adding a state to the statechart that reflects the amount of time between an agent's decision to purchase the product and the time they receive it.

1. Prepare a place for another state between *PotentialUser* and *User* by moving the *User* state toward the bottom of the screen.

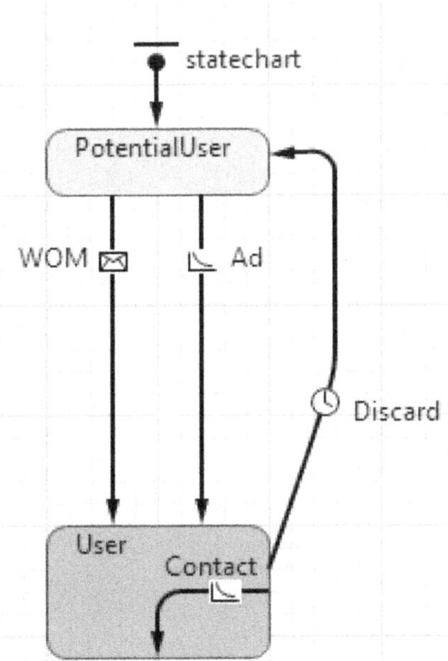

2. Disconnect the *User* state from the transitions.

    Select the *WOM* and *Ad* transitions, move their end points toward the top of the screen, and disconnect the *Discard* transition from *PotentialUser*. Afterward, you'll notice the disconnected transitions are drawn in red.

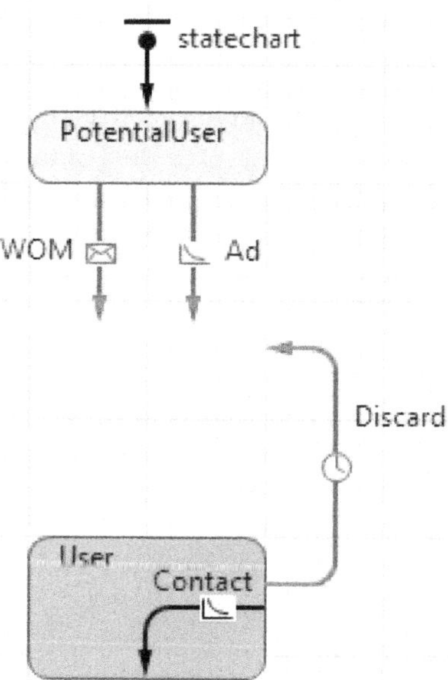

3. Add another **State** ⚪ from the **Statechart** palette to the middle of the consumer's statechart and name it *WantsToBuy*. Consumers in this state have decided to purchase the product, but they have not done so.

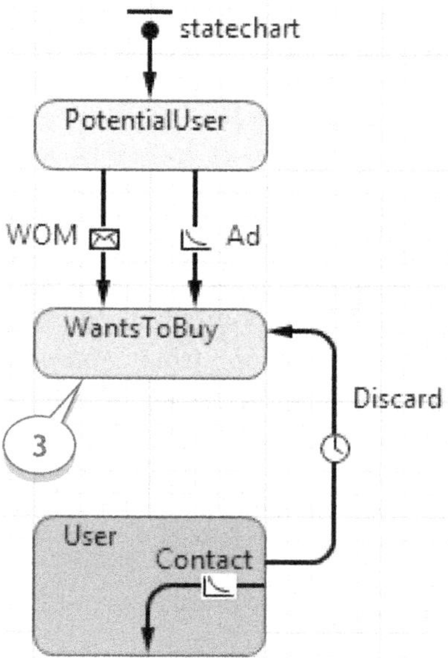

4. Reconnect transitions to the middle state: the *WOM*, *Ad*, and *Discard* transitions should now end in the *WantsToBuy* state.

5. Modify *WantsToBuy* similar to other states:
   Fill color: *gold*
   Entry action: *shapeBody.setFillColor(gold)*

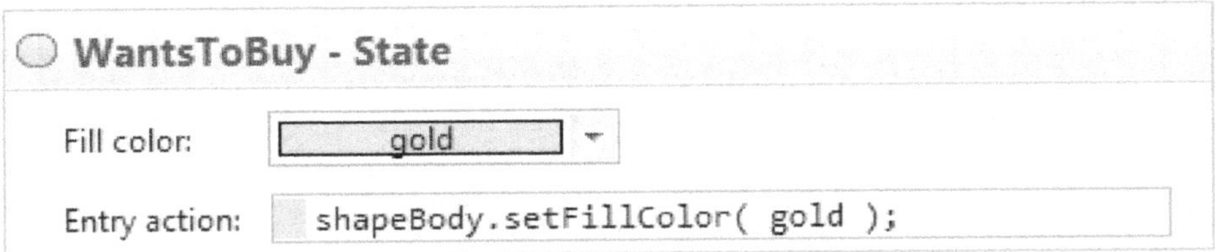

6. Add a transition from *WantsToBuy* to *User* state to model the product shipment and name it *Purchase*.

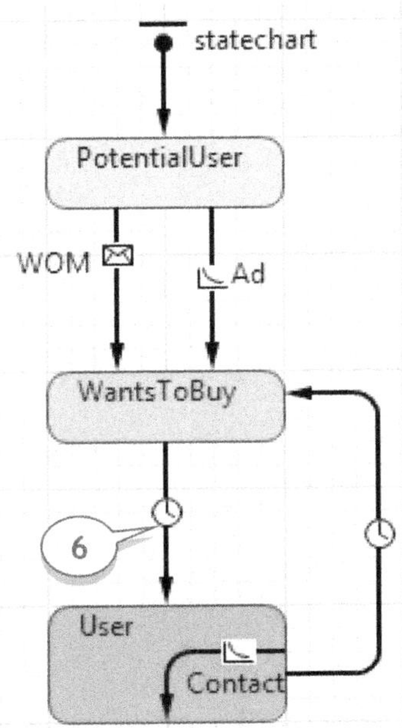

7. Let's assume it typically takes a user two days to get the product. This means once the consumer's statechart enters the state *WantsToBuy*, it will proceed to the state *User* with a two-day delay. With this in mind, set 2 days timeout for the *Purchase* transition:

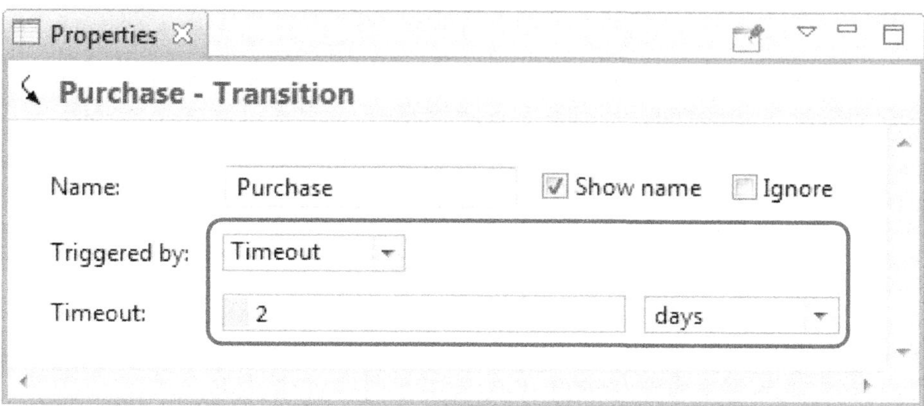

8. Define one more statistics function to count the product's market-driven demand. In the editor of *Main*, click the *consumers*, go to the **Statistics** properties section, and add a statistics item: *NWantToBuy* with condition `item.inState(Consumer.WantsToBuy)`

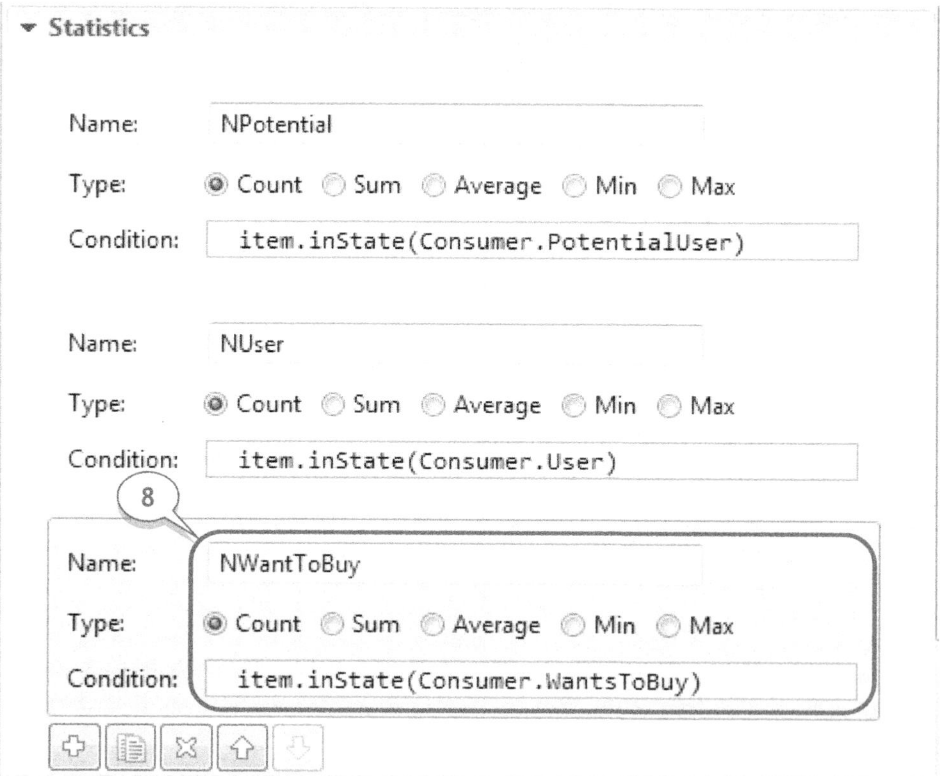

9. On *Main*, select the time stack chart, and add another data item to be displayed with the chart: *consumers.NWantToBuy()* with the title *Want to buy* and color *gold*.

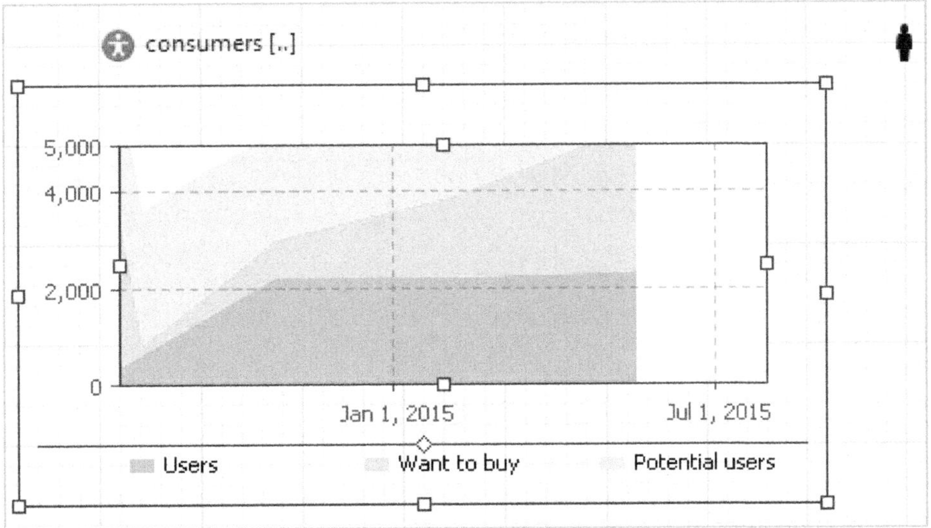

10. Make the newly-defined data item second in the list by selecting the item's section and clicking the "up" button .

11. Run the model, and you'll notice AnyLogic displays the number of consumers who are waiting for the product in yellow.

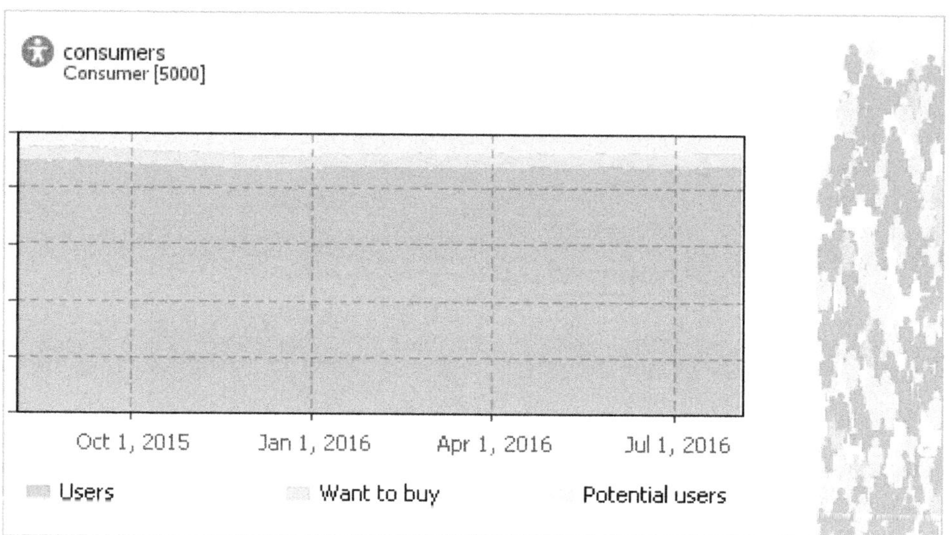
consumers
Consumer [5000]

Oct 1, 2015   Jan 1, 2016   Apr 1, 2016   Jul 1, 2016

Users   Want to buy   Potential users

Phase 7. Simulating consumer impatience

Our model needs to address the varying amounts of time that consumers are willing to wait for their product's delivery. If the delivery time exceeds the time a consumer is willing to wait, the consumer will reconsider their decision and return to being a potential user rather than one who wants to buy.

Let's start by defining two parameters in *Main*: maximum product delivery time (25 days) and the maximum consumer's waiting time (7 days).

1. Open the *Main* agent type diagram.

2. Since we don't want the model window to display the model's parameters at runtime, we can place them outside the model window's default display area.

   On *Main*, the model window is depicted with a blue rectangular frame. Elements inside the frame will be visible at the model runtime, but you can hide them by moving the graphical diagram's canvas slightly to the right and placing two parameters as shown in the figure below.

♦ **To move the graphical diagram's canvas, hold down the right mouse button as you move the mouse.**

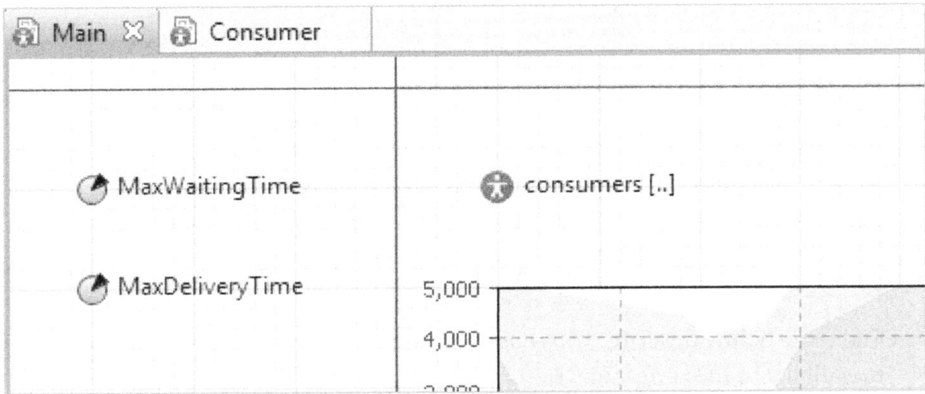

3. Configure the parameters. *MaxWaitingTime* defines the maximum time a consumer will wait for the product (in this case, seven days).

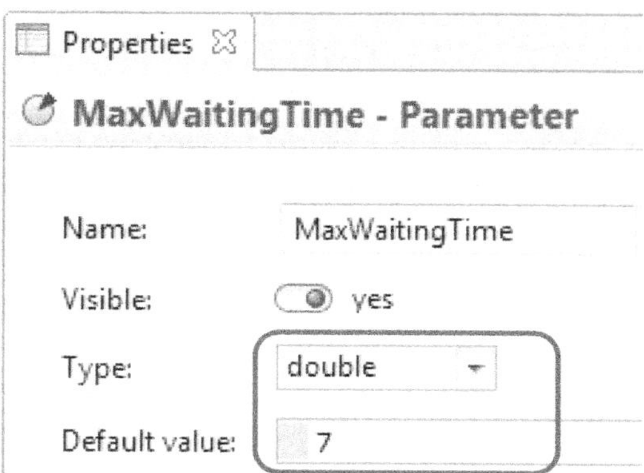

4. Set the other parameter, *MaxDeliveryTime* to 25 days to reflect our assumption it may take up to 25 days to deliver a product.

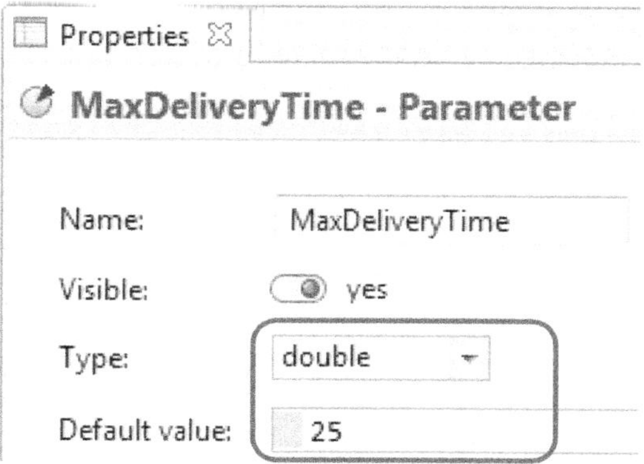

We assume it takes between one and 25 days – with an average of two days – to deliver the product. With that in mind, let's change the delivery time from a fixed two day delivery period to the stochastic expression that describes this pattern.

Probability distribution functions

The table below describes AnyLogic's frequently used distributions, but you'll find the full list in the program's Help section.

Probability distribution	Primary use
Uniform uniform(min, max)	You know the minimum and the maximum values but lack any knowledge about how the remaining values are distributed between them. In other words, you don't know if any values are more frequent than others and assume any location between min and max has the same chance of receiving a value.
Triangular triangular(min, mode, max)	You know the minimum and the maximum, and you have a guess about the most likely (modal) value. A triangular distribution is often used for service times or the duration of operations where you don't have enough samples to build a meaningful distribution shape.
Exponential exponential(lambda, min)	Describes the times between events in a Poisson process, i.e. when events occur independently at a constant average rate. Used as the inter-arrival time for input streams of customers, parts, calls, orders, transactions or failures in process models. In agent based models, an exponential distribution is used as timeout for rate transitions that model independent events in agents that are known to occur at a certain global average rate.

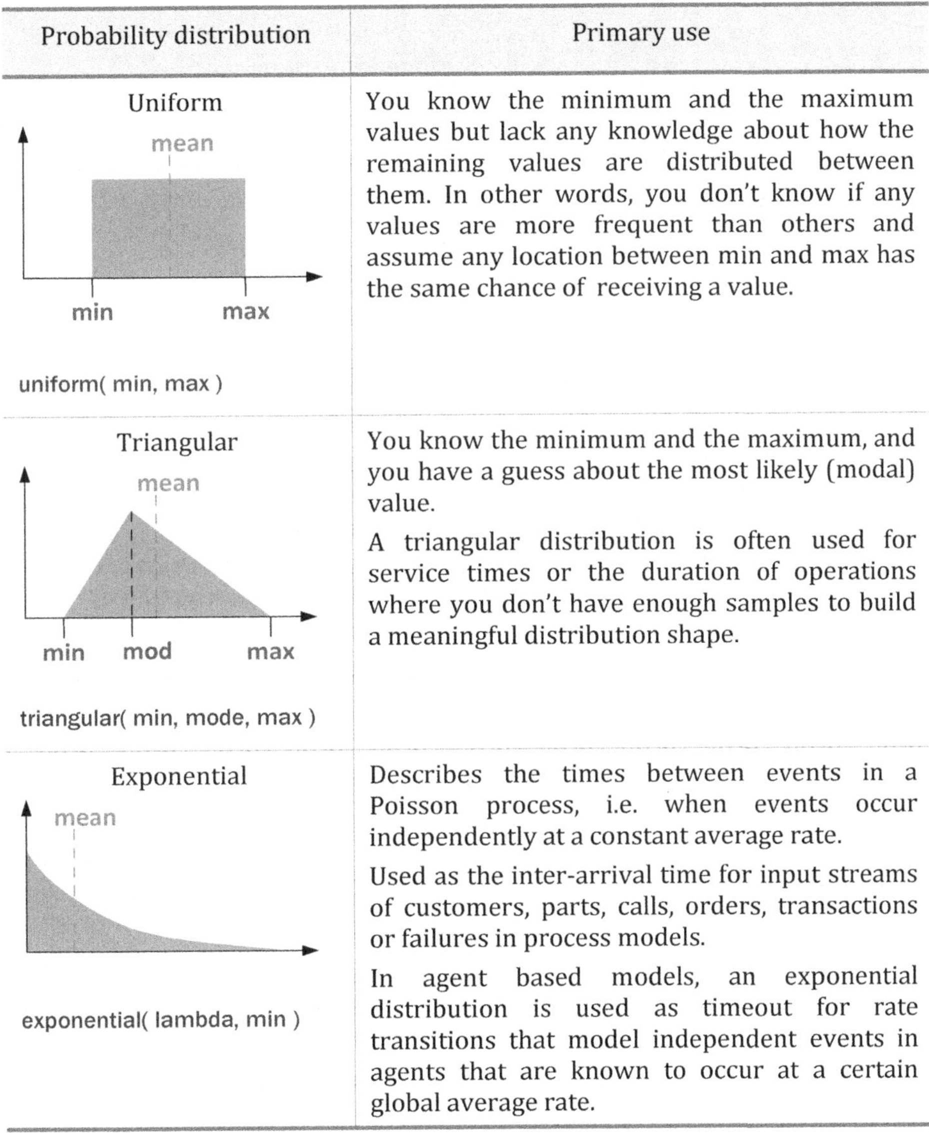

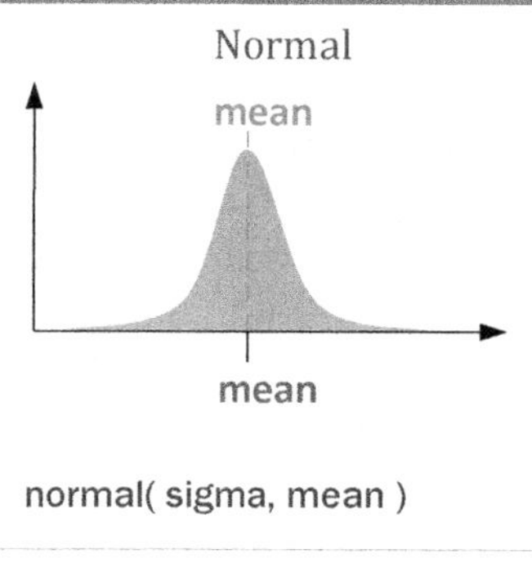 normal(sigma, mean)	Gives a good description of data that tend to cluster around the mean. Note that the normal distribution is unbounded on both sides, so if you wish to impose limits (e.g. to avoid negative values) you have to use its truncated form or use other distributions such as Lognormal, Weibull, Gamma, or Beta.
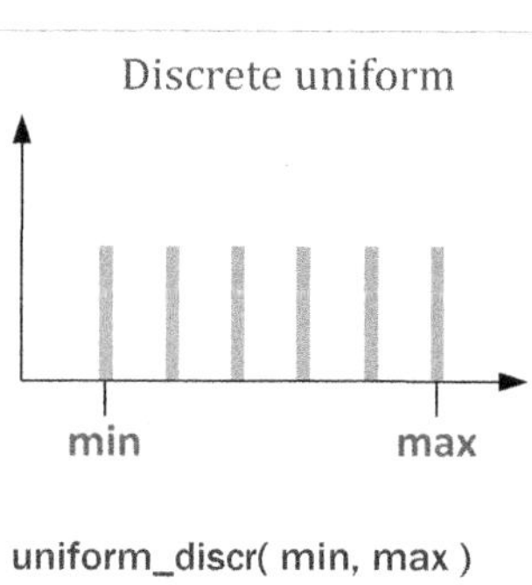 uniform_discr(min, max)	Used to model a finite number of outcomes that are equally probable, or when you have no knowledge about which outcomes are more likely to occur. Note that both the minimum and maximum values are included in the set of possible results, so a call of *uniform_discr(3, 7)* may return 3, 4, 5, 6, or 7. (Borshchev, 2013)

As you can see from the table, a triangular probability distribution is the easiest way to define the required time pattern.

5. Open the *Consumer* diagram and select the *Purchase* transition. We want to change the transition's timeout expression, and we'll do that by using a wizard to choose the distribution function and insert the function's name in the property. To substitute the existing value, use your mouse to select the existing **Timeout** expression.

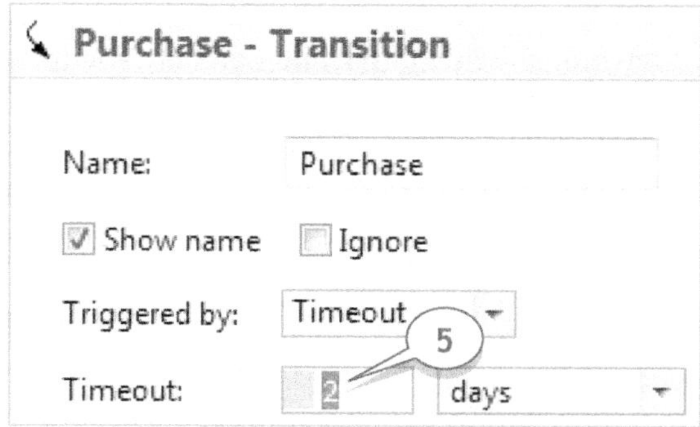

6. Click the **Choose Probability Distribution...** toolbar button.

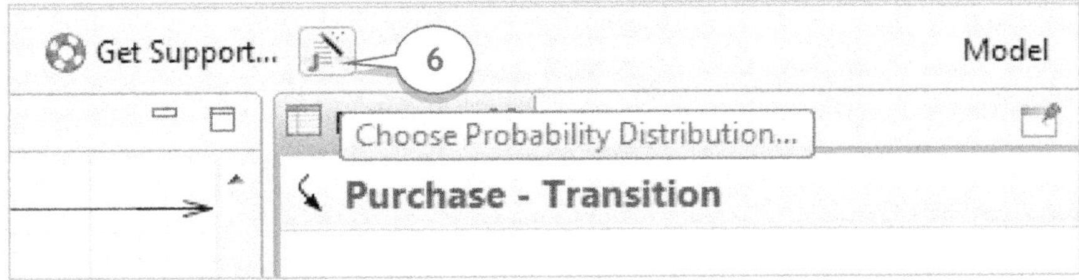

7. You'll see the **Choose Probability Distribution...** dialog box.

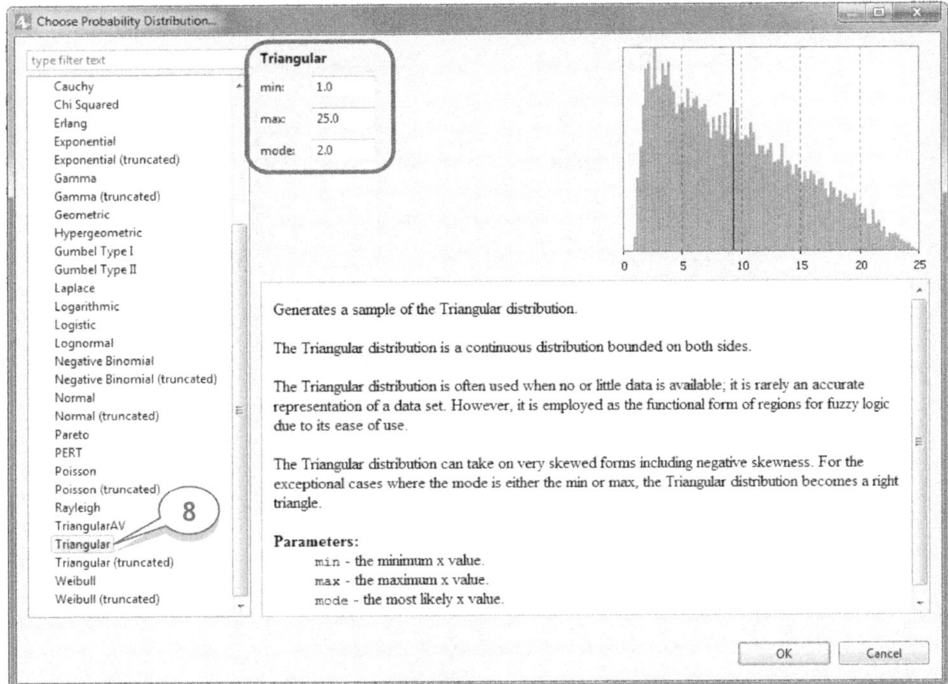

8. The **Choose Probability Description** screen allows you to view the list of supported distributions, and you can click any name in the list to view the distribution's description. Choose *triangular* in the list. Set **min**, **max** and **mode** parameters equal to 1, 25, 2 respectively. In the upper right, you'll see PDF instantly built for the distribution with the specified parameters. Click **OK** when finished.

9. You'll see the expression *triangular(1, 25, 2)* automatically inserted as the timeout value. Let's modify the line to *triangular(1, main.MaxDeliveryTime, 2)*

Here *main* is how we access the *Main* agent from the consumer agent.

10. Draw the last transition *CantWait* that goes from *WantsToBuy* to *PotentialUser* state. This transition will model how a consumer's impatience causes them to change their purchase decision, and the *Consumer* diagram will look like this:

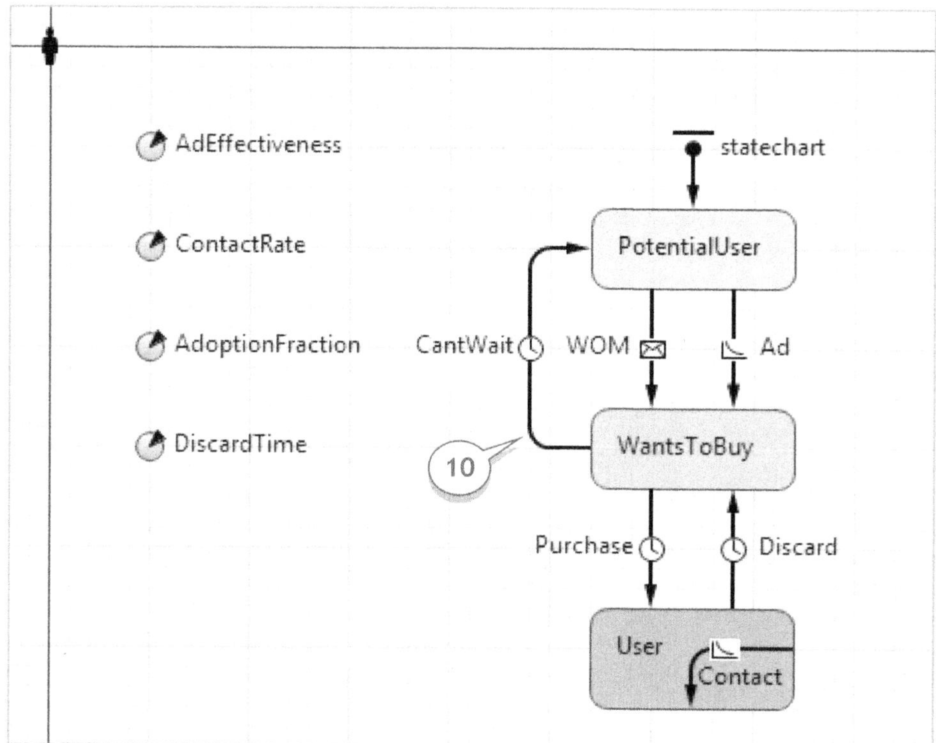

11. Modify the transition properties so it is triggered by **Timeout** which equals *triangularAV(main.MaxWaitingTime, 0.15)* **days**

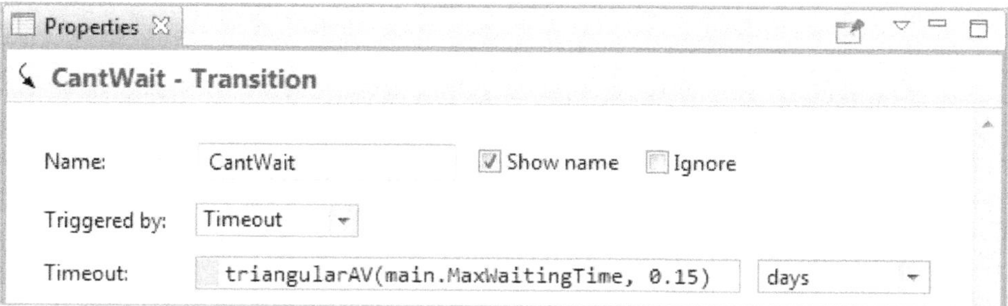

Rather than setting the maximum waiting time equal to constant *MaxWaitingTime*, we assume it follows a triangular distribution with an average of one week and a possible variation to up to 15 percent.

We could easily define maximum waiting time and maximum delivery time as constant parameters, but we want to vary these numbers dynamically and see how these changes affect the system's behavior. One way we can add interactivity to our model is by adding controls and linking them to the model parameters.

Controls

AnyLogic's *controls* may help you add interactivity to your model. You can use them to set up parameters before the model execution and change the model on-the-fly. The control may run code or make changes to the model's parameters.

You can also associate an arbitrary action such as calling a function, scheduling an event, sending a message, or stopping the model with a control. The action is executed each time the user touches the control. The control's value is typically available as *value* in the control's **Action** code field and also is returned by the control's *getValue()* function.

The table below briefly describes each control.

Control	Description
Button Stop the agent	Enables the user to interactively influence the model. You can define a specific action (in the button's **Action** property) the model will perform every time the user clicks the button at the model runtime.
Check Box Show density map	Control that can be selected or deselected, and which displays its state to the user. Check boxes are often used to change values of *boolean* variables and parameters.
Edit Box 36.6	A text control that allows the user to type a small amount of text. You can link this control to a variable or a parameter of type *String*, *double* or *int*. In this case, when the user changes the content of the edit box, the linked variable/parameter immediately receives this content as its value.

Radio Buttons ○ choice 1 ○ choice 2 ○ choice 3	Groups of buttons in which only one button at a time can be selected. You can link this control to a variable or a parameter of type *int*. In this case when the user chooses another option from the group of buttons, the linked variable/parameter immediately gets an index of this option as its value. The first button defined in the **Radio Buttons** table has index 0, the second has index 1, and so forth.
Slider 0 34 100	Lets the user graphically select a numeric value within a bounded interval by sliding a knob. Commonly used for modifying values of numeric variables and parameters at the model runtime. If it's hard to set precise *double* values, you can use text input in edit boxes instead of sliders.

AnyLogic Professional also supports four other controls:

- **Combo Box**
- **List Box**
- **File Chooser**
- **Progress Bar**

We'll add a slider control that will let us select a numeric value within a bounded interval. Sliders are often used to modify values of numeric variables and parameters.

12. Go back to *Main* diagram. Open the **Controls** palette and drag two **Sliders** on to the diagram below the chart. We'll eventually link the sliders to our two parameters.

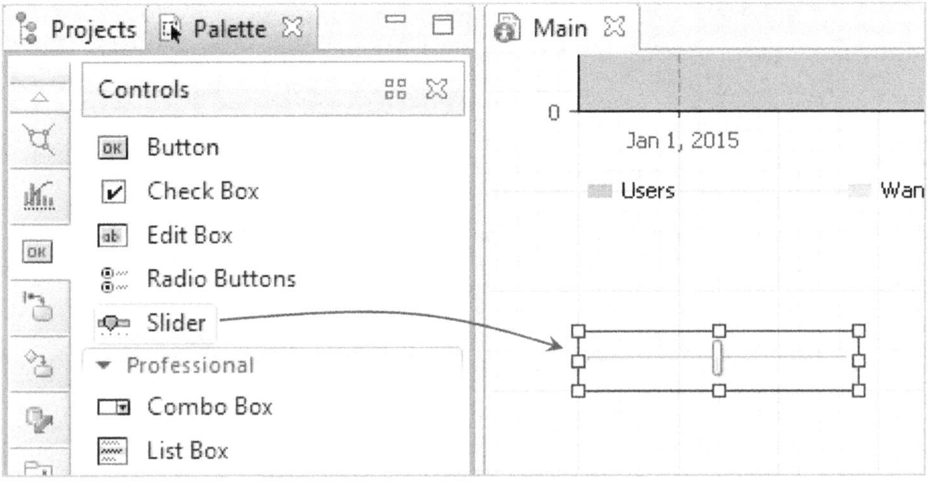

13. Modify the slider's properties:

- Select the checkbox **Link to** and select the parameter *MaxWaitingTime* to the right.

- Set the slider's **Minimum** and **Maximum values**. The parameter value can vary within the range you define here, and we'll set 2 as **Minimum** and 15 as **Maximum value**.

- Finally, click the **Add labels…** button to display the slider's minimum, maximum, and current values at runtime (the *min*, *value*, and *max* text shapes will appear beneath the slider).

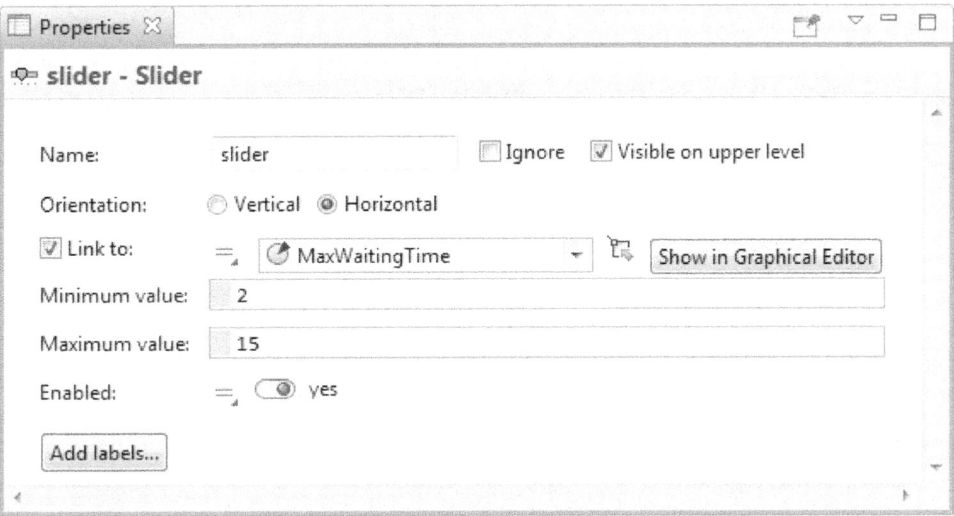

14. Add another slider below and configure it as follows:

slider1 - Slider

Name:	slider1 ☐ Ignore
Orientation:	○ Vertical ● Horizontal
☑ Link to:	MaxDeliveryTime
Minimum value:	5
Maximum value:	25

Some controls have built-in labels, but you should use the **Text** shape to manually create them for the sliders.

15. Open the **Presentation** palette, drag two **Text** *Aa* shapes on to the diagram, and place them above the sliders. Let's configure the titles of these controls.

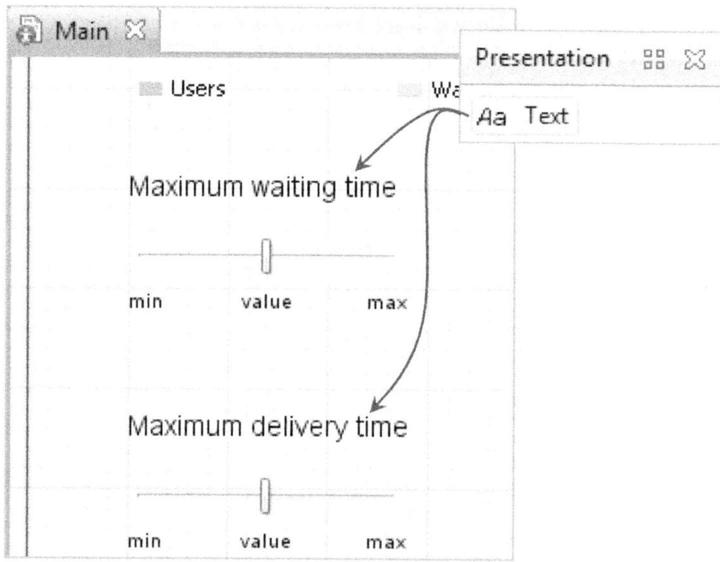

16. In the properties view, in the **Text** section, enter the text that the model will display. Using text shapes, name one slider *Maximum waiting time* and the other slider *Maximum delivery time*.

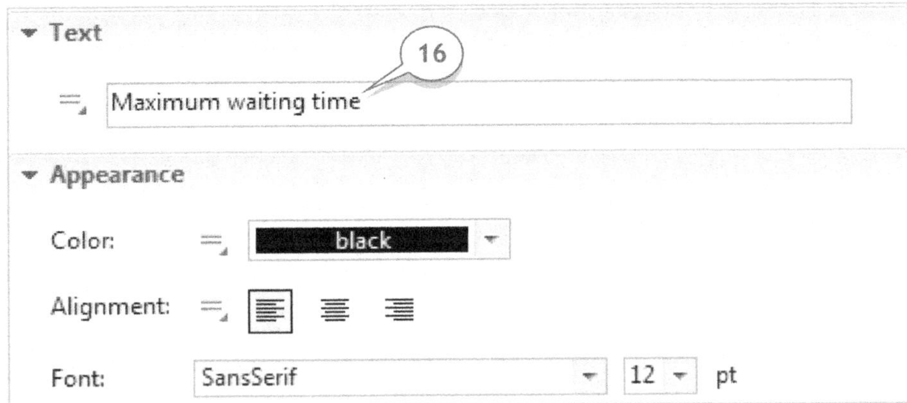

17. In the properties section, under **Appearance**, you can customize the text's color, alignment, font, and point size.

The labels that display the slider's minimum, current, and maximum values are also **Text** *Aa* shapes. Their dynamic properties will display the slider's minimum, current and maximum values at the model's runtime, and you can edit their labels like you would edit any text shape.

You can also move the *consumers* element to the left beyond the presentation window frame.

18. Run the model and observe the behavior. As you use the sliders to change the maximum waiting time or delivery time, you'll see your changes reflected in consumer behaviors and whole adoption dynamics.

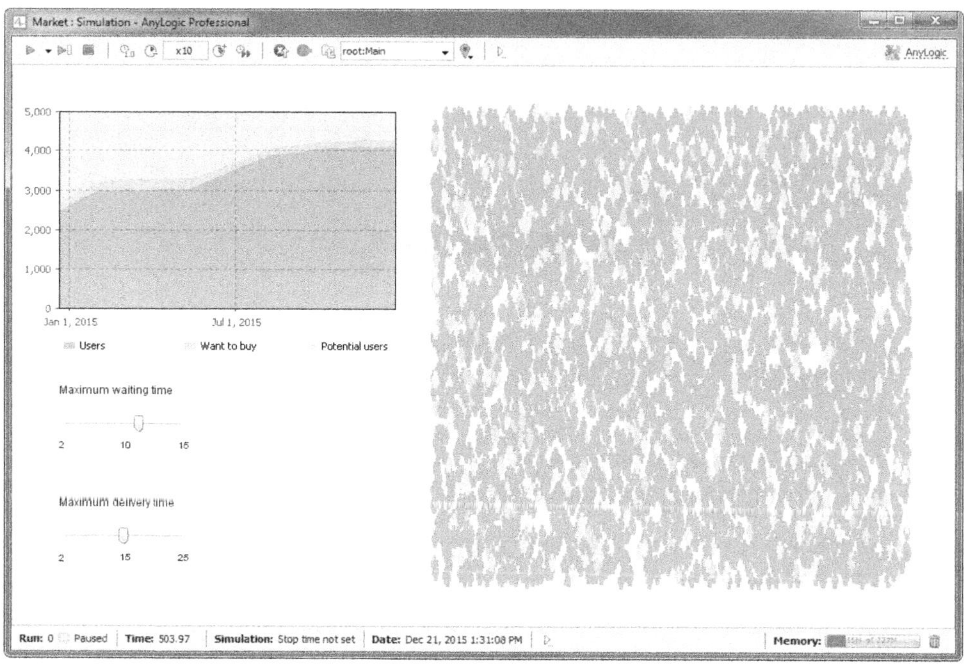

Phase 8. Comparing model runs with different parameter values

In this phase, we want to run the model and observe the adoption process under different settings. We could manually change the parameter values, run the model and save the results, but it's much easier to use AnyLogic's built-in experiments to compare outputs.

First, we'll build an experiment that allows us to manually vary the *ContactRate* parameter and compare the model behavior. We want our experiment to investigate data from a period that exceeds a year, and we'll use 500 days.

Compare Runs experiment

This interactive experiment allows you to enter the model parameters, run a simulation, and add the simulation's output to the charts for later comparison.

The experiment's default user interface includes the input fields and the output charts. The parameters define the input, and the parameters' control type depends on the settings of their **Value editor**.

1. Open the *Main* diagram and add a **Data Set** ⊡ from the **Analysis** ⊪ palette. Name it *usersDS*.

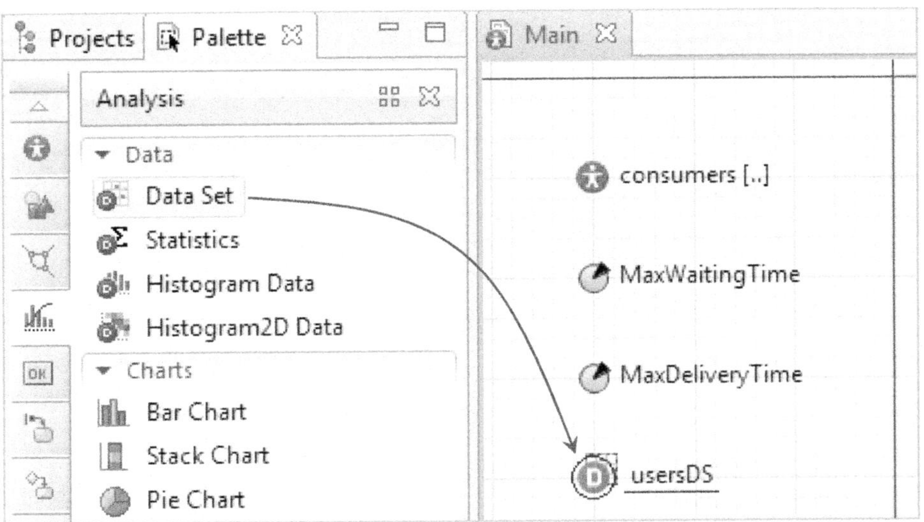

Data Set is capable of storing 2D (X,Y) data of type *double*. We want this dataset to store the history of product sales dynamics. We'll store data samples, each with a timestamp and the current number of the product users.

2. To store the timestamps, leave the dataset's option **Use time as horizontal axis value** selected.

3. Set the value that the dataset will store. In the **Vertical axis value** property, type: *consumers.NUser()*.

4. The dataset keeps a limited number of recent latest data items, and we'll limit our sample size to 500. Set the dataset to **Keep up to** *500* **latest samples**. Set it to **Update data automatically** with the default **Recurrence time**: *1*. We'll add one data sample for one day of the model's lifetime.

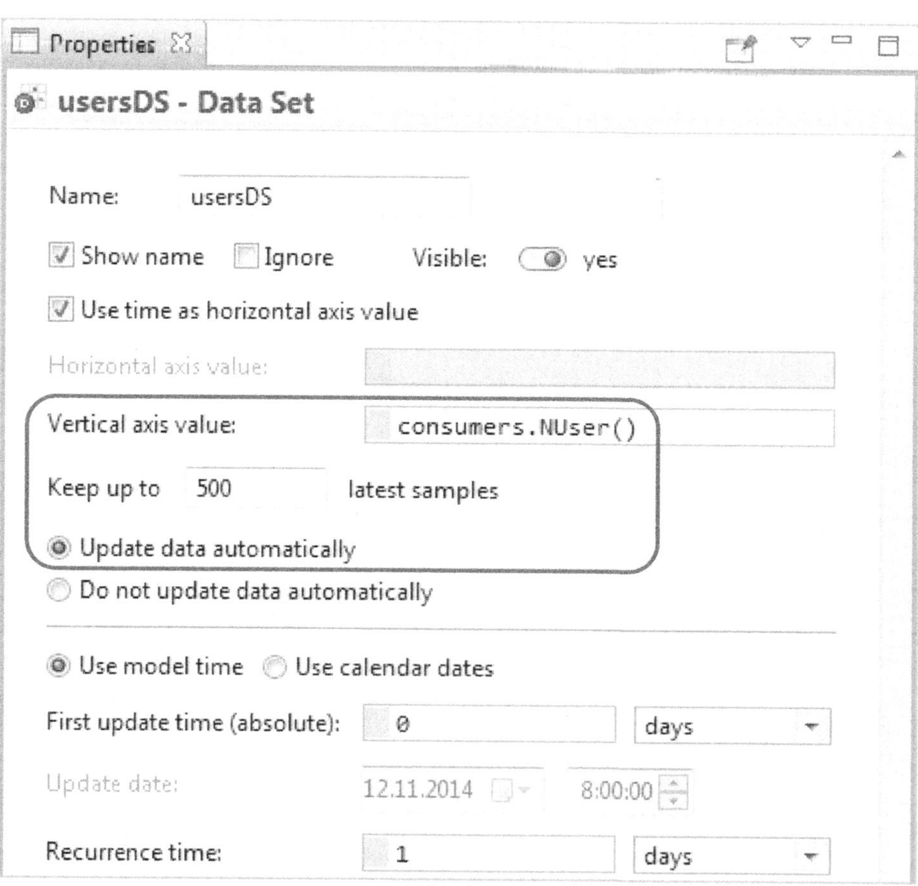

You now have the dataset that will store the history of the key variable (the number of product users). It obtains data samples by calling the statistics function *NUser()* that we created for the agent population *consumers*.

5. Next, make changes in the **Value editor** section for both parameters on *Main* diagram (*MaxWaitingTime* and *MaxDeliveryTime*). Choose *Slider* as **Control type**, set **Min** and **Max** values the same as we have in the sliders on *Main*, and if you want, change the default label (say, *Maximum waiting time*).

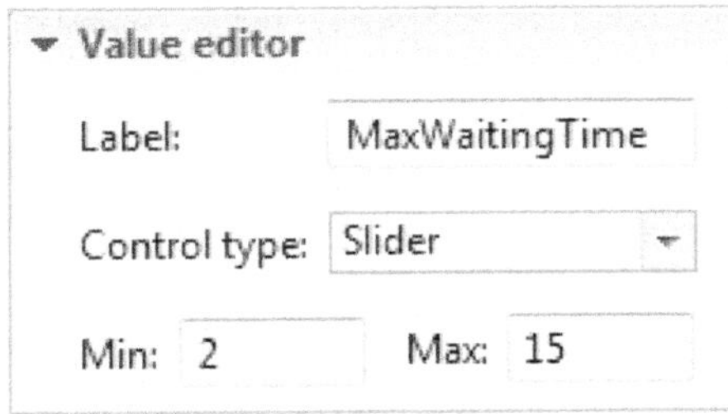

Now we're ready to create a Compare Runs experiment.

6. Open the **Projects** view, right-click the model item, and select **New > Experiment** from the context menu. The **New experiment** wizard will pop up.

7. Select **Compare Runs** experiment from the list of experiment types and click **Next**.

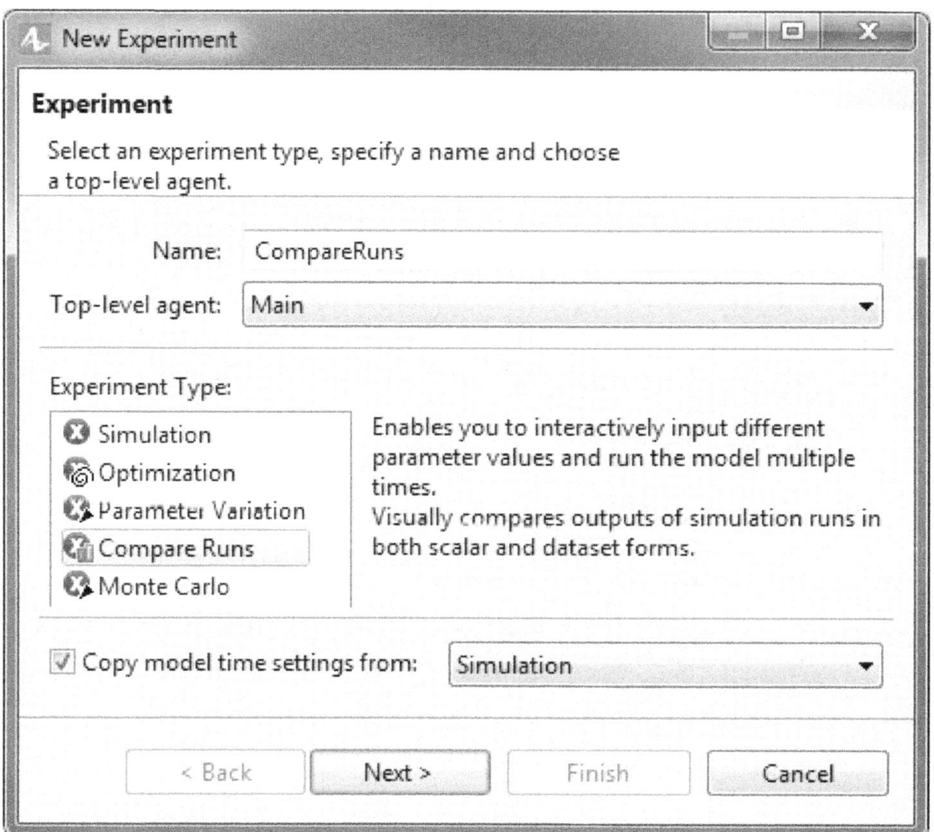

8. On the **Parameters** page, add both parameters to the **Selection** column. To add a parameter, select it in the **Available** list on the left and click the ▶ arrow. You can also click the ⏩ button to add all the parameters. Click **Next** after both parameters are in **Selection**.

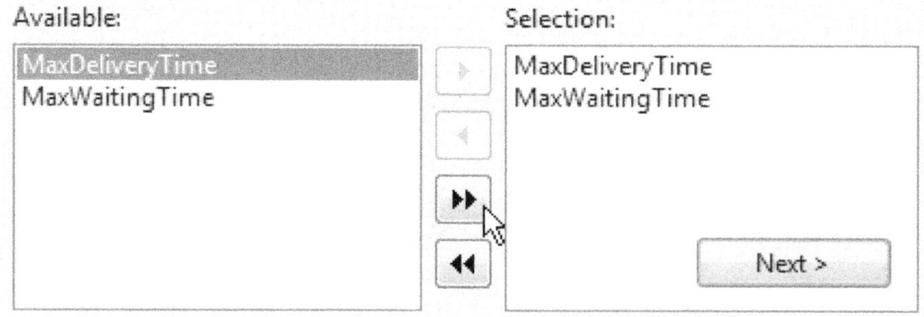

9. On the wizard's following page, configure the output charts for this experiment. The chart will display the data collected by the dataset *usersDS*. In the **Charts** table, do all of the following:

   a.   In the **Type** column, select **dataset**.

   b.   In the **Chart Title** column, type *Users*.

   c.   In the **Expression** column, refer to the dataset you defined in *Main* as *root.usersDS* where *root* is the model's top-level agent (*Main*)

10. Click **Finish**.

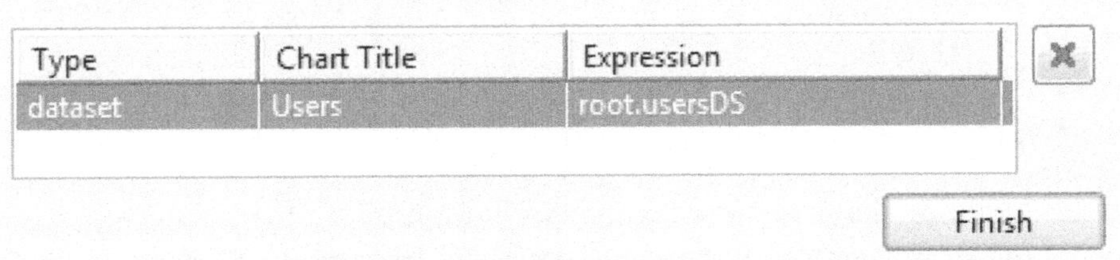

The *CompareRuns* experiment diagram should open automatically, and you'll see the default user interface we created with the wizard.

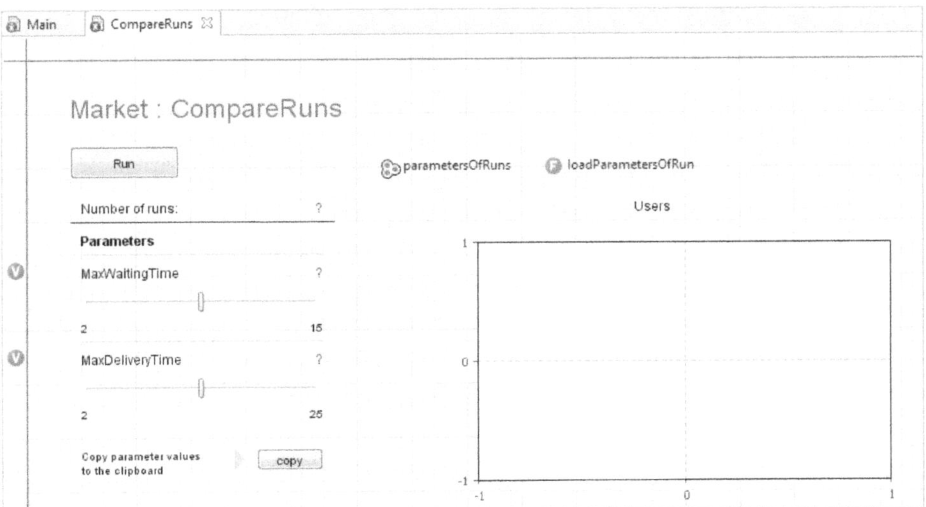

11. We want our experiment to simulate the model for just 500 days. To do this, select *CompareRuns* experiment in the **Projects** tree. In the experiment properties, open the **Model time** properties section, and type *500* in the **Stop time** field.

12. Run the experiment. Select the newly-created experiment from the **Run** list: **Market / CompareRuns**, or right-click the *CompareRuns* experiment in the **Projects** tree and select **Run** ● from the context menu.

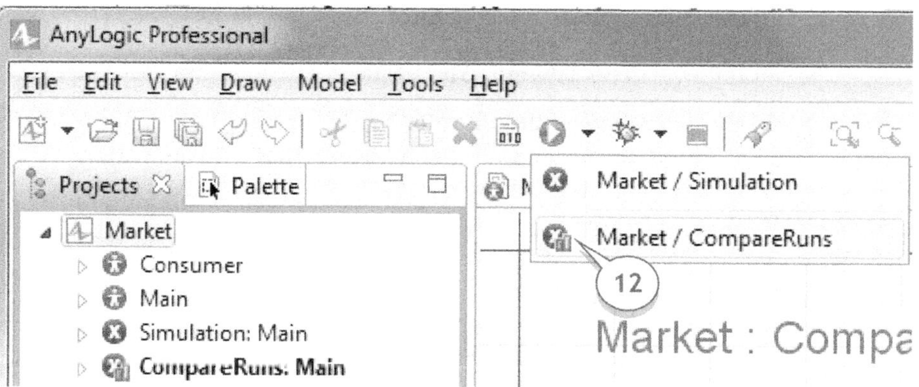

13. In the model window, click the **Run** button to see the result associated with the default parameter values. Afterward, change the parameter values and click **Run** again to observe the system behavior for the new settings. The chart displays all the results for your review.

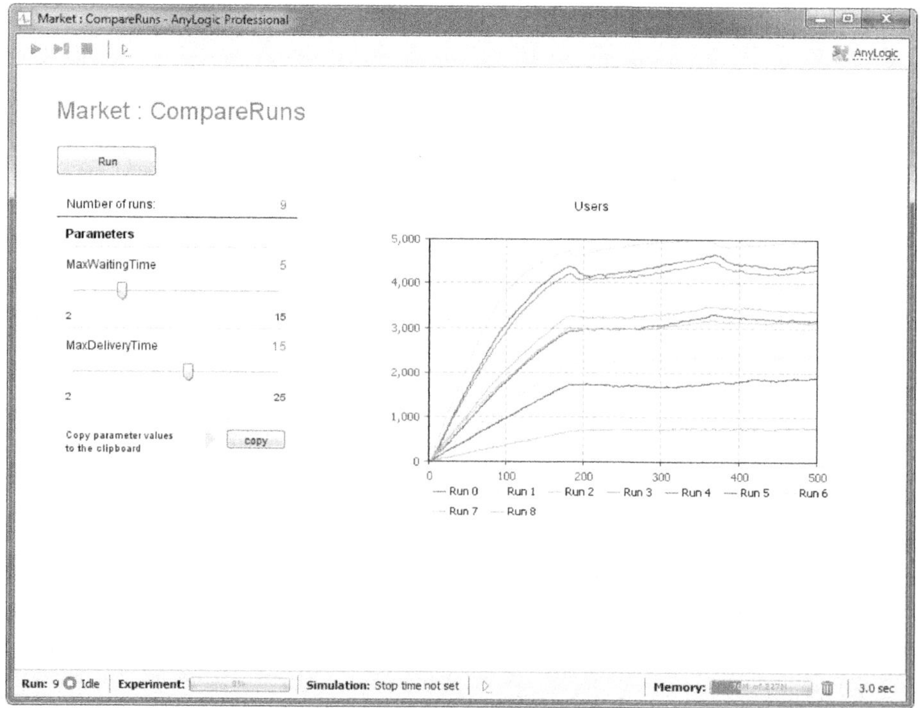

14. Each curve in a chart corresponds to a specific simulation run, and you can click any item in the chart's legend to highlight the curves that correspond to the run. The controls on the left will show the values that led to this result. To deselect a curve, click on its legend a second time.

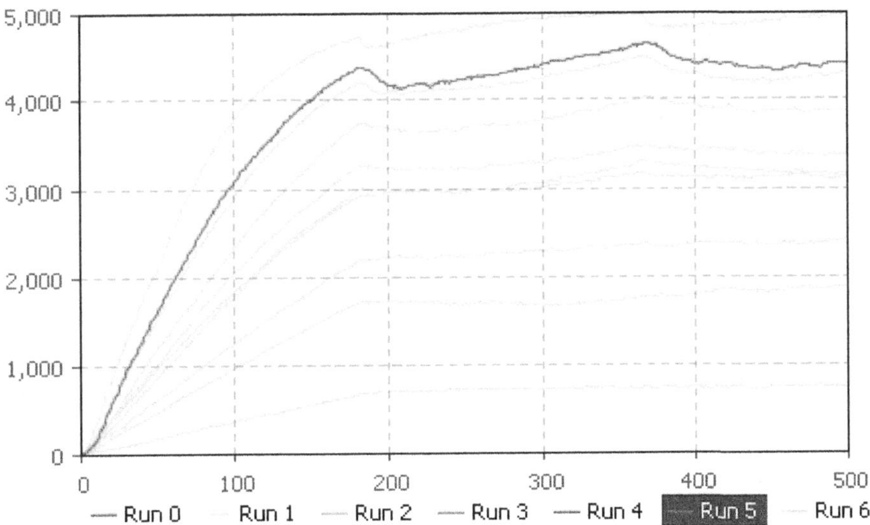

15. You can copy the datasets by clicking in the legend and selecting **Copy all** or **Copy selected** from the context menu.

Now that you've finished developing the agent-based *Market* model, you can extend it by making the consumer's logic more sophisticated (for example, by introducing competing products). You can find a similar model *Statechart for Choice of Competing Products* in the *Models from the "Big Book of Simulation Modeling"* section of AnyLogic example models. To view the models, choose **Examples** from the **Help** menu.

System Dynamics modeling

"System dynamics is a perspective and set of conceptual tools that enable us to understand the structure and dynamics of complex systems. System dynamics is also a rigorous modeling method that enables us to build formal computer simulations of complex systems and use them to design more effective policies and organizations."

John Sterman, "Business Dynamics:
Systems Thinking and Modeling for a Complex World"

The *system dynamics* method was created in 1950s by MIT Professor Jay Forrester. Drawing on his science and engineering background, Forrester sought to use the laws of physics, in particular the laws of electrical circuits, to investigate economic and social systems.

Today, system dynamics is typically used in long-term, strategic models, and it assumes high levels of object aggregation: SD models represent people, products, events, and other discrete items by their quantities.

System dynamics is a methodology to study dynamic systems. It suggests you:

- Model the system as a causally closed structure that defines its own behavior.

- Discover the system's feedback loops (circular causality) balancing or reinforcing. Feedback loops are the heart of system dynamics.

- Identify stocks (accumulations) and flows that affect them.

Stocks are accumulations and characterize the system state. They are the memory of the system and sources of disequilibrium. The model works only with aggregates - the stock's items are indistinguishable. Flows are the rates at which these system states change.

If you're having difficulty distinguishing between stocks and flows, consider how we measure them. Stocks are usually expressed in quantities such as people, inventory levels, money, or knowledge, while flows are typically measurements of quantities in a given time period such as clients per month or dollars per year.

This chapter will to teach you how to use AnyLogic to develop system dynamics models. If you want more information about the system dynamics approach, we recommend *Business Dynamics: Systems Thinking and Modeling for a Complex World* by John Sterman.

SEIR model

We're about to build a model that displays the spread of a contagious disease among a large population. Our sample model will have a population of 10,000 people – a value we call *TotalPopulation* – of which one person is infectious.

- During the infectious phase, a person comes into contact with an average of *ContactRateInfectious* = 1.25 people each day. If an infectious person comes into contact with a susceptible person, the susceptible person's probability of infection is *Infectivity* = 0.6.

- After a susceptible person is infected, the infection latent phase lasts for *AverageIncubationTime* = 10 days. We'll use the word *exposed* to describe people who are in the latent phase.

- After the latent phase, infectious phase starts. This phase lasts for *AverageIllnessDuration* = 15 days.

- Persons who have recovered from the disease are immune to a second infection.

Phase 1. Creating a stock and flow diagram

1. Create a new model by selecting **File > New > Model** from the menu, and then name it *SEIR*. Select **days** as the **Model time units**.

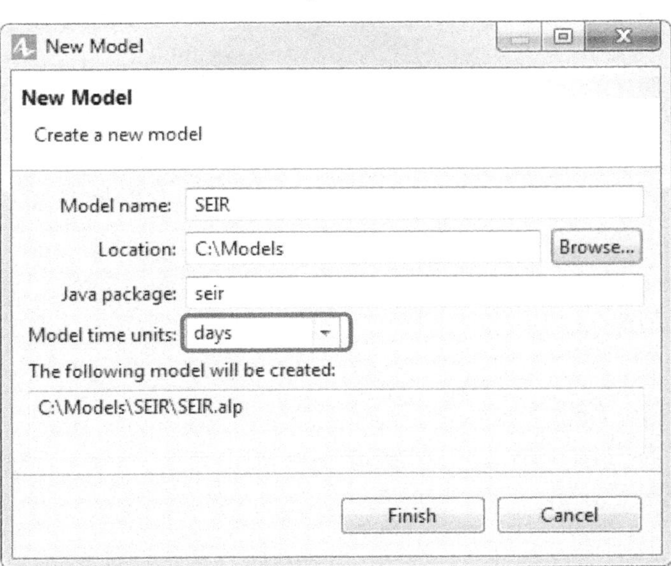

Let's start with drawing stock and flow diagram. To model an epidemic's progress, we need to reduce our population diversity. In this example, we'll consider four important characteristics:

- *Susceptible* - people who are not infected by the virus

- *Exposed* - people who are infected but who can't infect others

- *Infectious* - people who are infected and who can infect others

- *Recovered* – people who have recovered from the virus

SEIR is an acronym that represents the four stages: Susceptible-Exposed-Infectious-Recovered. The terminology and the overall structure of the problem is taken from the ("Compartmental models in epidemiology". n.d.) -- namely, from the SEIR (Susceptible Exposed Infectious Recovered) model.

There are four stocks in our model - one for each stage.

2. Open the **System Dynamics** palette. Drag the **Stock** ☐ from the **System Dynamics** palette on to the diagram. Name it *Susceptible*.

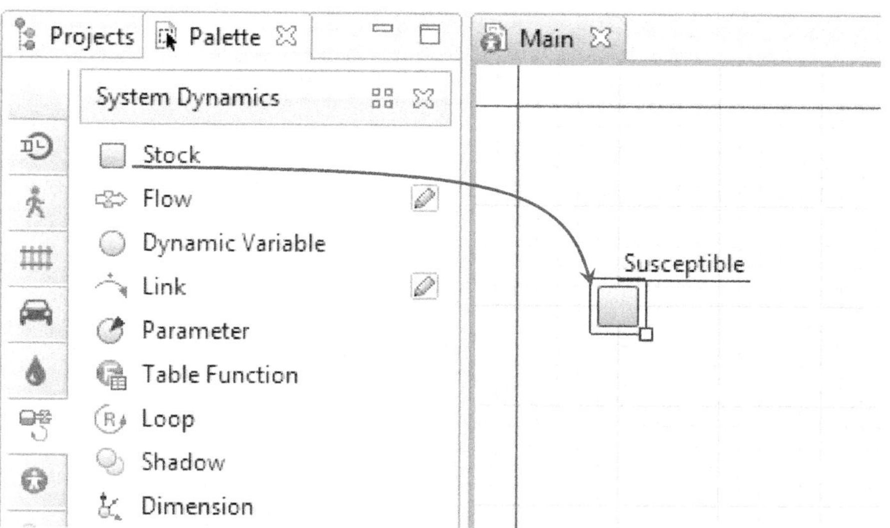

3. Add three more stocks. Place them as shown in the figure and name them *Exposed*, *Infectious*, and *Recovered*.

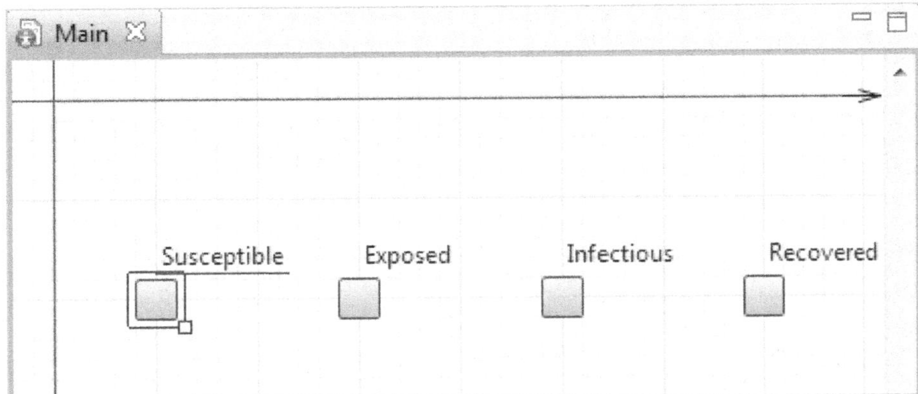

Stocks and flows

In System Dynamics, *stocks* (also known as levels, accumulations, or state variables) represent real-world stocks of material, knowledge, people, money, etc. *Flows* define their rate of change - how stock values change and define the system's dynamics. Here are some examples of stocks and flows:

Stock	Inflows	Outflows
Population	Births Immigration	Deaths Emigration
Fuel tank	Refueling	Fuel consumption

Flow may flow out of one stock and flow in another. Such a flow is outflow for the first stock and inflow for the second one at the same time:

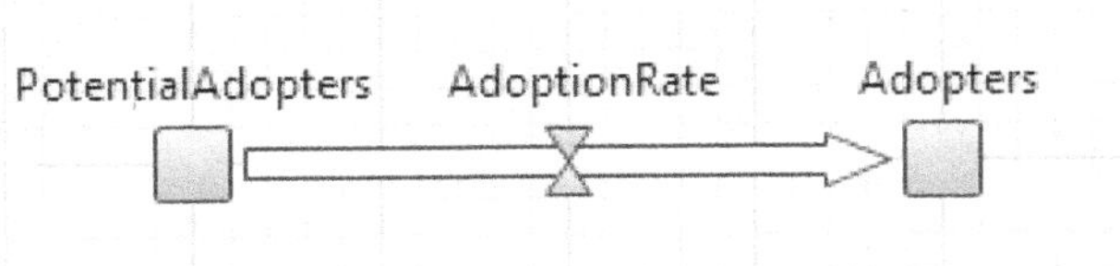

Flow may flow into a stock from nowhere. In this case the cloud (denoting "source") is drawn at the flow's starting point.

And symmetrically, flow may flow out from a stock to "nowhere". In this case the cloud (denoting "sink") is drawn at the flow's end point.

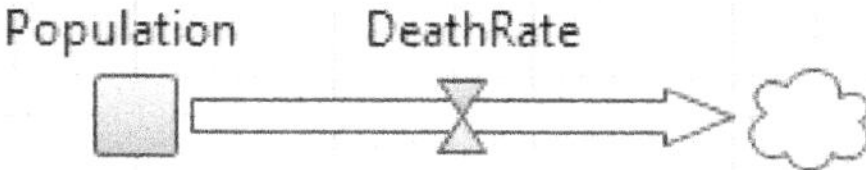

The flow's arrow shows its direction.

In our model, susceptible people are exposed to the virus, become infectious, and then recover. It's a progression that requires our model to use three flows to drive people from one stock to the next.

4.   Add the first flow that flows from the stock *Susceptible* to *Exposed*. Double-click the stock where the flow flows out (*Susceptible*), and then click the stock where it flows in (*Exposed*).

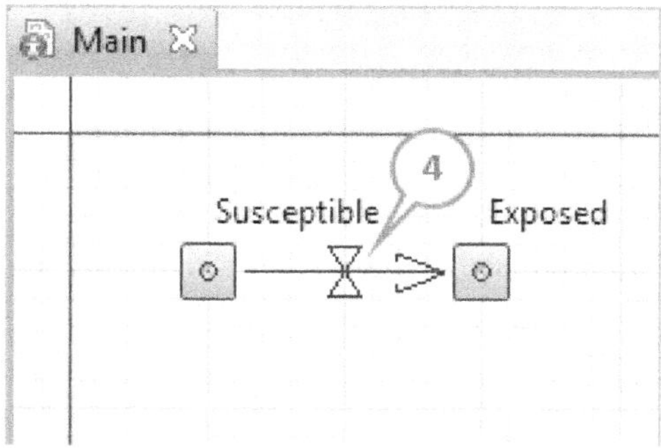

5.   Name the flow *ExposedRate*.

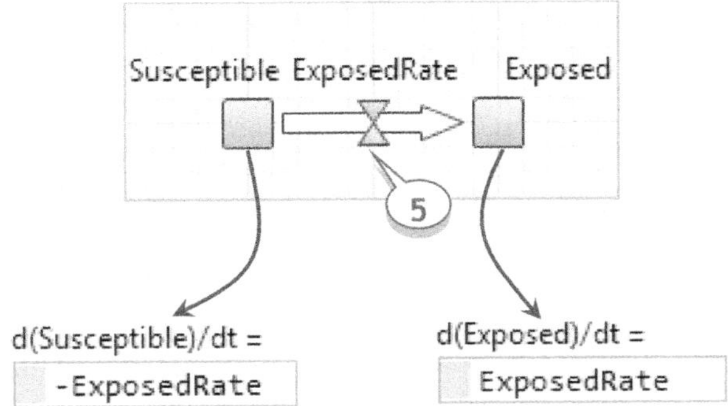

6. You can look at the formulas of *Susceptible* and *Exposed* stocks. Since our *ExposedRate* flow reduces the value of *Susceptible* stock and increases *Exposed*, the formulas should be the same as in the figures below. AnyLogic automatically created these formulas when you added the flow.

Formulas of stocks

AnyLogic automatically generates a stock's formula according to the user's stock-and-flow diagram.

Stock value is calculated according to flows flowing in and out from the stock. The value of inflows – the flows that increase stock value – are added and the value of outflows – flows that reduce the stock – are subtracted from the stock's current value:

inflow1 + inflow2 … - outflow1 - outflow2 …

In the classic system, dynamics notation only flows can appear in the formula. The formula is non-editable and no other elements other than flows flowing in and out the stock can appear in the formula.

7. Add a flow from *Exposed* to *Infectious*, and then name it *InfectiousRate*.

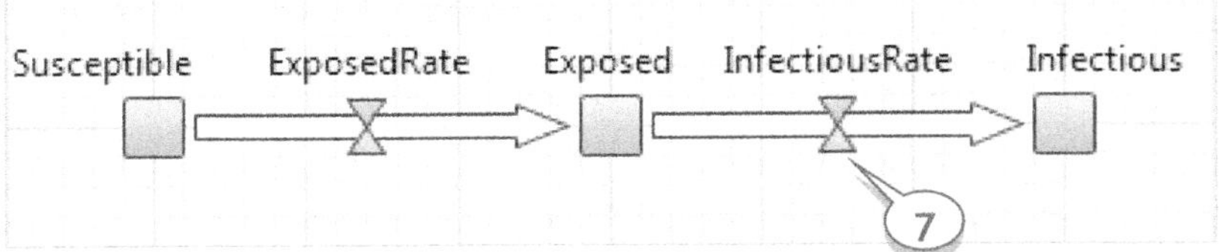

8. Add a flow from *Infectious* to *Recovered*, and then name it *RecoveredRate*.

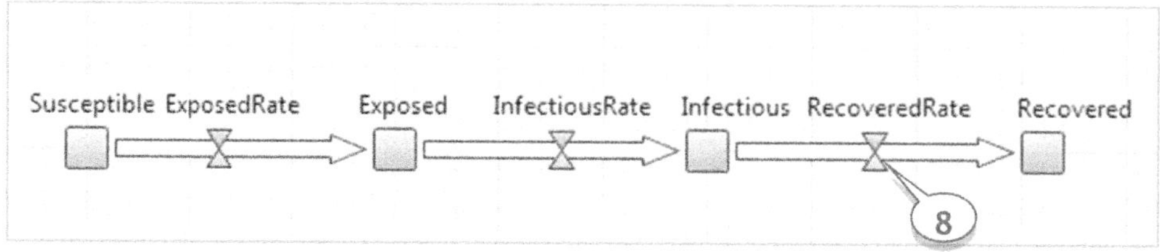

9. Rearrange the flow names as shown in the figure below. To do this, select a flow and then drag its name.

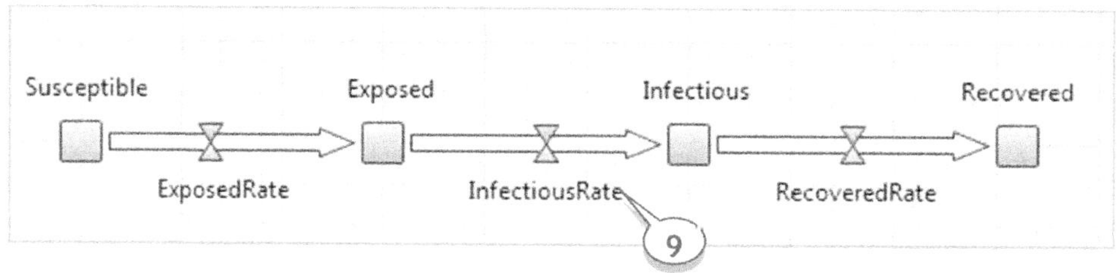

10. Now, let's define the parameters and dependencies. Add five **Parameters** ,
rename them, and define their default values according to the information below:

- *TotalPopulation* = 10 000

- *Infectivity* = 0.6

- *ContactRateInfectious* = 1.25

- *AverageIncubationTime* = 10

- *AverageIllnessDuration* = 15

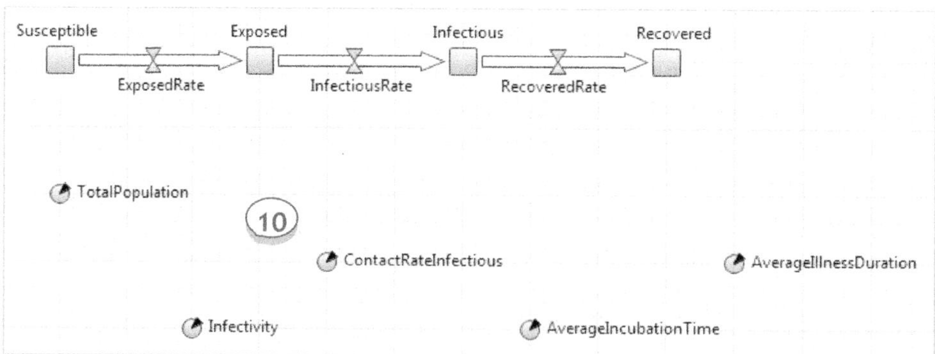

11. Define the number of infected people by specifying *1* as the **Initial Value** of the stock *Infectious*.

12. Define the **Initial Value** for the stock *Susceptible*: *TotalPopulation-1*.

You may press Ctrl+space (Mac OS: Alt+space) and then select the parameter's name from the Code Completion assistant.)

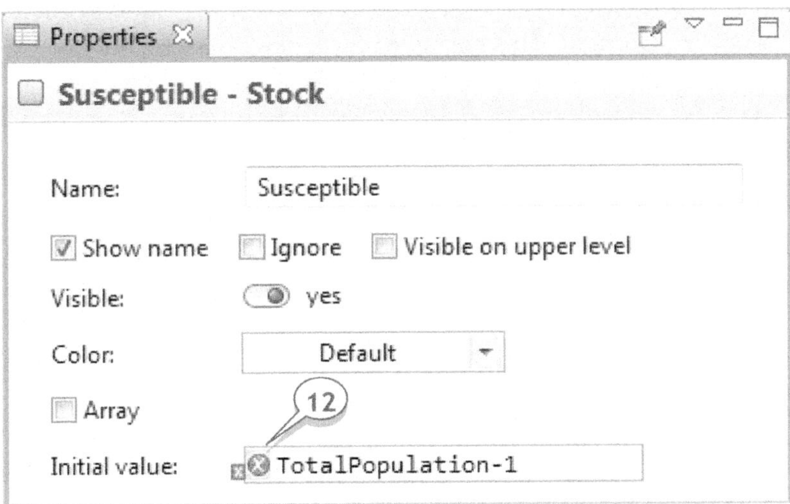

You'll see the red sign to the expression's left. The reason for the problem is you've defined a dependency between two elements in the stock and flow diagram (the stock *Susceptible*'s initial value depends on the parameter *TotalPopulation*), but this dependency is not defined graphically as it should be.

Dependency links

Stock and flow diagrams have two types of dependencies:

- An element (stock, flow, auxiliary, or parameter) is mentioned in a flow or auxiliary's formula. This link type is drawn with a solid line:

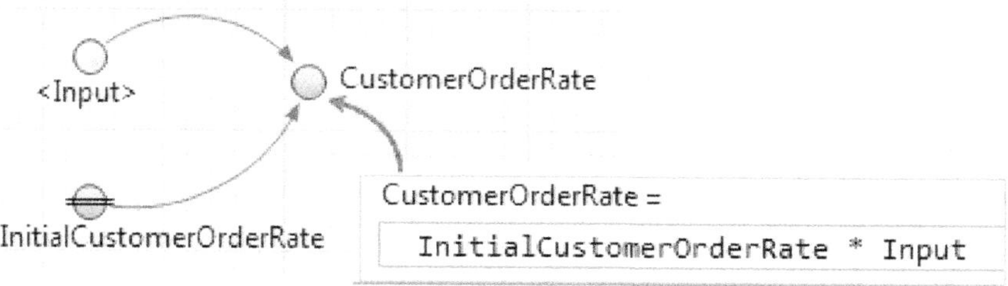

- An element is mentioned in the stock's initial value. This link type is drawn with a dotted line:

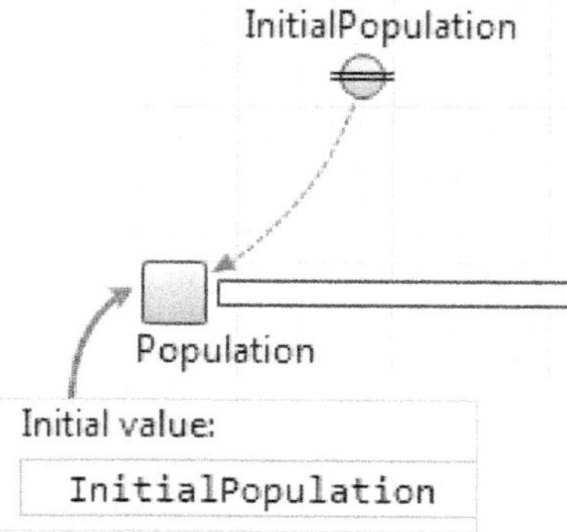

You should use *links* to graphically define dependencies among a stock and flow diagram's elements.

If an element *A* is mentioned in the equation or element *B*'s initial value, you should first connect these elements with a link from *A* to *B* and then type the expression in *B*'s properties.

13. Draw a dependency link from *TotalPopulation* to *Susceptible*:

In the **System Dynamics** palette, double-click the **Link** element, click *TotalPopulation*, and then click the stock *Susceptible*. You should see the link with small circles drawn on its end points:

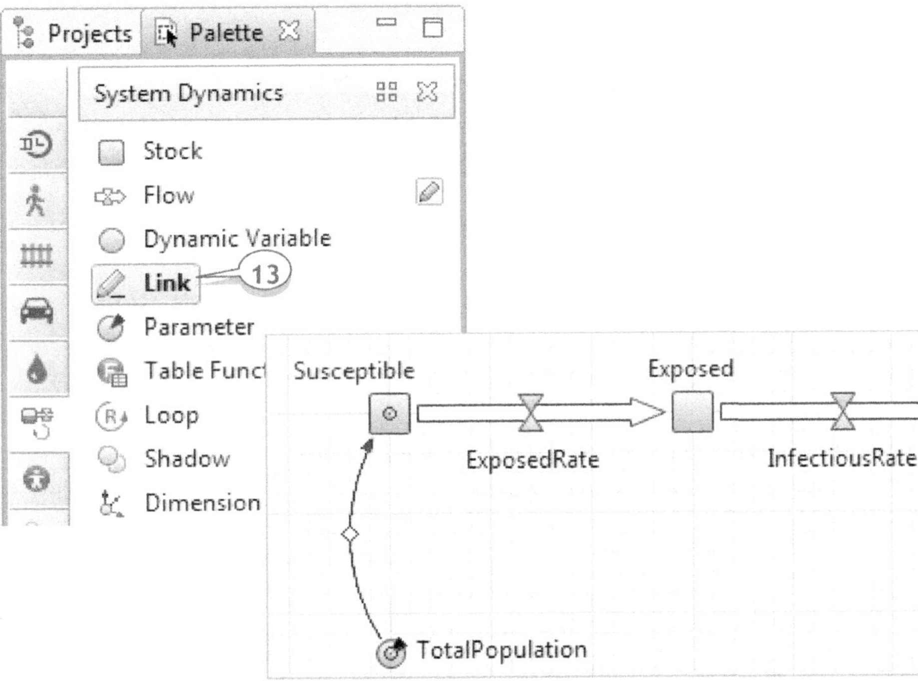

14. Let's define the formula for the flow *ExposedRate*.

Click the flow and define the following formula using the Code Completion assistant:

*Infectious*ContactRateInfectious*Infectivity*Susceptible/TotalPopulation*

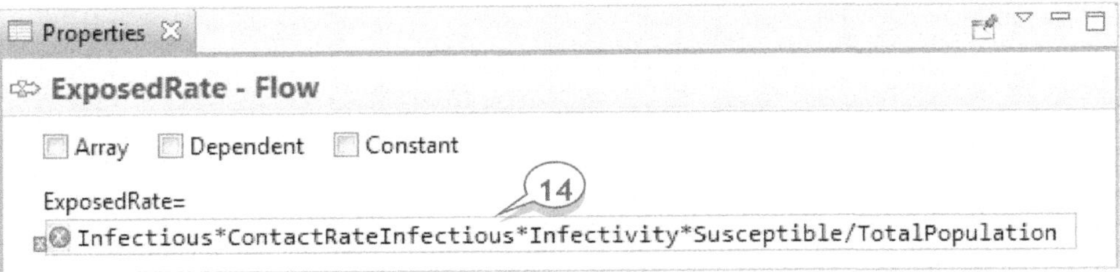

We need to draw dependency links from the mentioned variables and parameters to this flow. You may find it tedious to manually draw the links, so we'll show you how to add links using AnyLogic's link auto-creation mechanism.

15. Right-click *ExposedRate* flow in the graphical diagram, and choose **Fix Variable Links > Create Missing Links** from the context menu. Afterward, you should see the links in the stock and flow diagram:

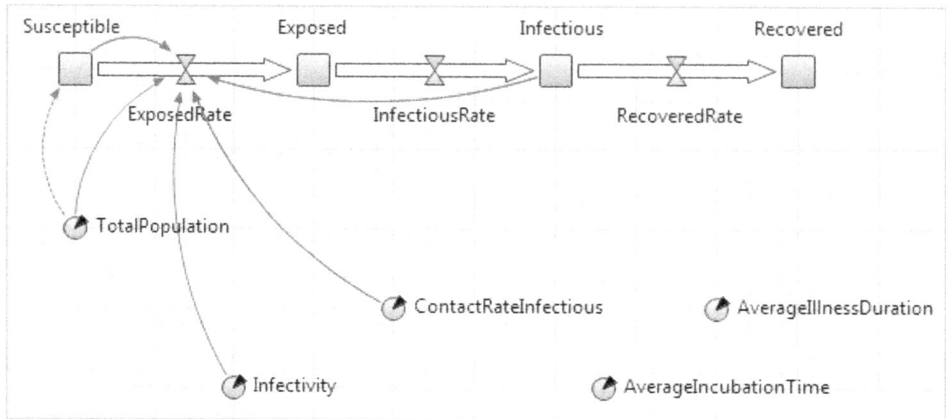

16. Define the following formula for *InfectiousRate*:
    Exposed/AverageIncubationTime

17. Define the following formula for *RecoveredRate*:
    Infectious/AverageIllnessDuration

18. Draw the missing dependency links, and your stock and flow diagram should resemble the following image:

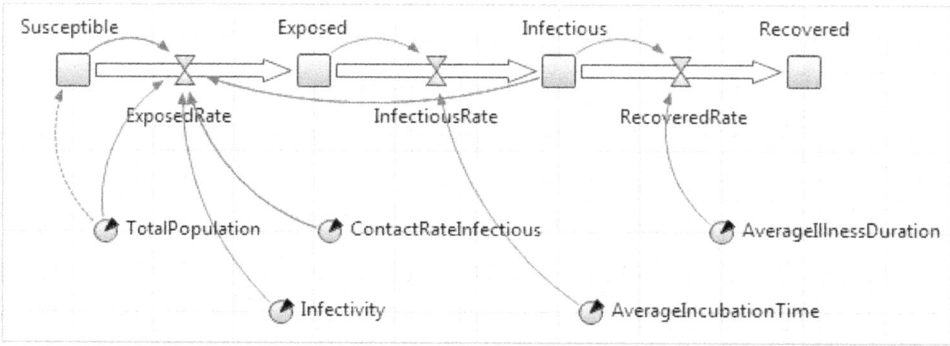

19. Adjust the appearance of dependency links. Modify the links' bend angles to make the diagram match the figure below. To adjust the link's bend angle, select it, and then drag the handle in the middle of the link.

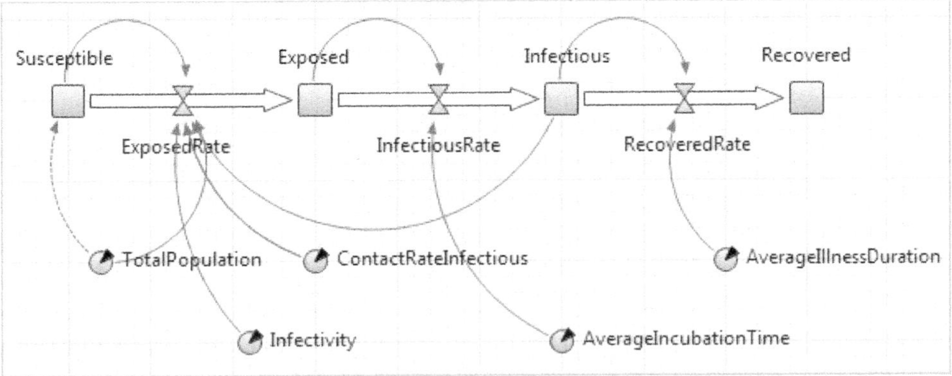

20. Run the model and inspect the dynamics using the variables' inspect windows. To open a variable's inspect window, click the variable to select it. To resize the window, drag its lower right corner.

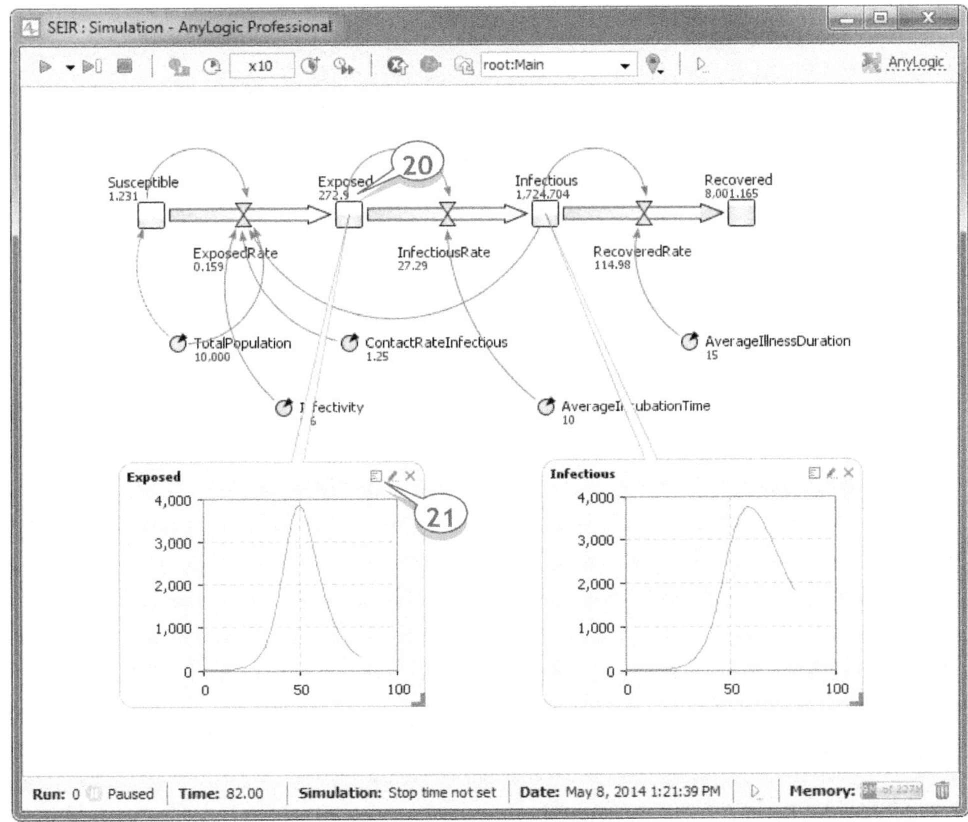

21. To switch the inspect window to the plot mode, click the leftmost icon in its toolbar.

22. Increase the model execution speed to make the simulation go faster.

Phase 2. Adding a plot to visualize dynamics

Feedback loops: balancing and reinforcing

System dynamics studies causal dependencies in systems. There are two types of feedback loops: *reinforcing* and *balancing*.

Here are some hints how to know the loop type (taken from Wikipedia).

To determine if a causal loop is reinforcing or balancing, start with an assumption such as "*VariableN* increases," and then follow the loop.

The loop is:

- *reinforcing* if, after going around the loop, you get the same result as the initial assumption.

- *balancing* if the result contradicts the initial assumption.

You can also use the alternate definition:

- *reinforcing* loops have an even number of negative links (zero also is even)

- *balancing* loops have an uneven number of negative links.

We'll add a loop identifier for one loop to show you.

1. Drag the **Loop** element from the **System Dynamics** palette on to the diagram, and then place it as shown in the figure.

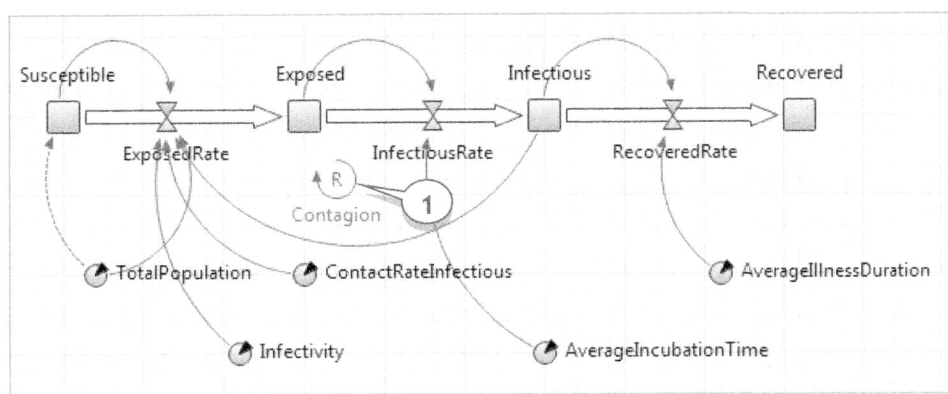

2. Go to the loop's **Properties**, change its **Type** to **R** (stands for Reinforcing), leave the default **Clockwise Direction**, and specify the text AnyLogic will display near the loop icon: *Contagion*.

Loop identifiers

Loop is a graphical identifier with a label that briefly describes the loop's meaning and an arrow that shows the loop's direction.

Rather than defining the causal loop, it provides information about how your stock and flow diagram's variables affect one another. By adding loops, you can help other users understand the stock and flow diagram's influences and causal dependencies.

Contagion loop is reinforcing. An increase in *Infectious* leads to an increase of *ExposedRate*, which in turn leads to a greater increase of *Exposed*. All links in this loop are positive.

Please find out what are other loops in this stock and flow diagram. What are their directions and types?

Let's add a time chart to plot *Susceptible*, *Exposed*, *Infectious*, and *Recovered* people.

3. Drag the **Time Plot** from the **Analysis** palette on to the diagram, and extend the time plot as shown in the figure below.

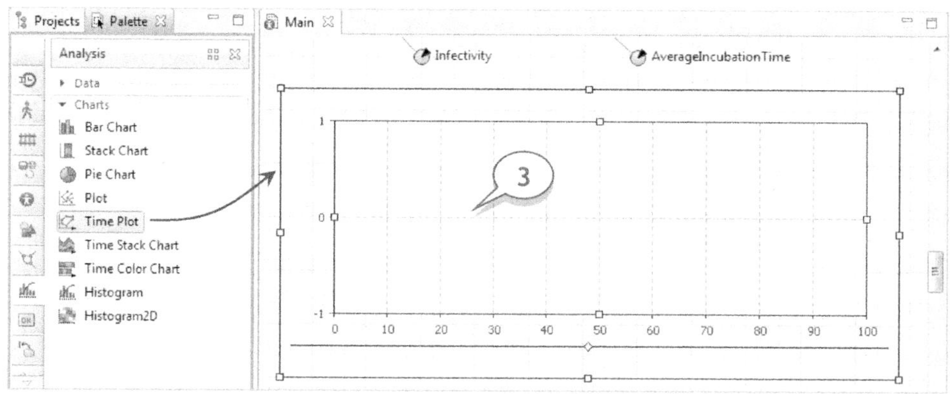

4. In the **Properties** view, go the section **Data** and click the button to add a new data item.

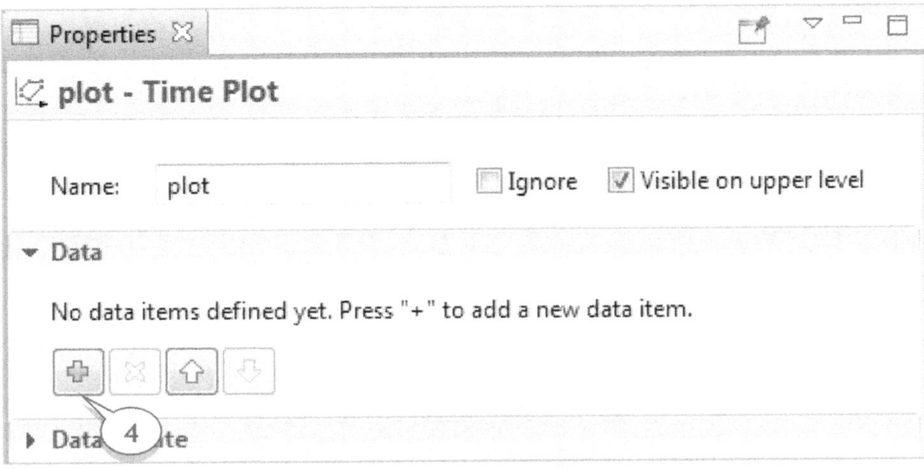

5. Modify the data item's properties:

    • **Title:** *Susceptible people* – title of the data item.

    • **Value:** *Susceptible* (use *Code Completion Master*).

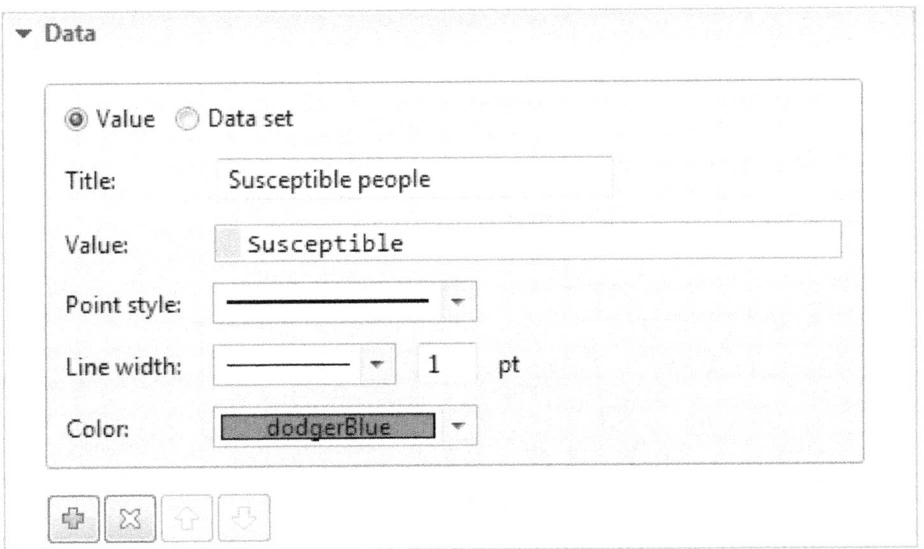

6. Add three data items to display the values of stocks *Exposed*, *Infectious*, and *Recovered* in the same way - and don't forget to define the corresponding **Titles**.

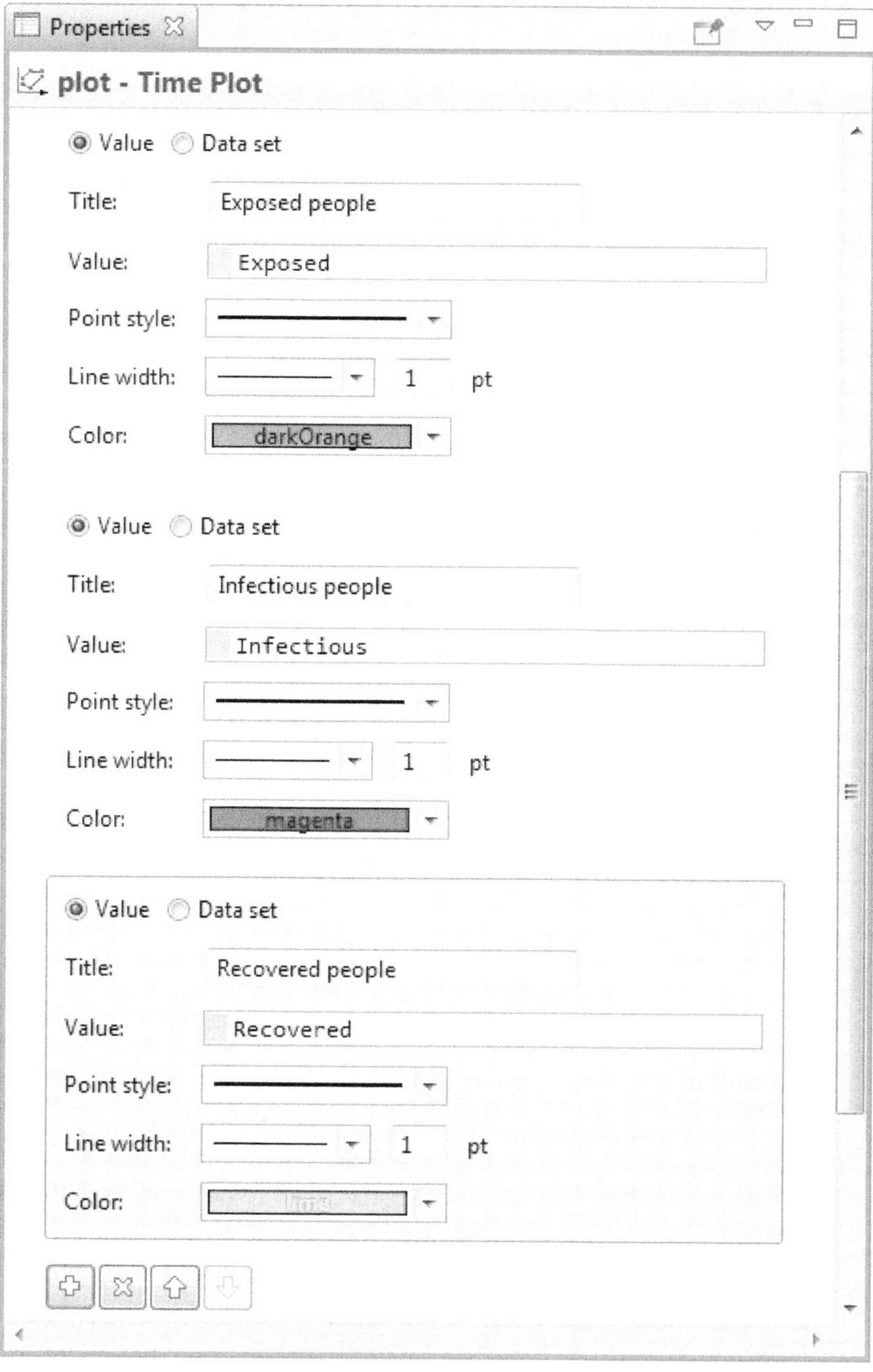
Properties
plot - Time Plot
Value   Data set
Title: Exposed people
Value: Exposed
Point style:
Line width: 1   pt
Color: darkOrange
Value   Data set
Title: Infectious people
Value: Infectious
Point style:
Line width: 1   pt
Color: magenta
Value   Data set
Title: Recovered people
Value: Recovered
Point style:
Line width: 1   pt
Color: lime

7. We've finished our last model. Now, run the model and use the chart you added to view its dynamics.

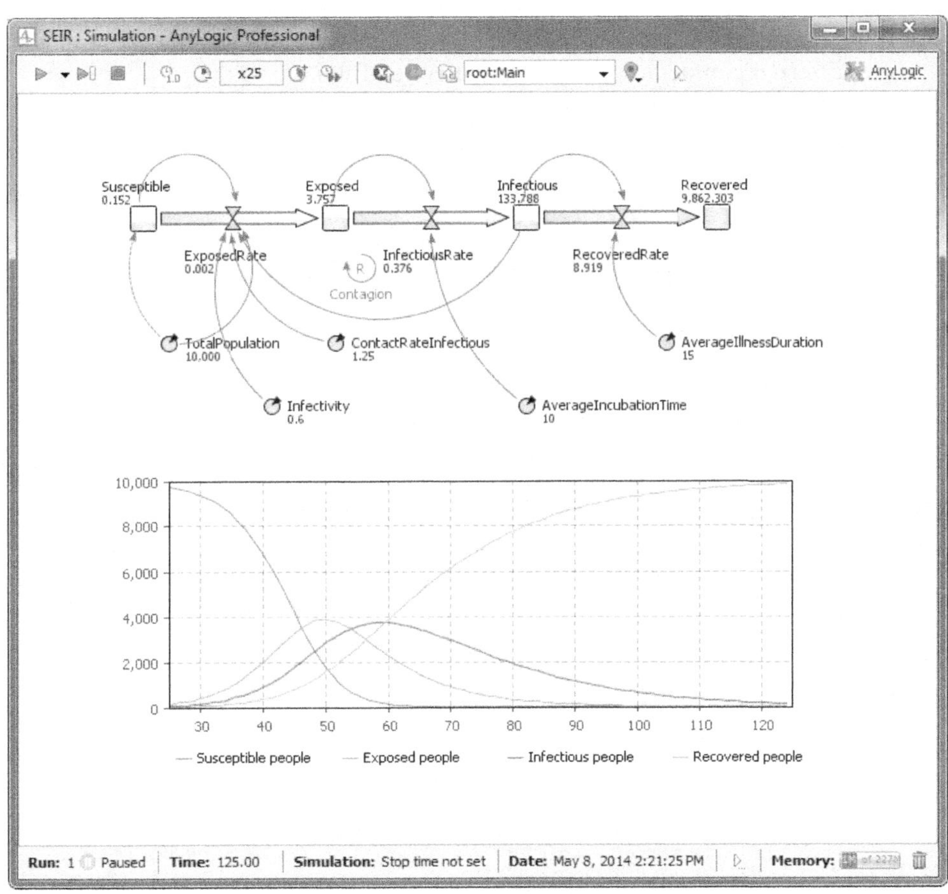

Phase 3. Parameter variation experiment

In this phase, we'll use AnyLogic's parameter variation experiment to determine how different contact rates affect the infection rate.

Parameter variation experiment

The parameter variation experiment allows us to create a complex model simulation that performs a series of single model runs that vary by one or many parameters. After the experiment is complete, AnyLogic can display each run's results on a single diagram to help us better understand how the varying parameters affected our model's results.

If we run our experiment with fixed parameter values, we can also assess the effect of random factors in stochastic models.

1. To add an experiment to the model, right-click the model item (*SEIR*) in the **Projects** tree, point to **New**, and then click **Experiment**.

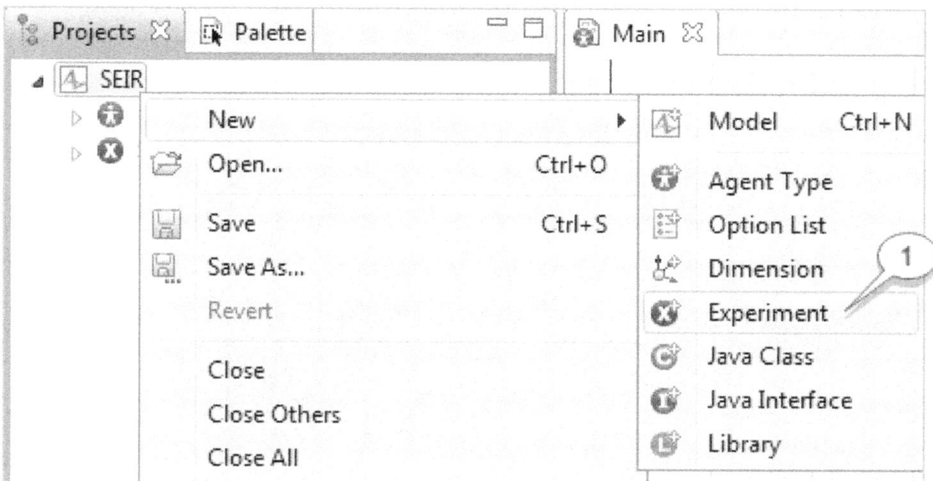

2. In the **New Experiment** wizard's **Name** field, type *ContactRateVariation*. AnyLogic will automatically select the *Main* agent type as the **Top-level agent**.

3. In the **Experiment Type** area, click **Parameter Variation**, and click **Finish**.

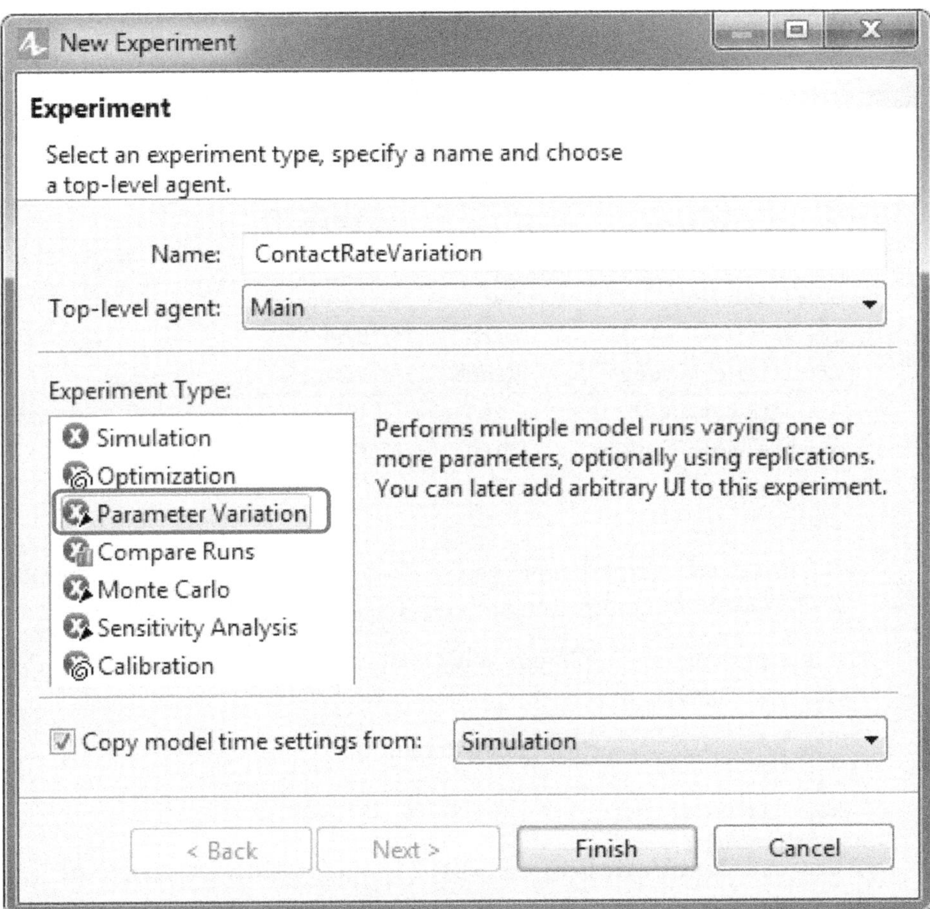

After you create the experiment, its diagram and properties will open.

4. In the experiment's properties, open the **Parameters** section. The parameters of the experiment's top-level agent (in our case, *Main*) display.

   By default, all parameters are set as *fixed*. These values will not change during the parameter variation experiment.

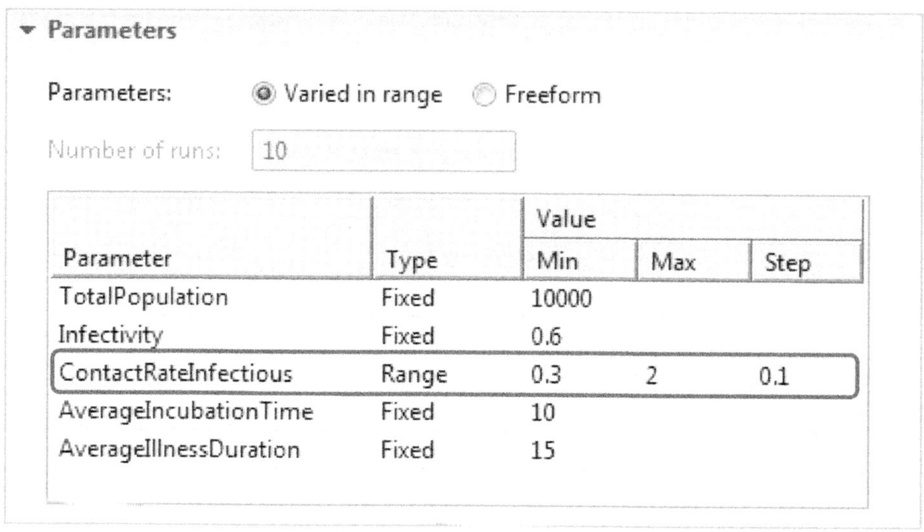

5. To ensure our experiment varies the contact rate, locate the table's *ContactRateInfectious* parameter and change its **Type** to **Range**.

6. Set the parameter's minimum and maximum values by setting **Min**: *0.3* and **Max**: *2* with a **Step** of *0.1*.

7. In the Properties area, click **Create default UI**.

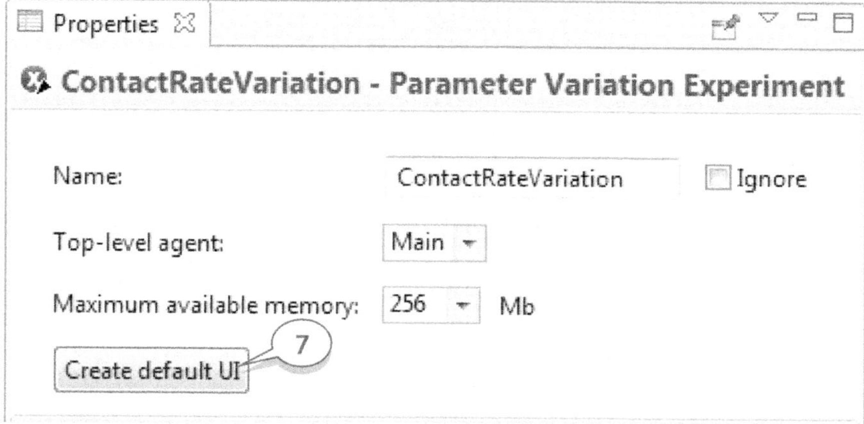

The experiment diagram will display the simple user interface.

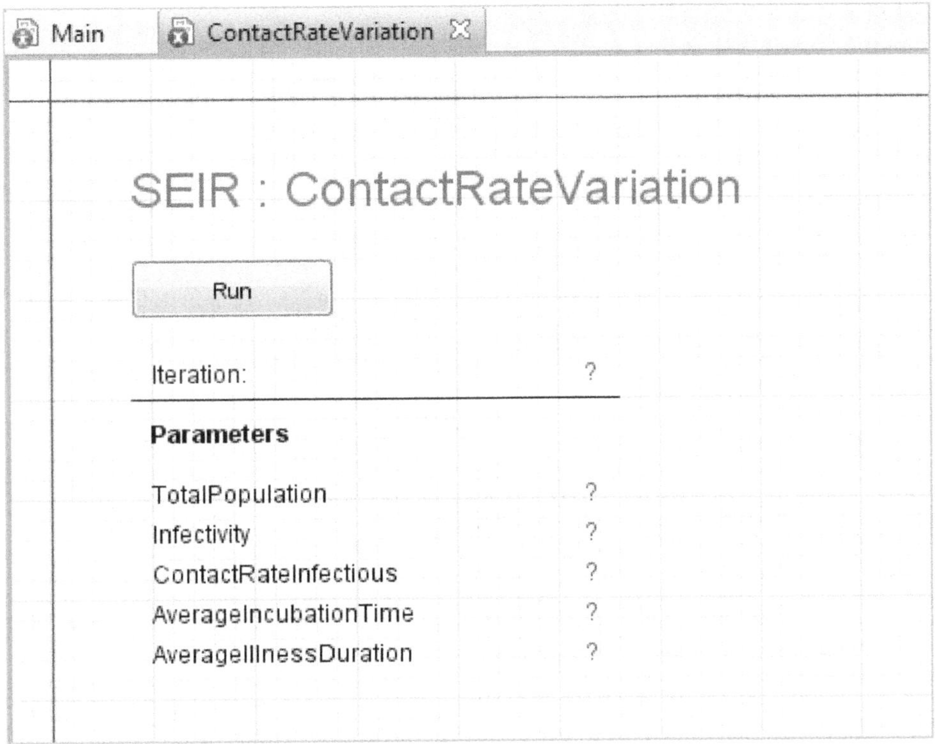

8. To ensure each run simulates exactly 300 days, we need to limit the model's lifetime to 300 days. Click *ContactRateVariation* in the **Projects** tree to open its properties. In the **Properties** view, open the **Model time** section, select **Stop at specified time** from the **Stop** list, and type *300* in the **Stop time** box.

Now, we'll add a time plot to display our experiment's results. Our first step is to gather data about the number of infectious persons.

9. Open the *Main* diagram, right-click the *Infectious* stock and then click **Create Data Set**.

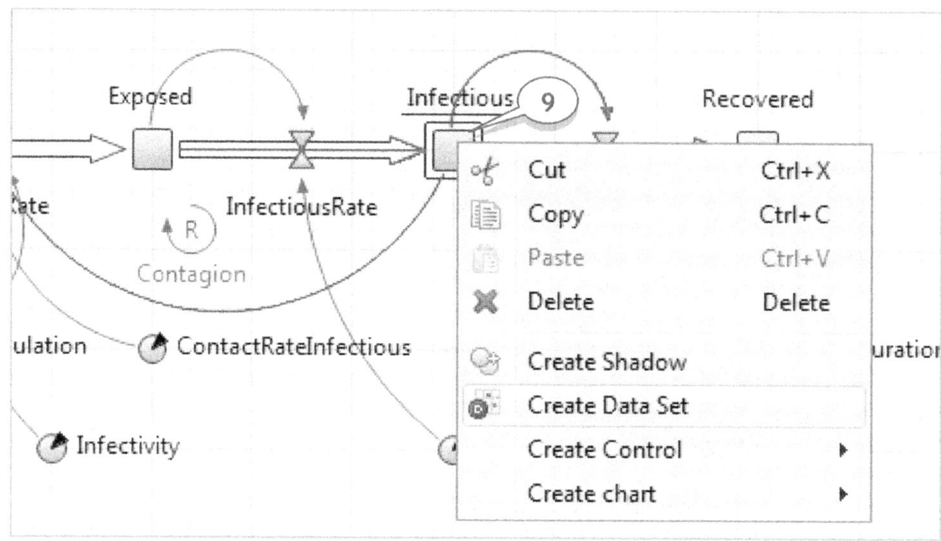

10. After the *InfectiousDS* data set displays, navigate to its properties. Since we want to view the infectious disease's dynamics, leave the **Use time as horizontal axis value** checkbox selected.

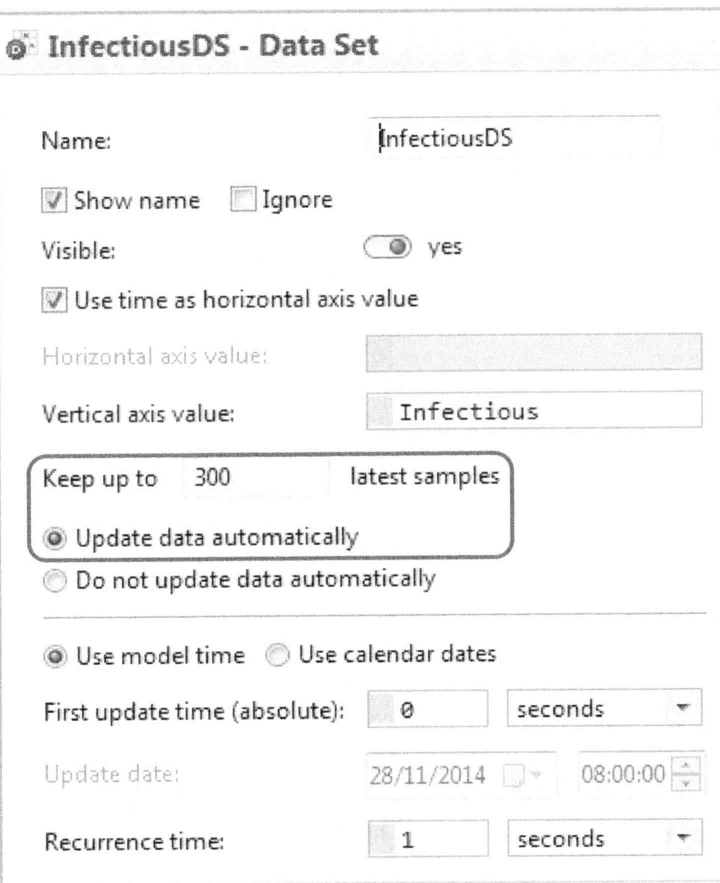

11. Select **Update data automatically** and leave **Recurrence time:** *1* to add one data sample to our dataset for each model life day.

12. To obtain data samples for the whole model run, set the dataset to **Keep up to** *300* **latest samples**.

We're ready to add a chart to the *ContactRateVariation* experiment diagram that will display our results.

13. Open *ContactRateVariation* diagram, and drag the **Time Plot** from the **Analysis** palette.

14. Open the time plot's properties. In the **Scale** section, ensure the time plot displays data for 300 model time units by setting the **Time window** to *300* **model time units**.

15. Enlarge the area available for the plot's legend by dragging the diamond handle toward the top of the screen.

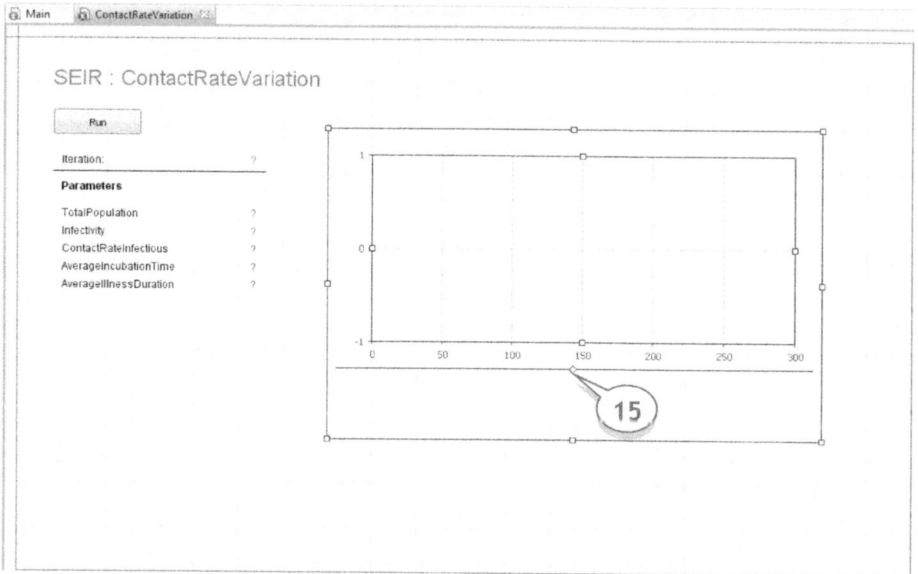

The plot's curves will each display the results from one model run: the history of disease spread for a contact rate collected by the *InfectiousDS* dataset.

16. Click *ContactRateVariation* in the **Projects** tree to open its properties, and then add data to the plot by navigating to the **Java actions** section and typing the following code in the **After simulation run** field:

```
plot.addDataSet( root.InfectiousDS,
"CR=" + format( root.ContactRateInfectious ) );
```

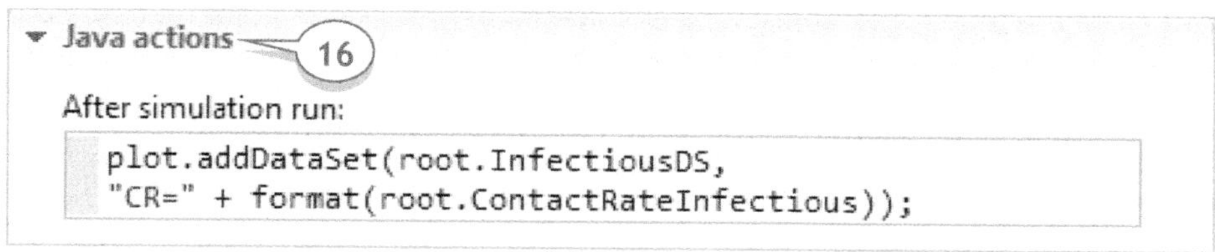

While we want our *plot* to display multiple curves - one for each simulation run – we can't add the data from each simulation run directly into the plot's **Data** properties. Each model run destroys the top-level agent and its data, and since our model can't store the accumulated data, we need to manually add each curve to the chart.

At the end of each simulation, AnyLogic stores the data in the *Main* agent's *InfectiousDS* dataset. The experiment's top-level agent is accessible as *root*, which means we access the data set as *root.InfectiousDS.*

We could use *addDataset(root.InfectiousDS)* to add a dataset to the chart with the default appearance and *"Data set"* title. However, we want AnyLogic to add a series of legends that will help us identify the plot's curves, and that's why we'll use another notation of *addDataSet()* function that has two arguments, *addDataSet(DataSet ds, String title).*

We construct a legend for the dataset from the *CR=* label (where CR stands for contact rate) and the *ContactRateInfectious* value. Since the model's top-level (root) agent defines this parameter, we'll access its value as *root.ContactRateInfectious* and use the function *format(double value)* to control how AnyLogic converts the values to text. For example, we want our chart's legend to display calculations such as 0.30001 as rounded values.

17. Open the *ContactRateVariation* experiment properties' **Advanced** section and then clear the **Allow parallel evaluations** checkbox.

18. We're ready to run the experiment and use our chart to observe the data we've gathered from multiple simulation runs. In the toolbar, on the ◓ **Run** list, select *SEIR / ContactRateVariation.*

19. In the presentation window, click **Run**.

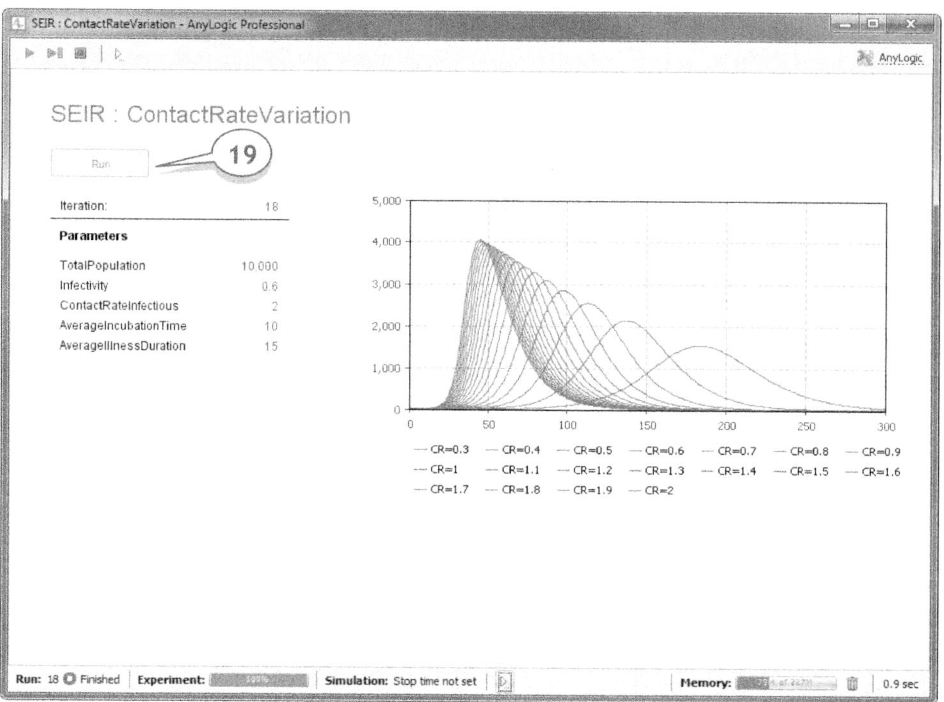

AnyLogic performs a series of runs that all use a different value for the *ContactRateInfectious* parameter and then add the simulation output to the chart.

If you review the Parameter variation experiment's results, you'll see how increased contact rates allow the infection to spread more quickly. You'll also see that the plot displays 18 iterations – in other words, 18 infection scenarios for contact rates that range from 0.3 to 2 – that represent the 18 steps in the parameter variation range that we defined earlier. You can highlight a curve by clicking its Contact Rate (CR) value in the legend.

Phase 4. Calibration experiment

In this phase, we'll tune our model's parameters to ensure its behavior matches a known (observed) pattern.

Since we can't directly measure two parameters – *Infectivity* and *ContactRateInfectious* – we need to determine their values before we use the model. The best way to do this is to use *calibration*, a process that uses a similar case's historical data and adjusted parameter values to help ensure our model reproduces the historical data.

Calibration experiment

- *Calibration experiment* uses the built-in OptQuest optimizer to locate the model parameter values that correspond to the simulation output that best fits the given data.

- Calibration experiment iteratively runs the model, compares the model's output to the historical pattern, and then changes the parameter values. After a series of runs, the experiment will determine which parameter values produce the results that best match the historical pattern.

We'll start by adding the historic data – the number of infected people over time – to our model. While the data samples are stored in a text file in the table form, AnyLogic's table function allows us to use this data to build the curve.

Table functions

- *Table function* is a function defined in the table form. The user defines a function by providing several (argument, value) pairs, and AnyLogic then uses a combination of the data and the selected interpolation type to build the table function. A function call that passes a value as a function argument will return a (possibly, interpolated) function value.

- You may need table functions to define a complex non-linear relationship which cannot be described as a composition of standard functions, or to bring experimental data defined as a table function to a continuous mode.

1. Open the *Main* diagram and add a **Table function** from the **System Dynamics** palette. Name it *InfectiousHistory*.

2. Open the *HistoricData.txt* file from *AnyLogic folder/resources/AnyLogic in 3 days/SEIR*. The *AnyLogic folder* is the location on your computer where you installed AnyLogic, such as *Program Files/AnyLogic 7 Professional*.

3. Copy the text file's contents to the Clipboard, go to the table function properties' **Table Data** section, and then click the **Paste from clipboard** button. The **Argument** and **Value** columns will automatically update.

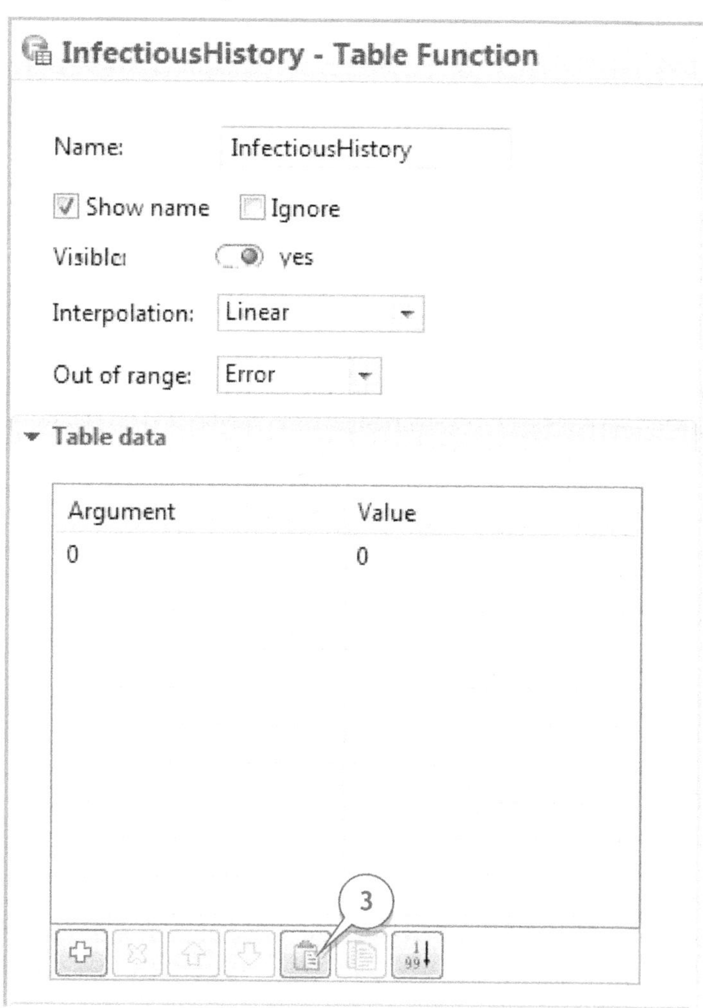

4. You can preview the curve built for the table function in the table function's properties' **Preview** section.

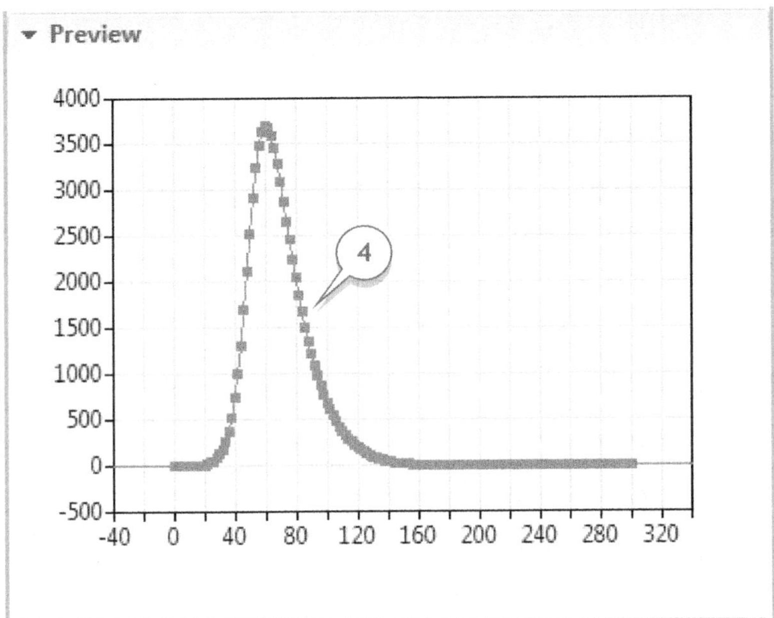

5. Set the **Out of range** option to **Nearest** to ensure the function correctly addresses cases where the function's argument exceeds the value of 300 that we defined in the **Table data**.

We're using the **Nearest** option to ensure the nearest valid argument extrapolates the function. This means that in all arguments to the left of the range, the function will take the value in the leftmost point. Conversely, in all arguments to the right of the range, the function will take the value in the rightmost point. The preview graph reflects the current inter- and extrapolation.

We're ready to create our experiment.

6. Right-click the model item (*SEIR*) in the **Projects** tree, point to **New**, and then click **Experiment**. In the **New Experiment** wizard, choose **Calibration** as the **Experiment type** and then click **Next**. This time, we'll use the wizard to set the parameters.

7. Change the parameter types we want to calibrate (*Infectivity* and *ContactRateInfectious*) from **fixed** to **continuous**, and then set the range's **Min** and **Max** values as shown in the figure below.

Parameters:

Parameter	Type	Value	Min	Max	Step
TotalPopulation	fixed				
Infectivity	continuous		0.005	1	
ContactRateInfectious	continuous		0.01	3	
AverageIncubationTime	fixed				
AverageIllnessDuration	fixed				

8. In the **Criteria** table shown below, enter the following information.

- **Title**: *Infectious curve match*

- **Match**: *data series*

- **Simulation output**: *root.InfectiousDS*

- **Observed data**: *root.InfectiousHistory*

- **Coefficient**: *1.0*

Criteria:

Title	Match	Simulation output	Observed data	Coef
Infectious curve match	data series	root.InfectiousDS	root.InfectiousHistory	1.0

Again, the top-level agent *Main* is available here as *root*. We use our dataset *InfectiousDS* to retain the model output at the end of a simulation run and compare it to the historic data from the *InfectiousHistory* table function.

While our model has one criterion, you can use coefficients if your model has several criteria.

9. Click **Finish**. The *Calibration* experiment diagram will display the configured user interface (UI).

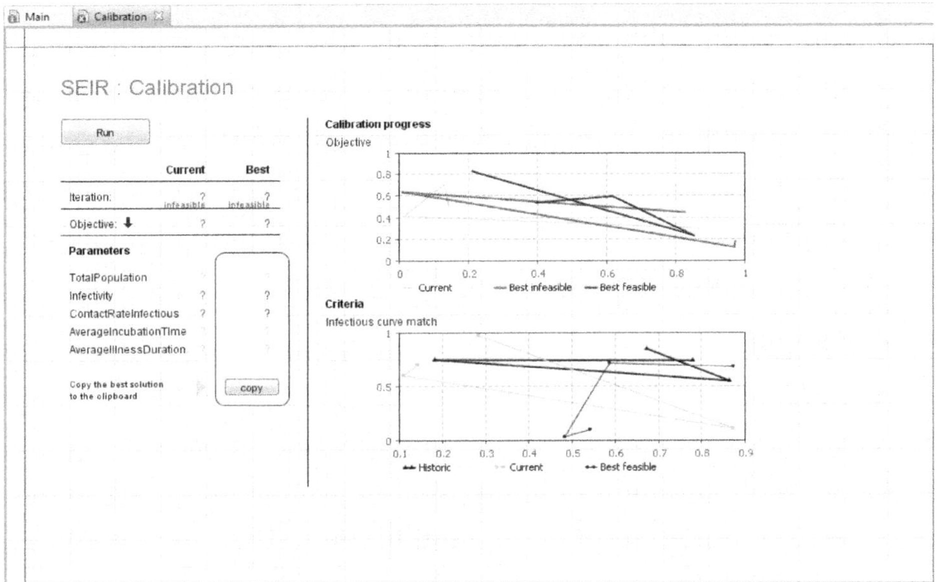

The image below shows the experiment's properties. Its objective is to minimize the difference between the model output and historical data.

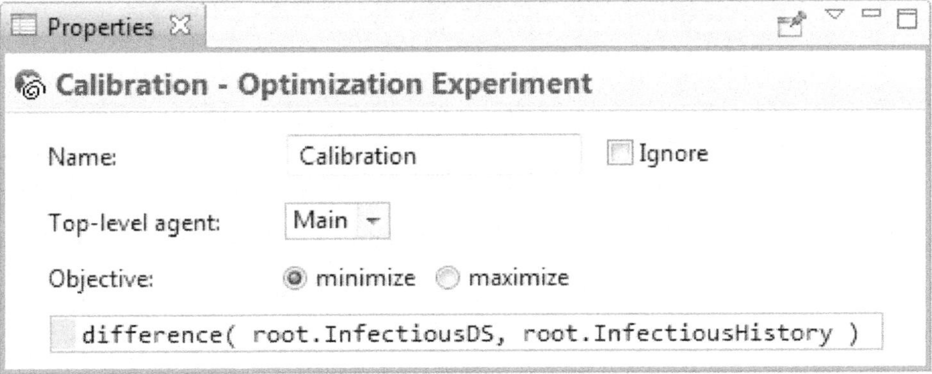

10. Open the calibration experiment properties' **Advanced** section and then clear the **Allow parallel evaluations** checkbox.

11. Run the calibration experiment by either right-clicking *Calibration* in the **Projects** view and then clicking **Run**, or by selecting *SEIR / Calibration* from the list of experiments in the **Run** toolbar menu.

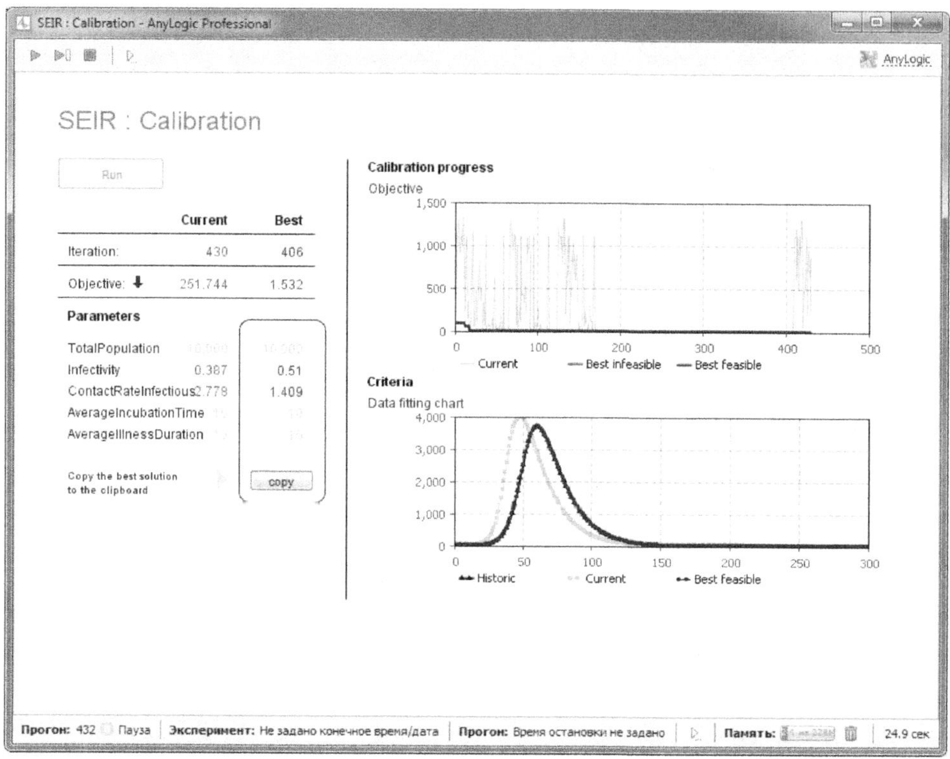

12. After the calibration is complete, you can copy the best fitting parameter values by clicking the experiment window's **copy** button and then paste them into the simulation experiment by clicking the **Paste from clipboard** button that you'll find on the *Simulation* experiment's properties page.

After you've pasted the parameter values into the experiment, you can then run the *Simulation* with the newly-calibrated parameter values.

Discrete-event modeling with AnyLogic

Discrete event modeling is nearly the same age as system dynamics. In 1961, IBM engineer Geoffrey Gordon introduced GPSS, considered to be the first software implementation of the discrete event modeling method. Today, a number of programs - including modern versions of GPSS - offer discrete event modeling.

> ◆ **Discrete event modeling requires a modeler to think about the system that he or she wants to model as a process - a sequence of operations that agents perform.**

A model's operations can include delays, service by various resources, process branch selections, splits and many others. As long as agents compete for limited resources and can be delayed, queues will be part of nearly all discrete event models.

The model is specified graphically as a process flowchart where blocks represent operations. The flowchart usually starts with "source" blocks that generate agents and inject them into the process and ends with "sink" blocks that remove them.

Agents – originally named *transactions* in GPSS or entities in other simulation software -- can represent clients, patients, phone calls, physical and electronic documents, parts, products, pallets, computer transactions, vehicles, tasks, projects, ideas, and so forth. *Resources* represent staff, doctors, operators, workers, servers, CPUs, computer memory, equipment, and transport.

Service times and agent arrival times are usually stochastic, and since they're drawn from a probability distribution, discrete event models are themselves stochastic. In simple terms, this means a model must run for a specific amount of time or complete a specific number of replications before it produces meaningful output.

Typical output expected from a discrete event model includes:

- Utilization of resources

- Time spent in the system or its part by an agent

- Waiting times

- Queue lengths
- System throughput
- Bottlenecks

Job Shop model

Our goal is to create a discrete-event model that will simulate a small job shop's manufacturing and shipping processes. The raw materials that are delivered to the receiving dock are placed into storage until processing takes place at the CNC machine.

Phase 1. Creating a simple model

We'll start by creating a simple model that will simulate the pallets' arrival at the job shop, their storage at the shipping dock, and their arrival at the forklift area.

1. Create a new model. In the **New Model** wizard, set the **Model name**: *Job Shop*, and **Model time units**: **minutes**.

2. Open the **Presentation** palette. The palette has several shapes that you can use to draw model animation, including a rectangle, a line, an oval, a polyline and a curve.

3. On the **Presentation** palette, select the **Image** shape and then drag it on to the *Main* diagram. You can use the **Image** shape to add images in several graphic formats -- including PNG, JPEG, GIF, and BMP – to your presentation.

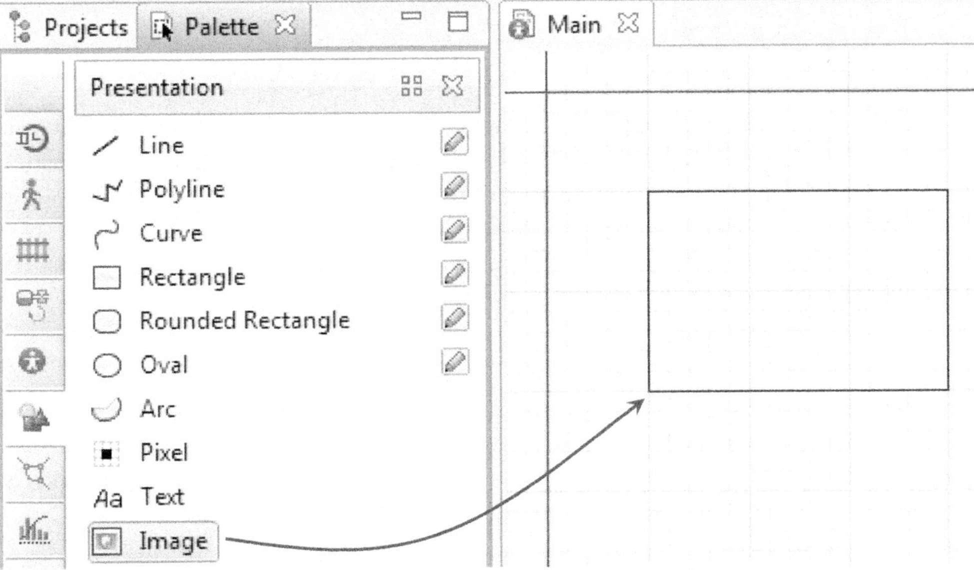

4. You'll see the dialog box that prompts you to choose the image file the shape will display.

5. Browse to the following location and then select the *layout.png* image:

   AnyLogic folder/resources/AnyLogic in 3 days/Job Shop

After you select the layout.png image, our diagram of the *Main* agent type should look like the following image:

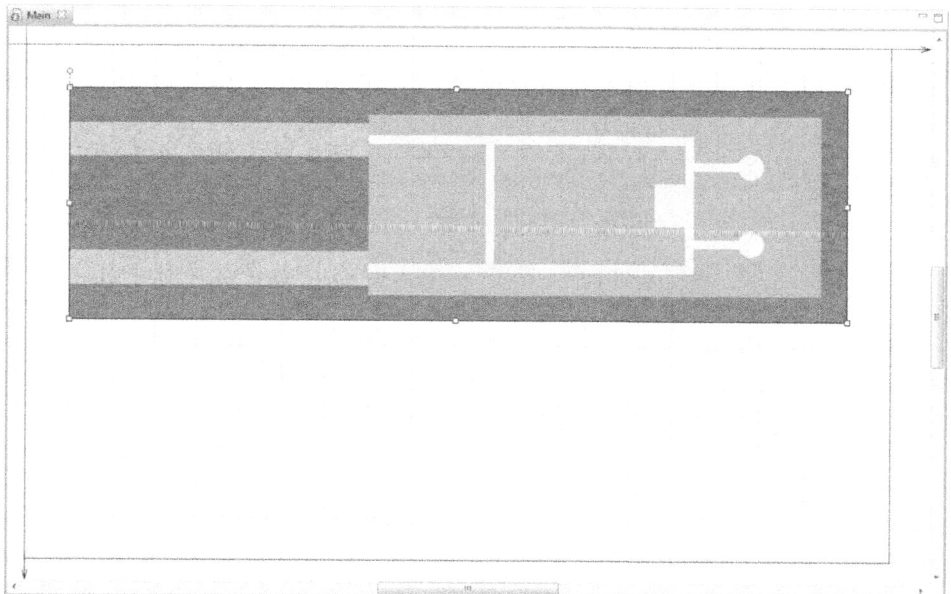

AnyLogic adds the image in its original size on to the *Main* diagram, but you can also change the image's width or length. If you distort the image's proportions as in the figure below, you can revert to the image's original size by opening the **Properties** view and clicking **Reset to original size**.

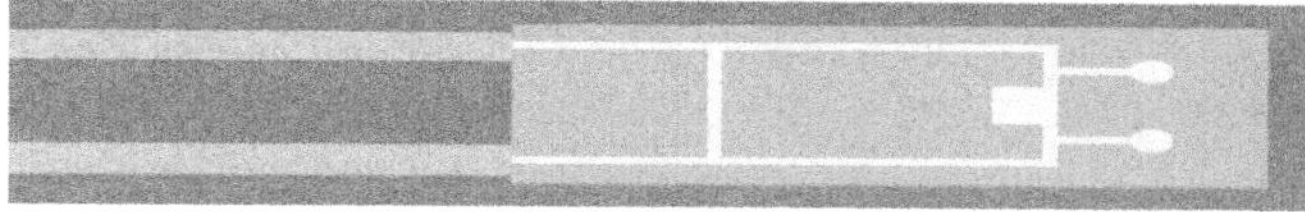

6. Select the image in the graphical editor. In the **Properties** view, select the **Lock** checkbox to lock the image.

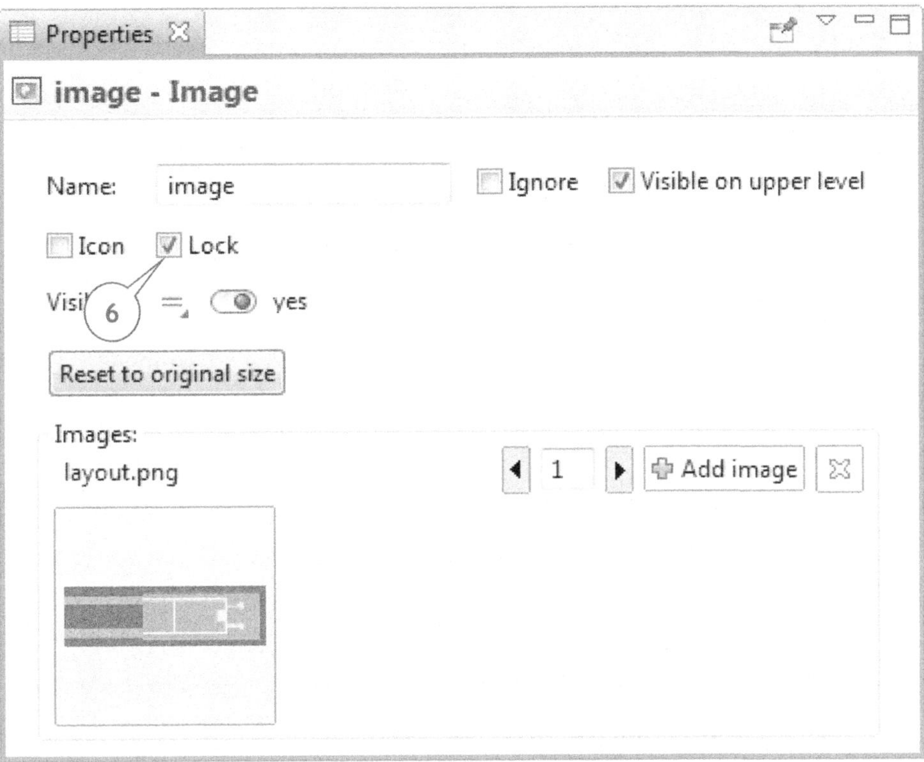

Locking shapes

- You can lock a shape to ensure it doesn't respond to your mouse click and you can't select it in the graphical editor. You'll find this very helpful as you draw shapes on top of layouts that represent facilities such as factories or hospitals.

- If you need to unlock a shape, right-click in the graphical editor and select **Unlock All Shapes** from the menu.

Space markup elements

Our next step is to use the **Space Markup** palette to place space markup shapes on top of the job shop's layout. The palette includes a **Path** element, three **Node** elements, an **Attractor** element, and **Pallet Rack** shapes.

Creating a network

Paths and *nodes* are space markup elements that define the locations of agents:

- A **Node** is a place where agents may reside or perform an operation.

- A **Path** is a route that agents can use to move between nodes.

Together, nodes and paths make up a *network* that a model's agents can use to move along the shortest paths between their origin and destination nodes. You'll usually create a network when your model's processes take place in a defined physical space and it has moving agents and resources. It is assumed that network segments have unlimited capacity, and the agents do not interfere with one another.

Now that you know a little bit about networks and their component parts, we're ready to create a network that will define the movement paths for our model's pallets. The first step is to use rectangular nodes to define specific areas on the job shop's layout.

Draw the rectangular node over the job shop's entrance, as shown in the figure below, to represent our model's pallet receiving dock.

7. Open the **Space Markup** palette, and drag the **Rectangular Node** element on to the *Main* diagram. Resize the node. The node should look as in the figure below.

8. Name the created node *receivingDock.*

9. Draw a node to define the location where the model's agents will park forklift trucks once the trucks are idle or the agents no longer need them to complete a task. Use another **Rectangular Node** to draw the parking area as shown in the figure below and then name this node *forkliftParking.*

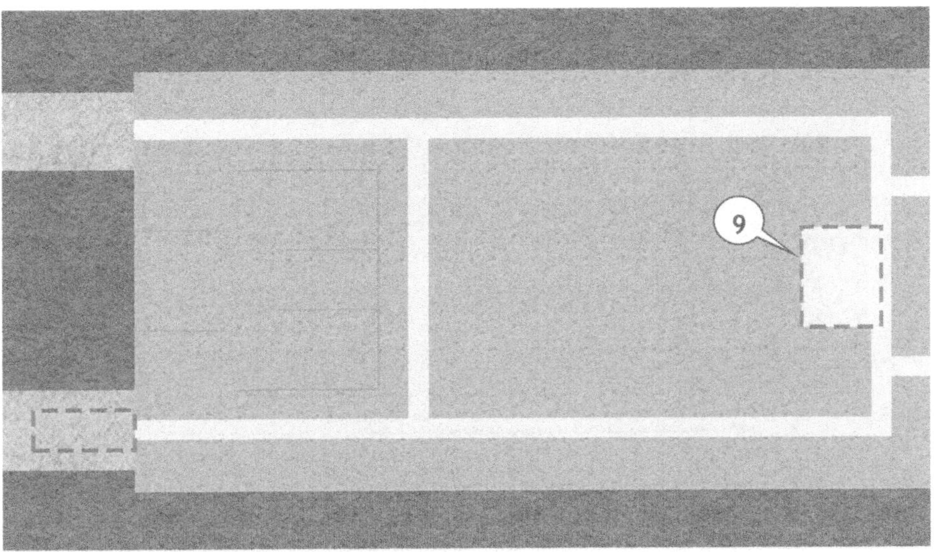

Let's draw a movement path to guide our model's forklift trucks.

10. Do the following to draw a movement path that will guide our model's forklift trucks:

    a.   In the **Space Markup** palette, double-click the **Path** element to activate its drawing mode.

    b.   Draw the path as shown in the figure below by clicking the *receivingDock* border, clicking in the diagram to add the path's turning point, and then clicking the *forkliftParking* node's border.

If you've successfully connected the nodes, the path's connection points will display cyan highlights each time you select the path.

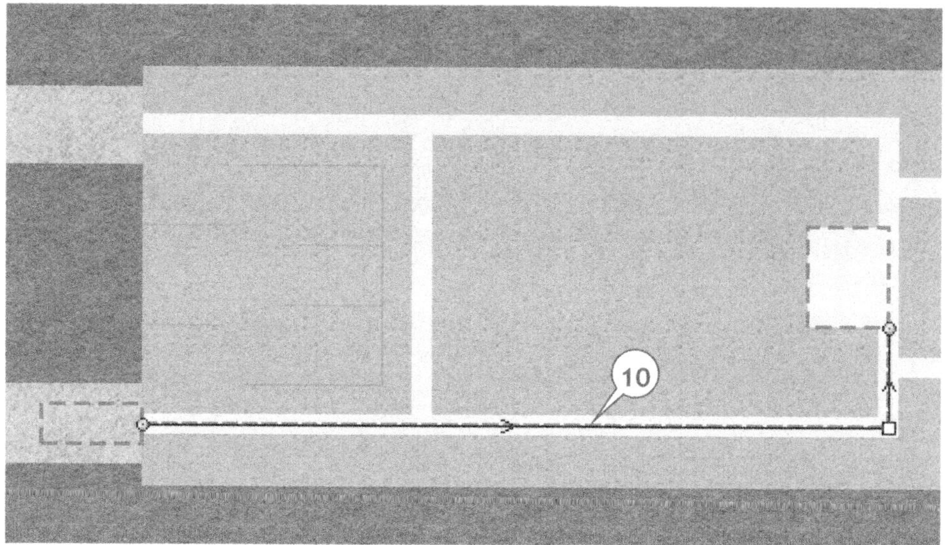

By default, paths in AnyLogic 7 are bidirectional. However, you can limit movement along a selected path to one direction by clearing the **Bidirectional** property and then defining the movement direction. You can view a given path's direction by selecting the path and then viewing the direction arrow that displays in the graphical editor.

11. Define your model's warehouse storage by dragging the **Pallet Rack** element from the **Space Markup** palette on to the layout and placing its aisle on the path. A correctly-placed pallet rack will display a green highlight that shows it is connected to the network.

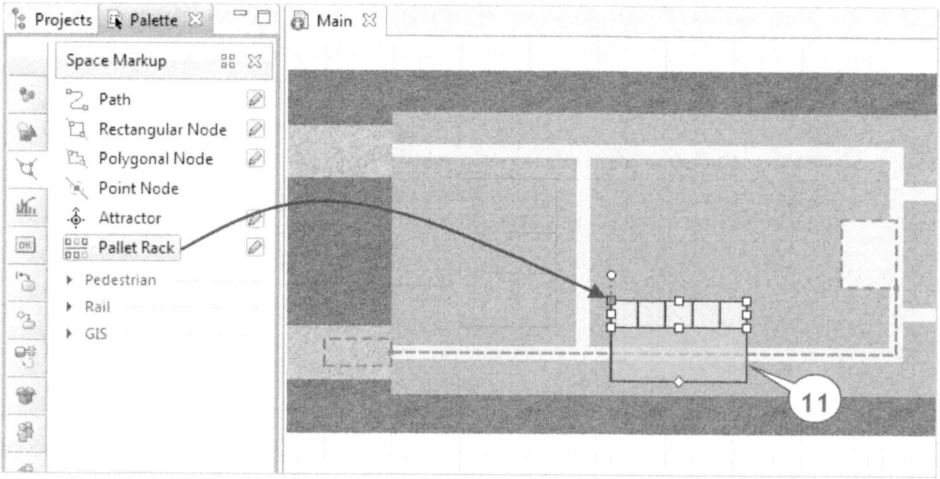

Pallet rack

The **Pallet Rack** 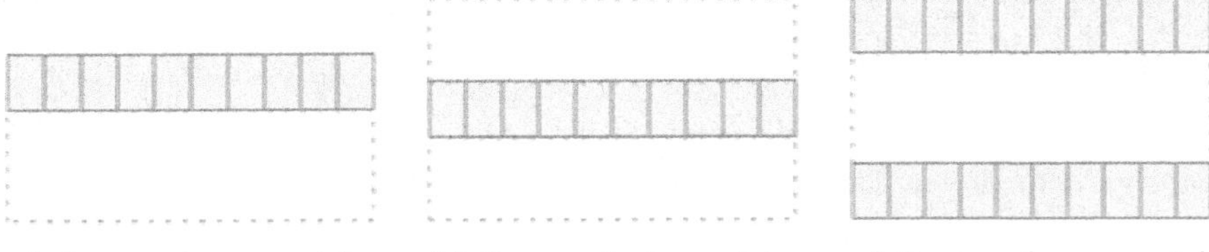 space markup element graphically represents the pallet racks you often see in warehouses and storage zones. As you can see below, the element has three alternative configurations.

During runtime, the **Pallet Rack** element manages the agents that the model stores in the single-level or multiple level cells that are available on side(s) of the aisle.

12. In the pallet rack's **Properties** area, do the following:

    a. Set **Type** to: *two racks, one aisle*

    b. **Number of cells**: *10*

    c. **Level height**: *10*

    In the **Position and size** section:

    d. **Length**: *160*

    e. **Left pallet rack depth**: *14*

    f. **Right pallet rack depth**: *14*

    g. **Aisle width**: *11*

13. After you've completed these changes, the pallet rack should resemble the pallet rack shown in the figure below. If necessary, move the pallet rack so that its center aisle lies on the path. Make sure the pallet rack is connected to the network by clicking it twice to select it. Your first click will select the entire network, and the second will select the pallet rack. The pallet rack should display a green highlight that shows it is connected to the network.

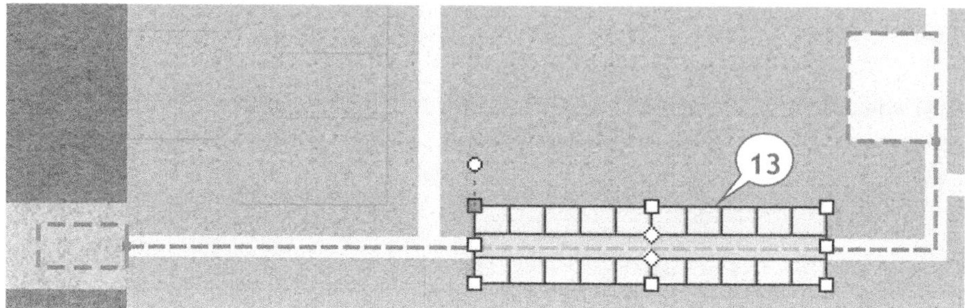

We've marked up our model's space by drawing the important locations and paths on top of our layout, and we'll now use the AnyLogic *Process Modeling Library* to model the processes.

Process Modeling Library

The blocks in AnyLogic's *Process Modeling Library* allow you to use combinations of *agents*, *resources*, and *processes* to create process-centric models of real-world systems. You learned about agents and resources earlier in this section, and we'll build upon that foundation by defining processes as operations sequences that include queues, delays, and resource utilization.

Your model's processes are defined by *flowcharts*, the graphical process representations you construct from the Process Modeling Library's blocks. In the following steps, you'll create the process flowchart.

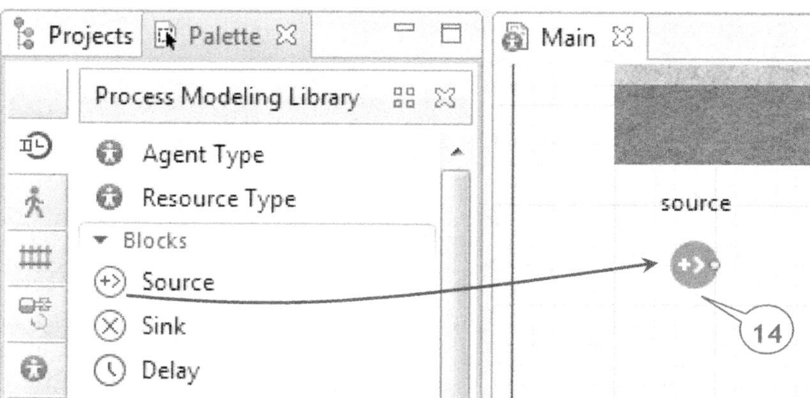

14. Drag the **Source** element from the **Process Modeling Library** palette on to the graphical diagram and name the block *sourcePallets*.

While the **Source** block usually acts as a process starting point, our model will use it to generate pallets.

15. In the *sourcePallets* block's **Properties** area, do the following to ensure the model's pallets arrive every five minutes and appear in the *receivingDock* node.

    a.   In the **Arrivals defined by** area, click **Interarrival time**.

    b.   In the **Interarrival time** box, type *5*, and select **minutes** from the list on the right to have pallets arrive every five minutes.

    c.   In the **Location of arrival** area, click **Network / GIS node** in the list.

    d.   In the **Node** area, click *receivingDock* in the list.

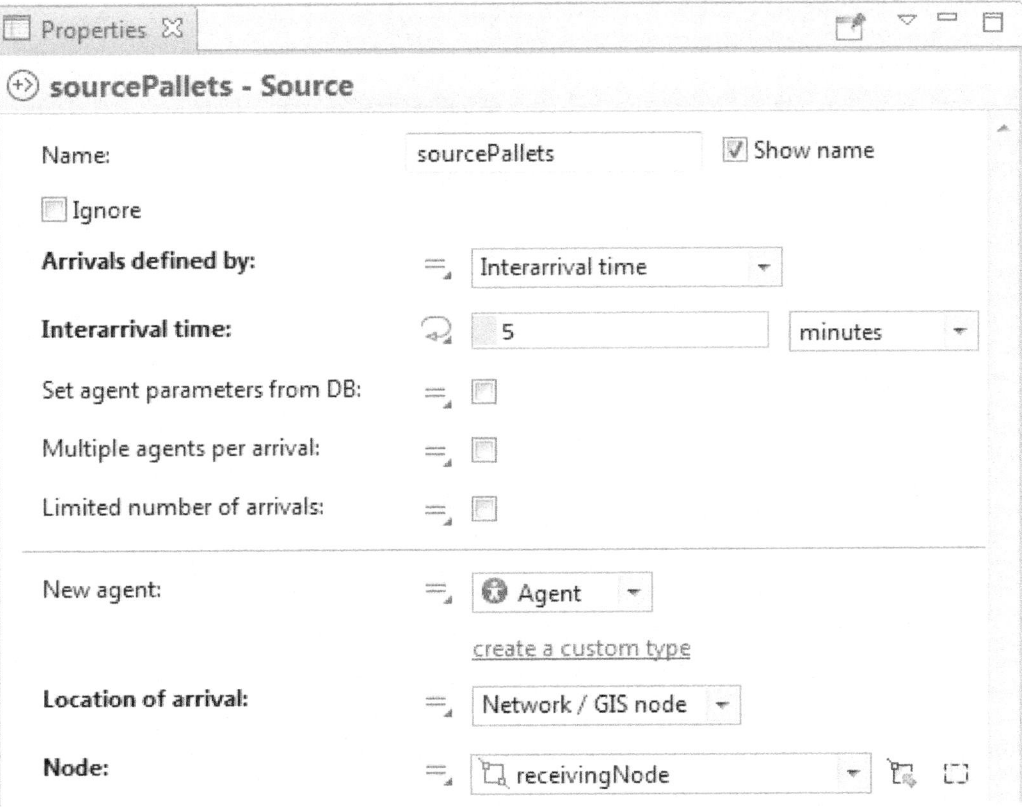

How to refer to model elements from block's parameters

The block's parameters offer two ways to select a graphical element:

- You can select a graphical element from the list of available and valid elements that displays beside the parameter.

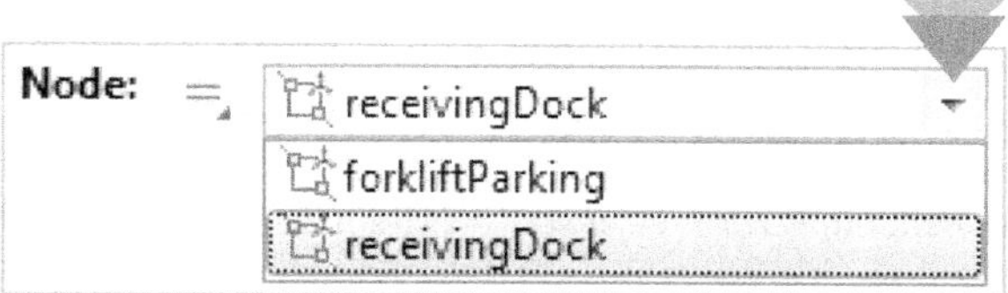

- You can select a graphical element by clicking the selection button that displays beside the list. If you click the selection button, it will limit your choices to the available and valid elements that you can select by clicking in the graphical editor:

Continue constructing the flowchart by adding other **Process Modeling Library** blocks:

16. Drag the **RackStore** block from the **Process Modeling Library** palette on to the diagram and place it near the *sourcePallets* block so they are automatically connected as shown in the diagram below.

The **RackStore** block places pallets into a given pallet rack's cells.

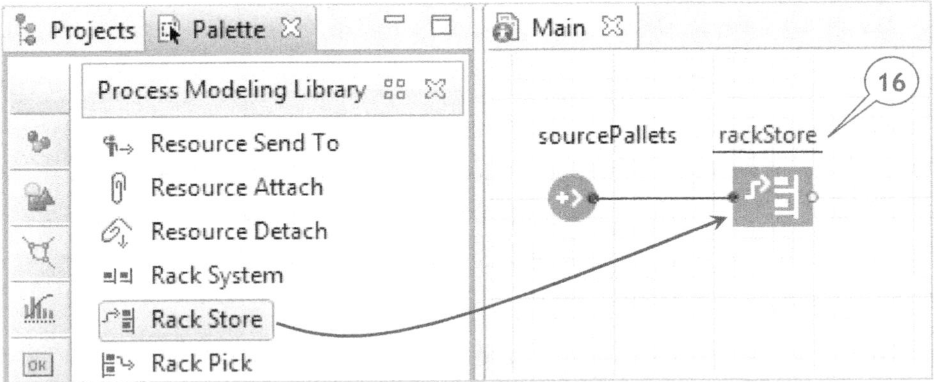

17. In the *rackStore* block's **Properties** area, do the following:

    a.   In the **Name** box, type *storeRawMaterial*.

    b.   In the **Pallet rack / Rack system** list, click *palletRack*.

    c.   In the **Agent location (queue)** list, click *receivingDock* to specify the location where agents wait to be stored.

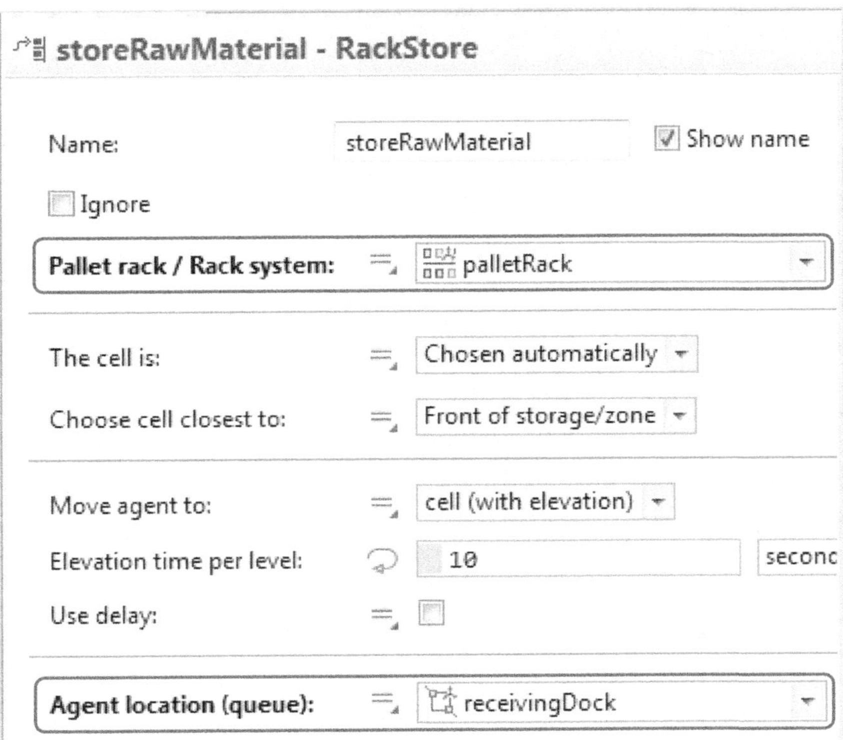

18. Add a **Delay** ⏱ block to simulate how pallets wait in the rack and then name the block *rawMaterialInStorage*.

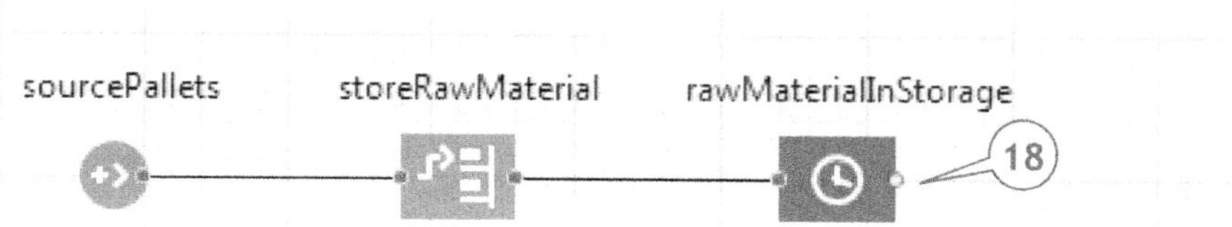

You've probably noticed that AnyLogic automatically connects the block's right port to the following block's left port. Each Process Modeling Library block has a left *input port* and a right *output port*, but you should only connect input ports to output ports.

19. In the *rawMaterialInStorage* block's **Properties** area, do the following:

   a.   In the **Delay time** box, type *triangular(15, 20, 30)* and select **minutes** from the list.

   b.   Select the **Maximum capacity** checkbox to ensure agents will not get stuck as they wait to be picked up from storage.

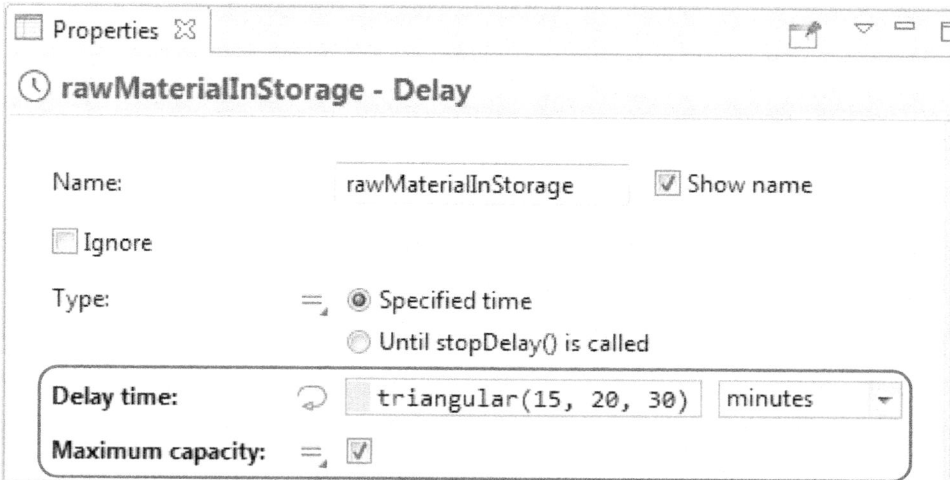

20. Add a **RackPick** block, connect it to the flowchart, and then name it *pickRawMaterial*.

In our model, the **RackPick** block removes a pallet from a cell in the pallet rack and then moves it to the specified destination.

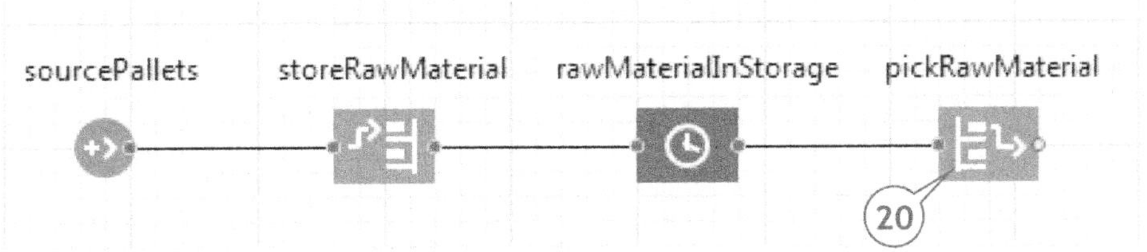

21. In the *pickRawMaterial* block's **Properties** area, do the following:

    a.   In the **Pallet rack / Rack system** list, click *palletRack* to select the pallet rack that will provide pallets to agents.

    b.   In the **Node** list, click *forkliftParking* to specify where the agents should park forklift trucks.

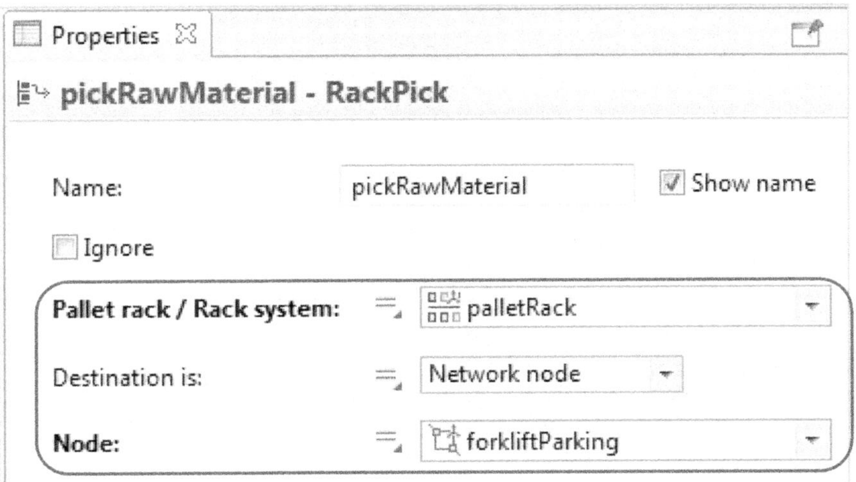

22. Add a **Sink** ⊗ block. The **Sink** block disposes agents and is usually a flowchart's end point.

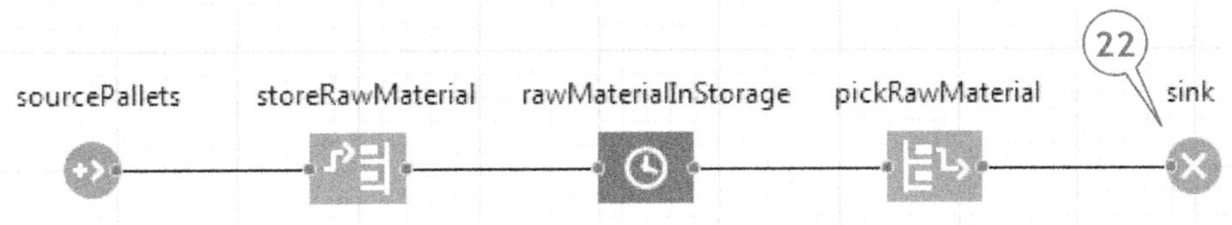

23. We've finished building this simple model, and you can now run it and observe its behavior. Run the model (*Job Shop / Simulation* experiment).

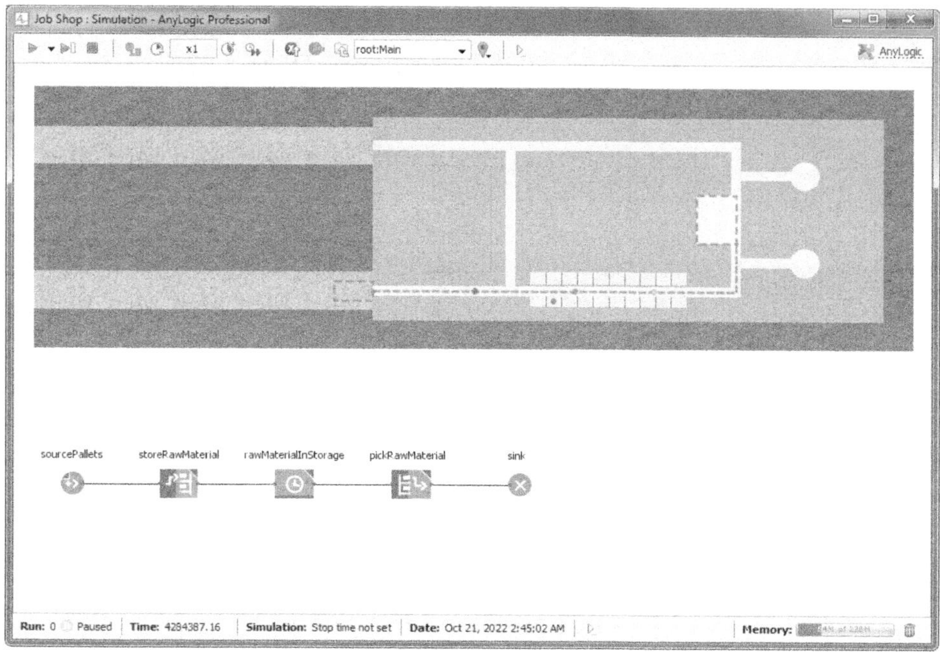

If the **Exception during discrete event execution** error message displays, you must connect your pallet rack to the network. You should select the pallet rack shape in the graphical editor, move it until the pallet rack's aisle displays a green highlight that shows it has connected to the network, and then rerun the model.

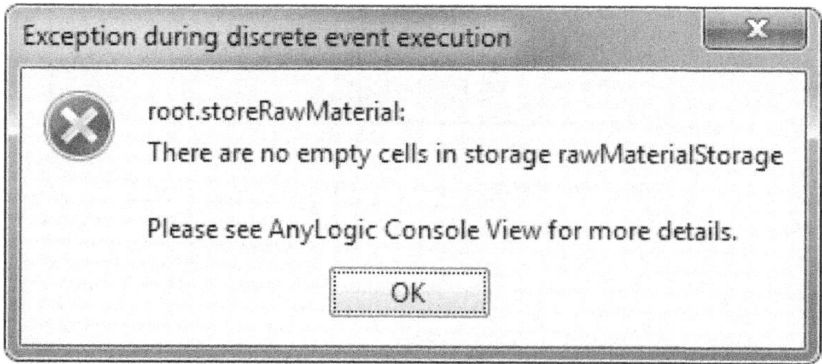

Phase 2. Adding resources

Let's continue developing our model by adding resources – forklift trucks – to store the pallets in the pallet rack and then move them to the production area.

Resources

Resources are objects that agents use to perform a given action. An agent must obtain the resource, perform the action, and then release the resource.

Some examples of resources include:

- A hospital model's doctors, nurses, equipment, and wheelchairs

- A supply chain model's vehicles and containers

- A warehouse model's forklift trucks and workers

There are three types of resources: *static*, *moving*, and *portable*.

- Static resources are bound to a specific location, and they cannot move or be moved.

- Moving resources can move independently.

- Portable resources can be moved by agents or by moving resources.

In AnyLogic, the Process Modeling library's **ResourcePool** block defines each set or pool of resources. Resource units can have individual attributes, and each resource has a graphical diagram where you can add elements such as statecharts, parameters, and functions.

Our model's resources are the forklift trucks that move pallets from the unloading zone to a pallet rack and then deliver pallets from the rack to the production zone.

1. On the **Process Modeling Library** palette, drag the **ResourcePool** block on to the *Main* diagram. You do not have to connect the block to the flowchart.

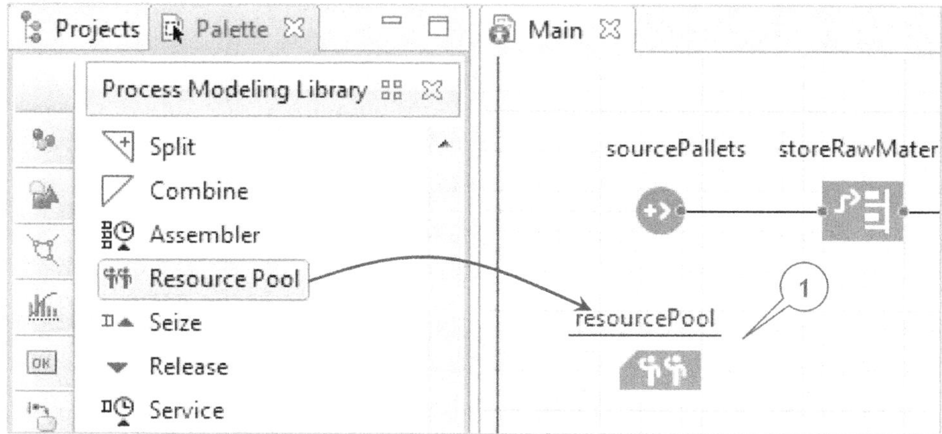

2. Name the block *forklifts*.

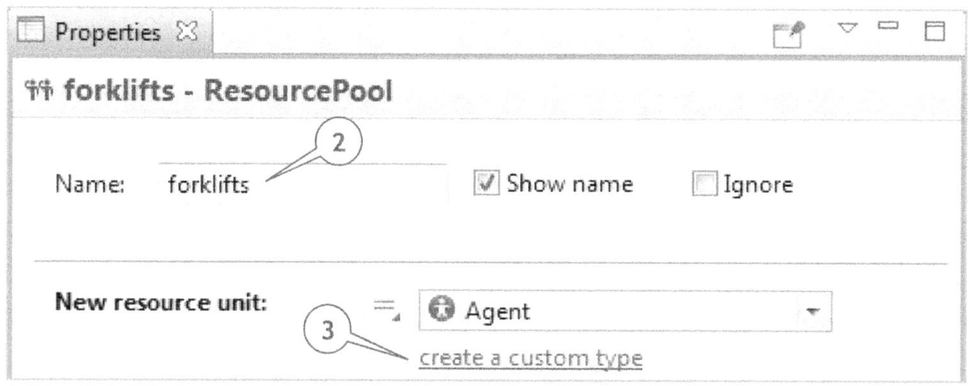

3. In the *forklifts* block's **Properties** area, click the button **create a custom type**. This way we create a new type of a resource.

4. In the **New agent** wizard:

   a.   In **Agent type name** box, type *ForkliftTruck*.

   b.   Click **Next**.

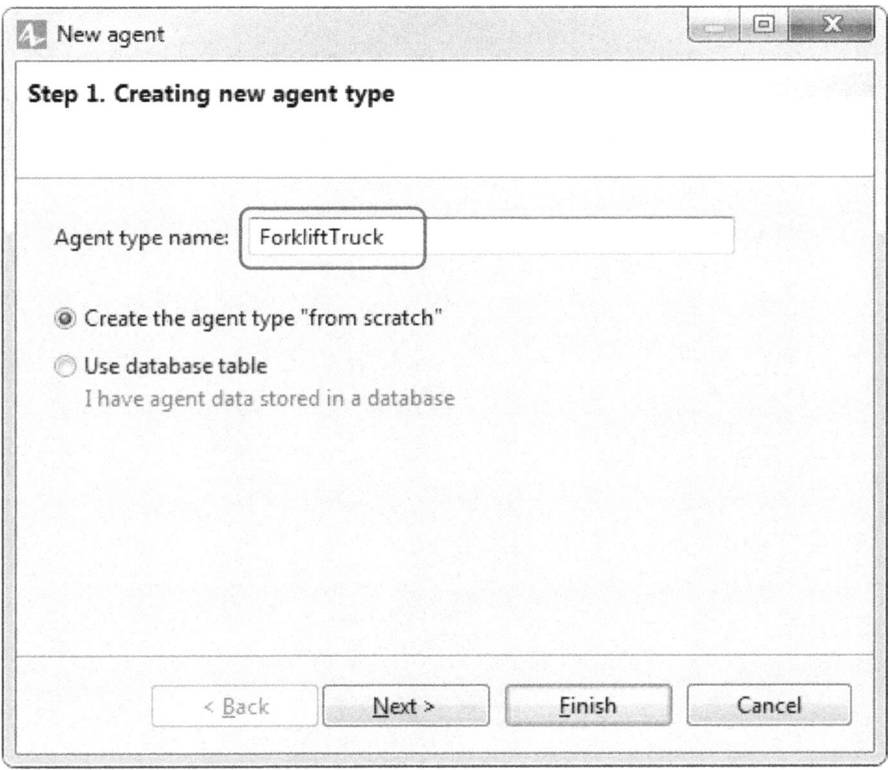

c.   On the next page, in the list in the left part of the wizard, expand the **Warehouses and Container Terminals** area, and then click the 3D animation figure **Fork Lift Truck**.

d.   Click **Finish**.

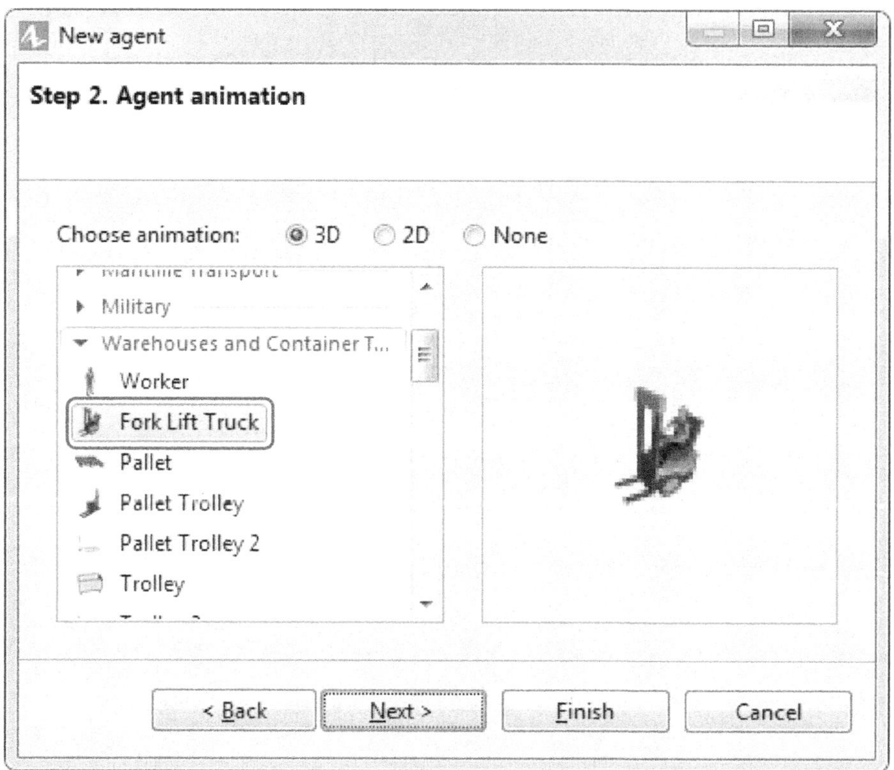

The *ForkliftTruck* agent type diagram will open and display the animation shape you selected in the wizard.

5. Click the **Main** tab to open the *Main* diagram.

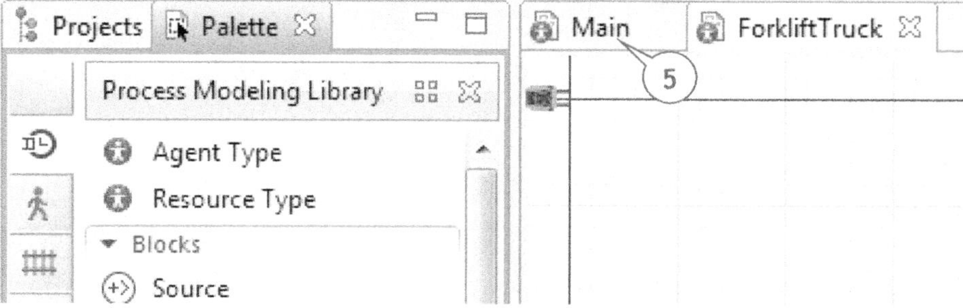

You'll see the *ForkliftTruck* resource type has been selected in the **ResourcePool** block's **New resource unit** parameter.

6. Modify the *forklifts* resource type's other parameters:

a. In the **Capacity** box, type **5** to set the number of forklift trucks in our model.

b. In the **Speed** box, type **1** and choose **meters per second** from the list on the right.

c. In the **Home location (nodes)** area, select the *forkliftParking* node. Click the plus button 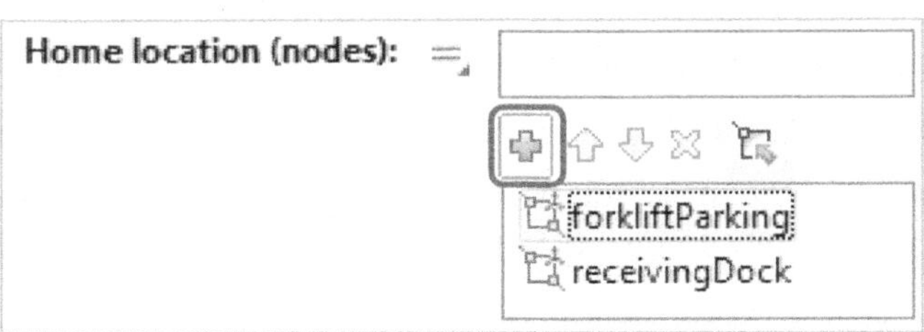 and then click **forkliftParking** in the list of the model's nodes.

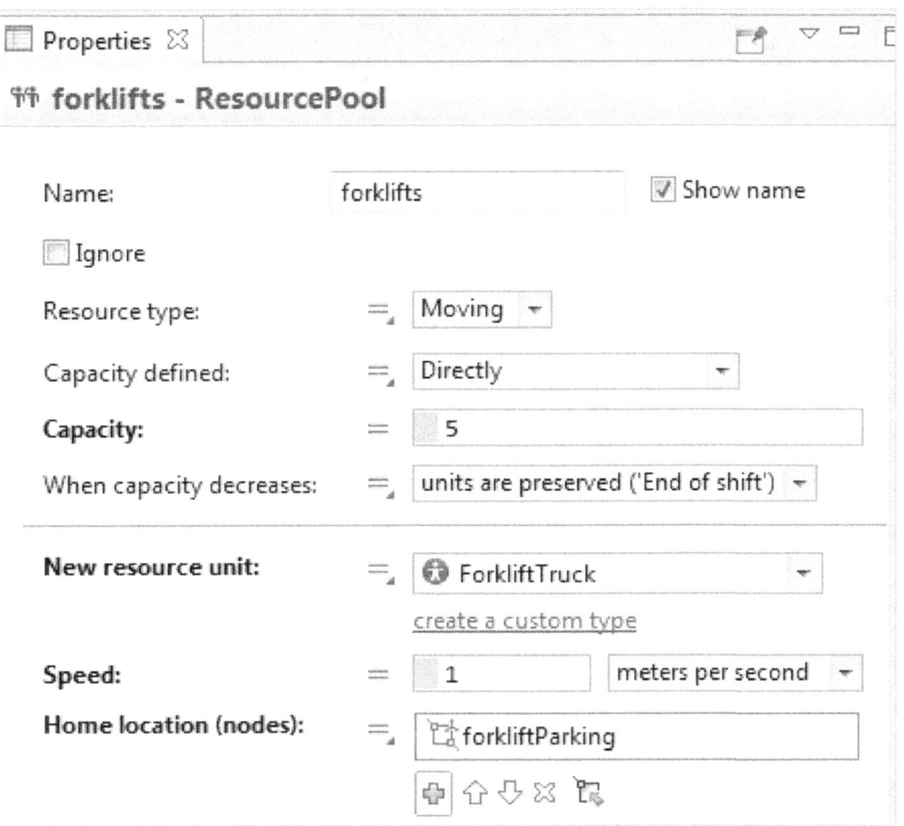

We've defined our resources, but we still need to make sure our model's flowchart blocks will use them during the simulated processes.

7.   In the *storeRawMaterial* block's **Properties** area, do the following:

   a.   Click the arrow to expand the **Resources** area.

   b.   Select the **Use resources to move** check box.

   c.   In the **Resource sets (alternatives)** list, select **forklifts** to ensure the flowchart block uses the selected resources -- in our case, the forklift trucks -- to move the agents. Click the plus button and then click **forklifts** in the list of the model's resources.

   d.   In the **Return home** area, select **if no other tasks** to ensure the forklift trucks return to their home location after they complete their tasks.

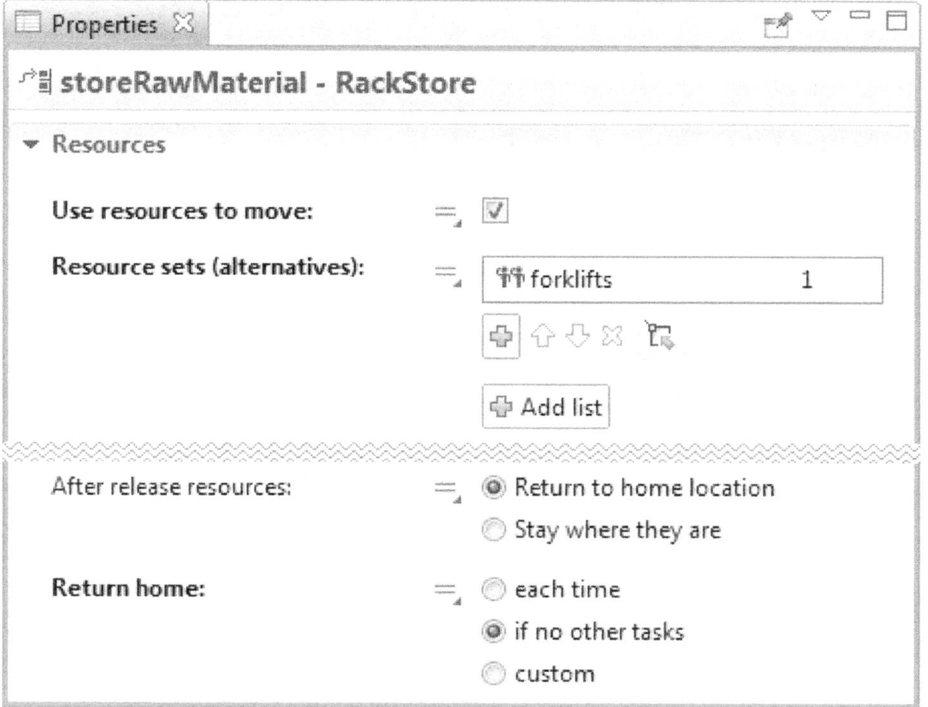

8.   In the *pickRawMaterial* block's **Properties** area, do the following:

   a.   Click the arrow to expand the **Resources** area.

   b.   Select the **Use resources to move** check box.

c.   In the **Resource sets (alternatives)** list, click **forklifts** to ensure the flowchart block uses the forklift trucks to move the agents.

d.   In the **Return home** area, click **if no other tasks** to ensure the forklift trucks return to their home location after they complete their tasks.

If our model's resources move an agent, **RackStore** (or **RackPick**) block seizes them, brings to the agent location, attaches to the agent, moves the agent to the cell, and then releases the resources.

9.   Run the model.

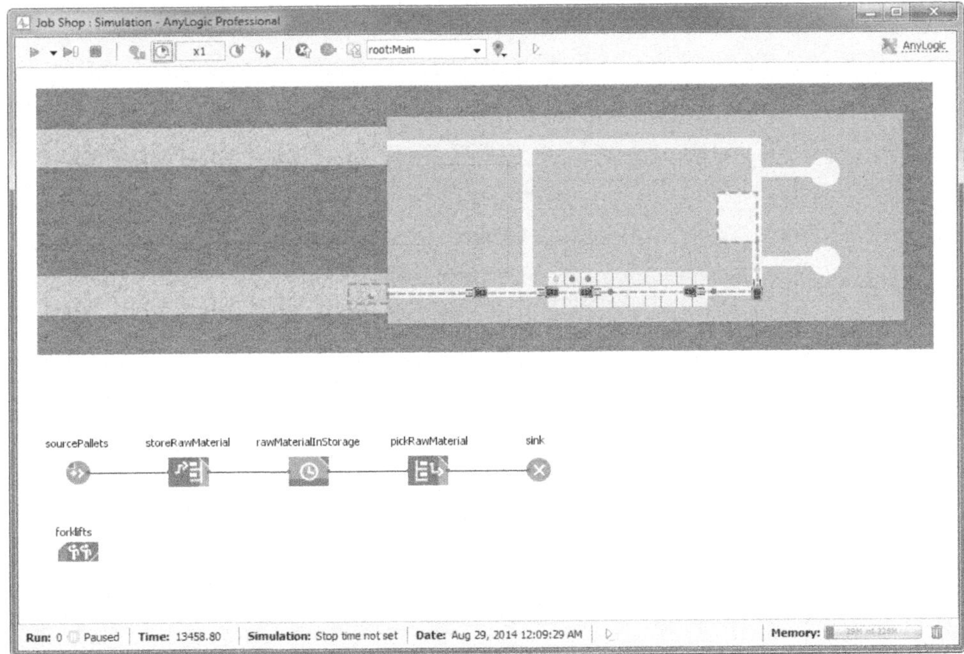

You'll see the forklift trucks pick up the pallets and store them in the pallet rack. After a brief delay, they move the pallets to the forklift truck parking area where the pallets will disappear.

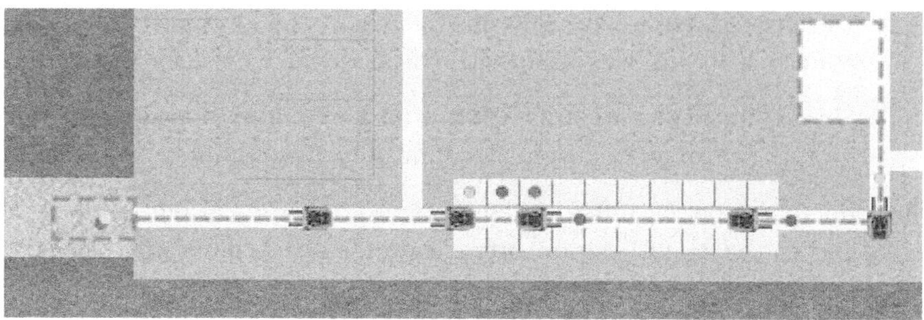

Phase 3. Creating 3D animation

You've now seen many of the features that help make AnyLogic such a powerful modeling tool. But there are others you haven't touched, and one of the most exciting is 3D animation.

Introducing Camera Objects

AnyLogic's camera objects allow you to define the view that displays in the 3D window. In essence, the camera object "shoots" the picture that you see.

You can also create several camera objects to show different areas of the same 3D scene or to show a single object from different points of view. If you use more than one camera object, you can easily switch from one view to another at runtime.

1. On the **Presentation**  palette, drag the **Camera** object on to the *Main* diagram so it faces the job shop layout.

2. Drag the **3D Window** element on to the *Main* diagram, and then place it below the process flowchart.

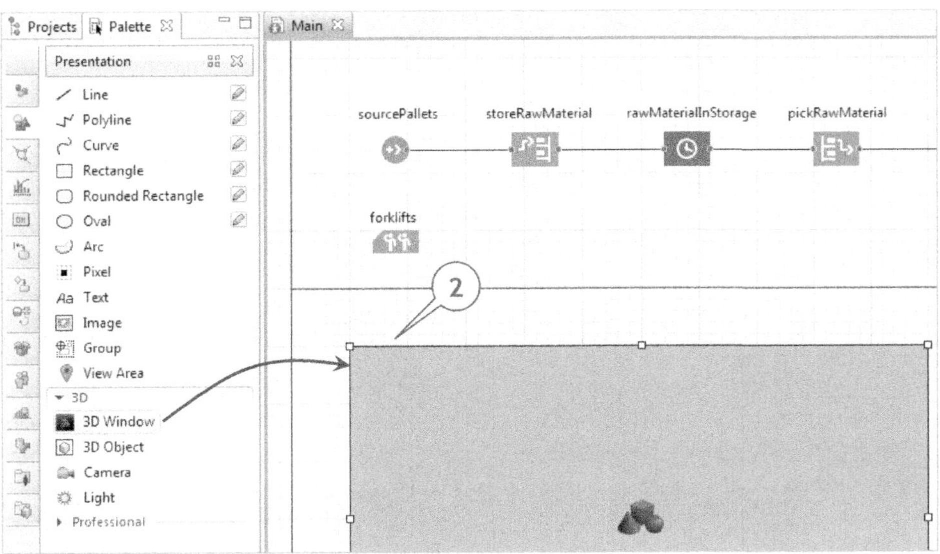

3D Window

In addition to having the option to add several cameras to your model, you can also add several 3D windows that will each display the same 3D scene from a different point of view.

3. Let the camera "shoot" the picture for the 3D window. In the 3D window's **Properties** area, click **camera** in the **Camera** list.

4. Prevent the camera from shooting the picture from under the floor by selecting the option **Limited to Z above 0** from the **Navigation type** list.

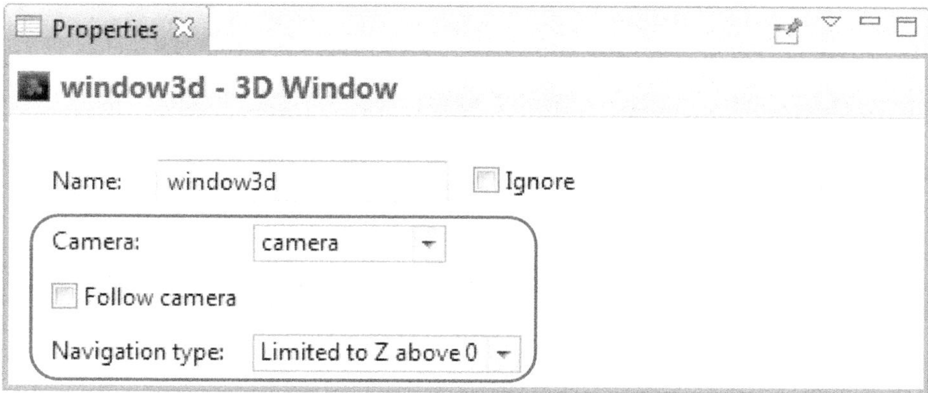

5. Run the model.

When you create a 3D window, AnyLogic adds a view area that allows you to easily navigate to the 3D view at runtime. To switch to this 3D view, click the toolbar's **Navigate to view area...** button and then click **[window3d]**.

The view area expands the 3D window to the model window's full size.

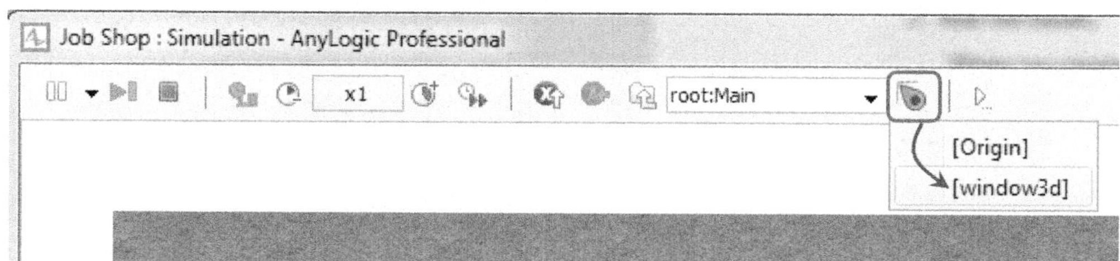

6. Do one or more of the following to navigate in 3D at runtime:

- To move the camera left, right, forward or backward, drag the mouse in the selected direction.

- To move the camera closer to or further from the scene's center, rotate the mouse's wheel.

- To rotate the scene relative to the camera, drag the mouse while you press and hold ALT and the left mouse button.

7. Choose the view you want to display at runtime, right-click (Mac OS: CTRL+click) inside the 3D scene, and then click **Copy the camera's location**.

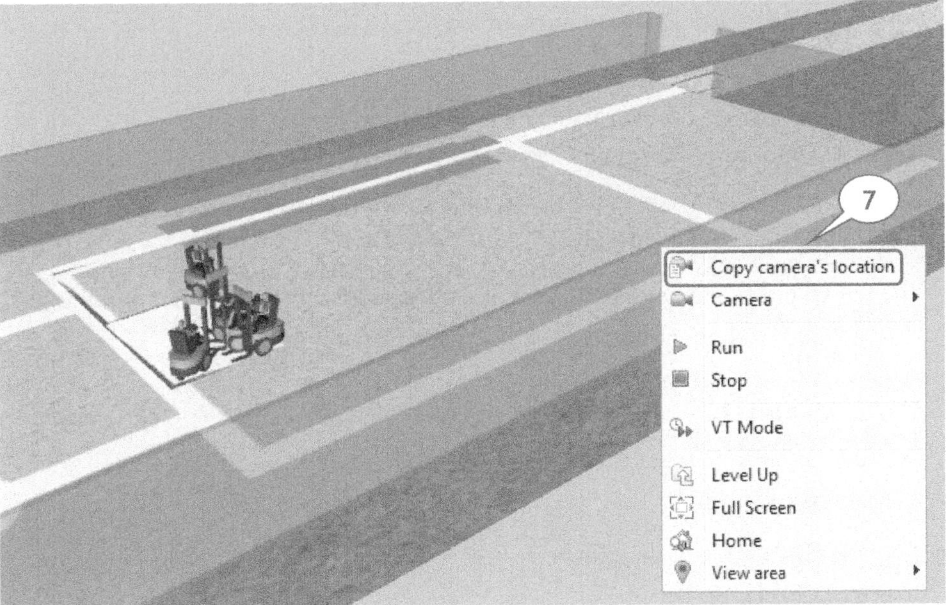

8. Close the model's window.

9. On the camera's **Properties** area, apply the camera location you selected during the previous step by clicking **Paste coordinates from clipboard**.

NOTE: If you can't locate the camera, you can use the **Projects** tree. It will display *camera* under the *Main* agent's **Presentation** branch.

10. Run the model to view the 3D view from the new camera position, and then close the model window.

11. Expand the **Space Markup** palette's **Pedestrian** area and then double-click the **Wall** element's icon to enable wall drawing mode.

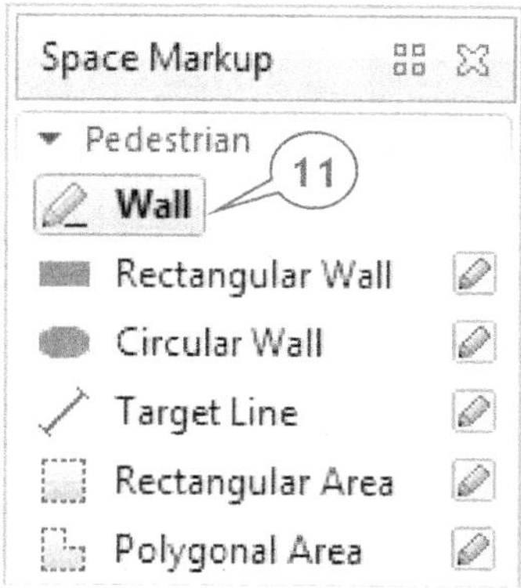

12. Do the following to draw walls around the job shop layout's working area:

    a.   Click the position in the graphical editor where you want to start drawing the wall.

    b.   Move the pointer in any direction to draw a straight line, and then click at any point where you want to change direction.

    c.   Double-click at the point where you want to stop drawing the wall.

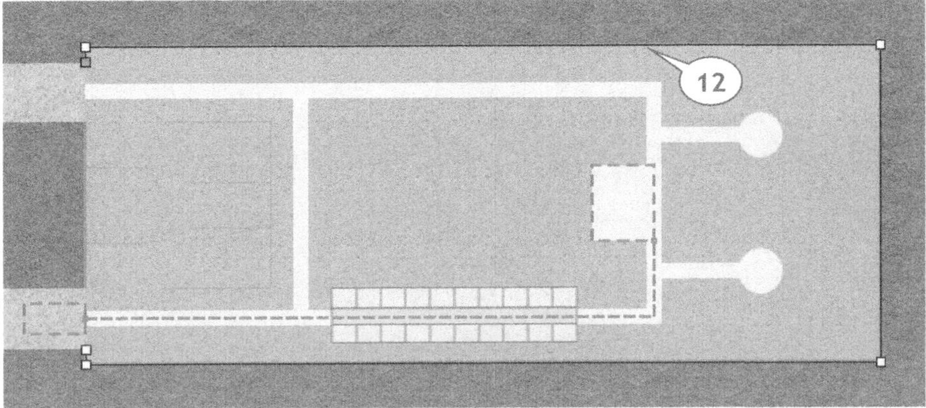

13. Do the following to change the wall's fill color and texture:

    a.   On the wall's **Properties** area, expand the **Appearance** section.

    b.   In the color menu, click **Other colors**.

    c.   In the **Colors** dialog, select the color that you want to apply to the wall from the palette or the spectrum.

        You can also set a transparency level (use **Transparency** slider in the **Colors** dialog) or customize the wall with any provided texture (click the **Textures...** item in the colors menu).

In this section, we're using walls to decorate our model. In a later tutorial where we'll model the actions of pedestrians at an airport, we'll see how walls can also be obstacles.

14. Go to the wall's **Position and size** section and change the **Z-Height** to *40*.

AnyLogic automatically sets the shape's height to 20 pixels to ensure it has volume in a 3D view, but we've now increased its height to 40 pixels.

15. Draw another wall between the exits and then change the settings in the second wall's **Properties** area to match the first wall.

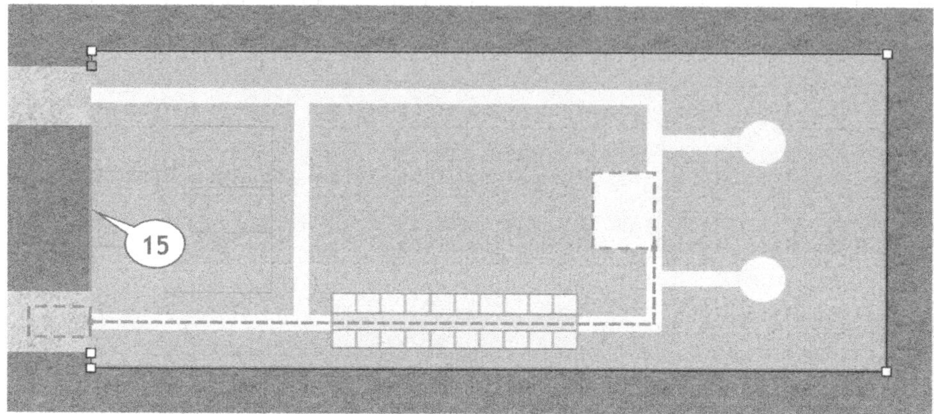

16. Run the model and view the 3D animation.

    You'll see that our model's animation uses cylinder shapes to represent pallets, but we'll correct the problem by creating an agent type that defines a custom animation for pallets.

17. In the *sourcePallets* block's **Properties** area, under the **New agent** list, click the **create a custom type** link.

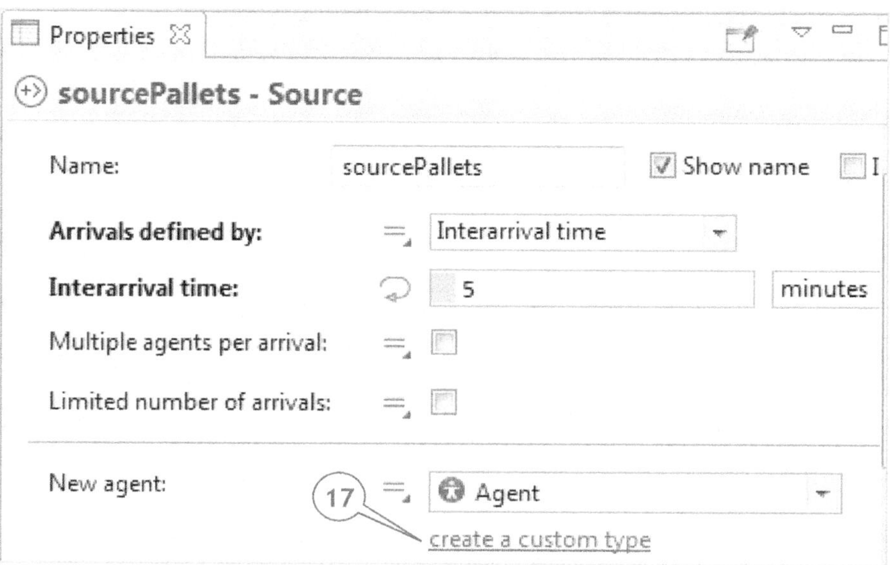

18. In the **New agent** wizard, do the following:

    a.   In the **Agent type name** field, type *Pallet*.

b. Click **Next**.

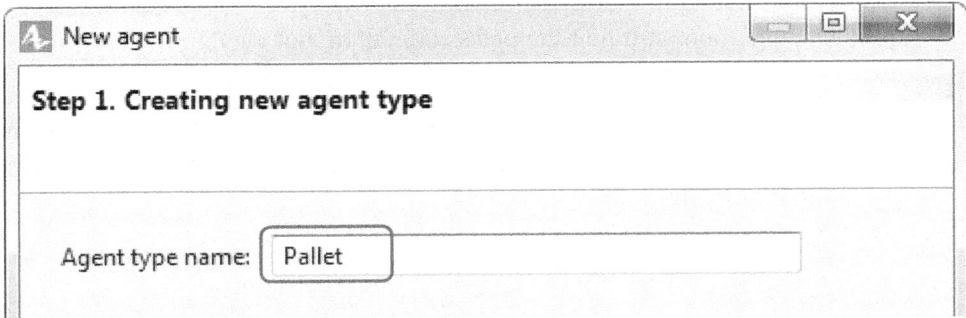

c. On the next page of the wizard, expand the **Warehouses and Container Terminals** section in the list on the left, and then click the 3D animation figure **Pallet**.

d. Click **Finish**.

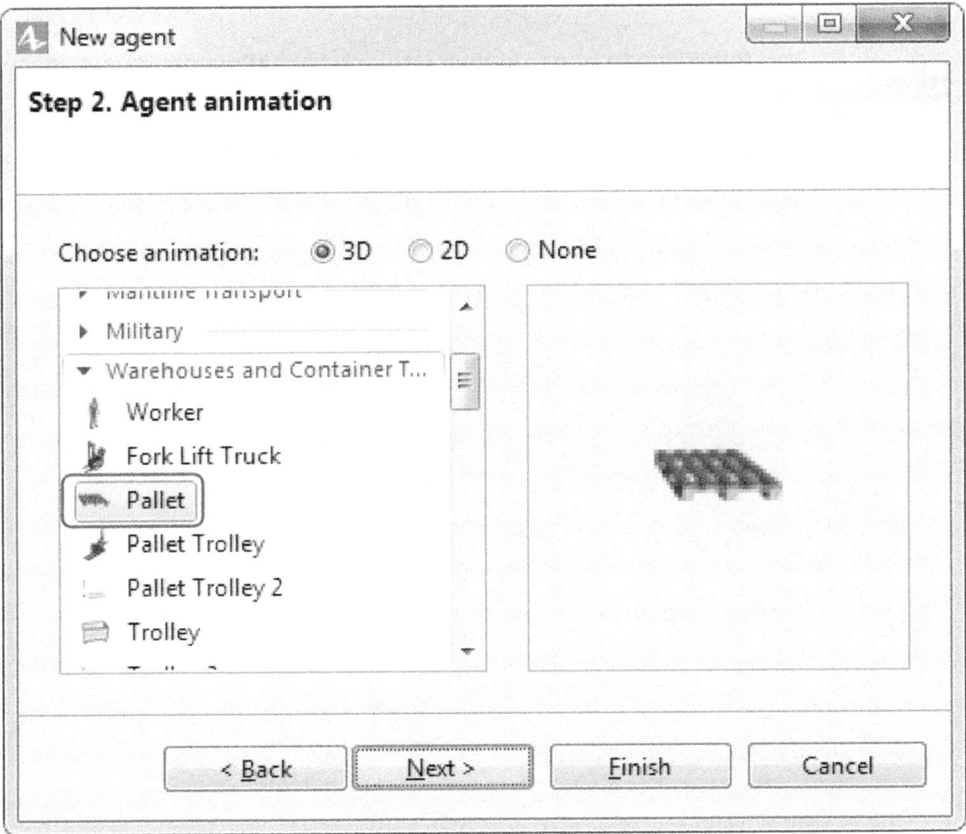

AnyLogic creates the *Pallet* agent type and opens the *Pallet* diagram that will display the animation that we selected in the wizard. Our next step will be to add product animation on top of the pallet animation, but we'll first enlarge the view to give us a closer look at the pallet.

19. Using the **Zoom** toolbar, enlarge the *Pallet* diagram to 500%, and then move the canvas to the right and down to view the axis' origin point and pallet animation shape.

Enlarging or reducing the view

AnyLogic's **Zoom** toolbar lets you enlarge or reduce the view of a graphical diagram:

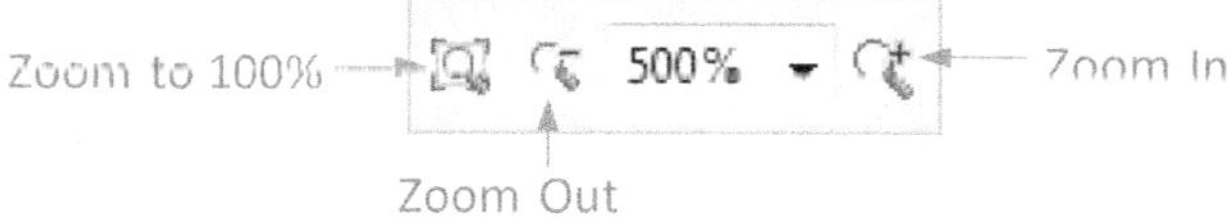

20. Do the following to start adding product animation on top of the pallet animation.

    a.   On the **3D Objects** palette, expand the **Boxes** area.

    b.   Drag the **Box 1 Closed** object on to the pallet's upper-left corner.

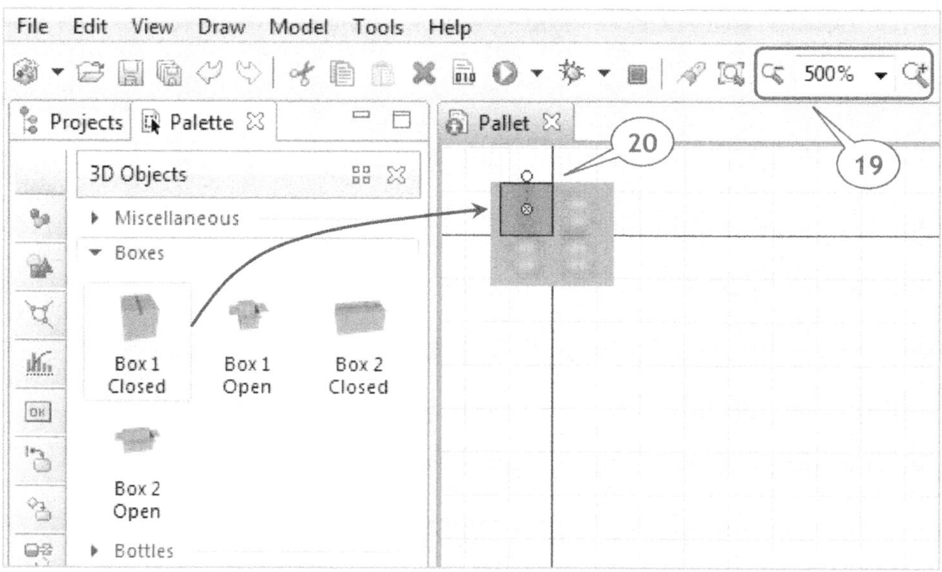

21. Since this box appears to be too large when compared to the pallet, let's change the box's **Scale** to *75%*.

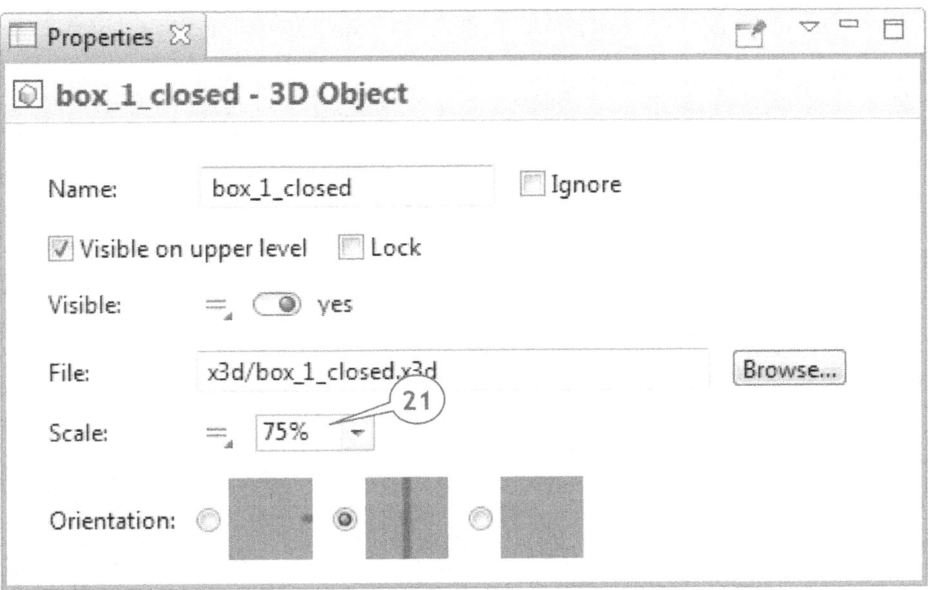

22. In the box's **Properties** area, expand the **Position** section, and then change the box's **Z** coordinate to *2*.

    Our change reflects the fact that we want to place boxes on the pallets and each pallet's height is about 2 pixels.

23. Add three boxes by copying the first box three times. To copy the box, select it and then press and hold CTRL as you drag the box.

    Our pallet now has four closed boxes, and you can now change the zoom level back to 100% by clicking the toolbar's **Zoom to 100%** button.

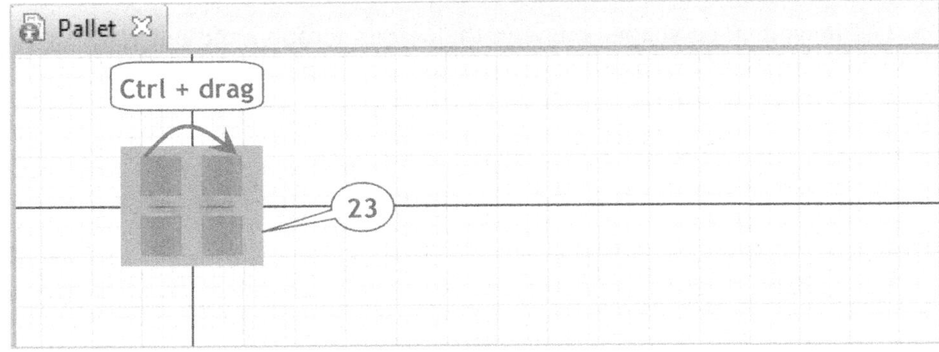

24. Return to the *Main* diagram.

If you open the *sourcePallets* block's **Properties** area, you'll see *Pallet* is selected as **New agent**. This block will generate agents of the *Pallet* type.

25. Run the model.

   You'll see pallet shapes have replaced the multicolored cylinders. However, if you zoom in the 3D scene, you'll notice that the forklift trucks aren't transporting pallets. We'll correct this problem by moving our model's pallet animation in a way that allows the forklift trucks to pick up the pallets.

26. In the **Projects** view, double-click the *ForkliftTruck* agent type to open its diagram and then move the *forkliftWithWorker* figure one cell to the right.

   The animation shape is now in the correct location and our model's pallets are aligned with the forklift trucks' forks.

27. Open *Main* diagram, and in the pallet rack's **Properties** area, in the **Number of levels** box, type *2*.

    TIP: Remember that your first click will select the network and your second click will select the network element.

28. In the *storeRawMaterial* flowchart block's **Properties** area, set the **Elevation time per level** parameter to *30* **seconds**.

29. In the *pickRawMaterial* block's **Properties** area, set the **Drop time per level** parameter to *30* **seconds**.

30. Run the model and you'll see a pallet rack with two levels.

Phase 4. Modeling pallet delivery by trucks

In this part of our tutorial, we'll add the trucks that deliver the pallets to the job shop. Let's start by creating an agent type to represent them.

1. On the **Process Modeling Library** palette, drag the **Agent Type** ⊕ element on to the *Main* diagram.

2. In the **New agent** wizard, do the following:

    a.   In the **Agent type name** box, type *Truck*.

    b.   Click **Next**.

    c.   On the next page of the wizard, expand the **Road Transport** section in the list on the left, and then click the 3D animation figure **Truck**.

    d.   Click **Finish**.

Let's add two more elements to our network: a node where the trucks will appear and the path that they will follow to the receiving dock.

3. Open the *Main* diagram,

4. Under the **Space Markup** palette, click the **Point Node** element and drag it on to the driveway entry.

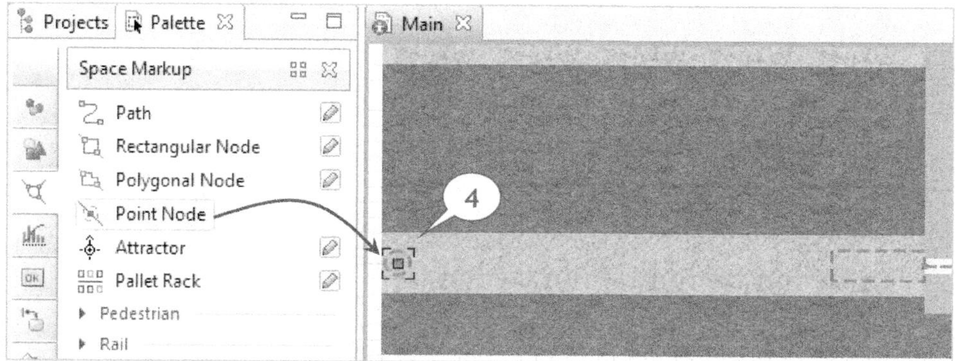

5. Name the node *exitNode*.

6. Draw a **Path** to connect the *exitNode* to the *receivingDock*.

Make sure all space markup elements connect to one network.

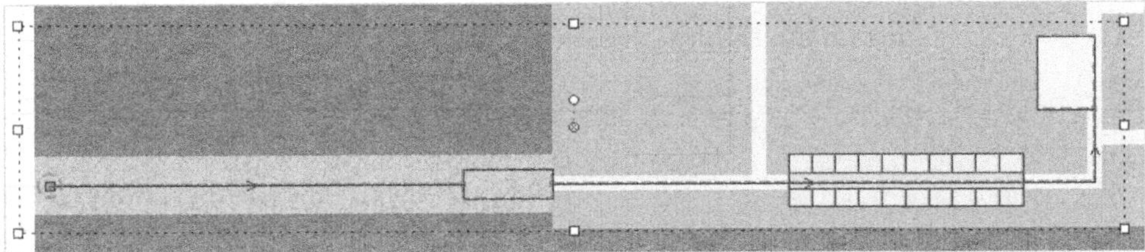

7. Create another process flowchart to define the truck movement logic by connecting the **Process Modeling Library** blocks in the following order:

⊕ **Source** – ⇥▛ **MoveTo** – ◷ **Delay** – ⇥▛ **MoveTo** – ⊗ **Sink**.

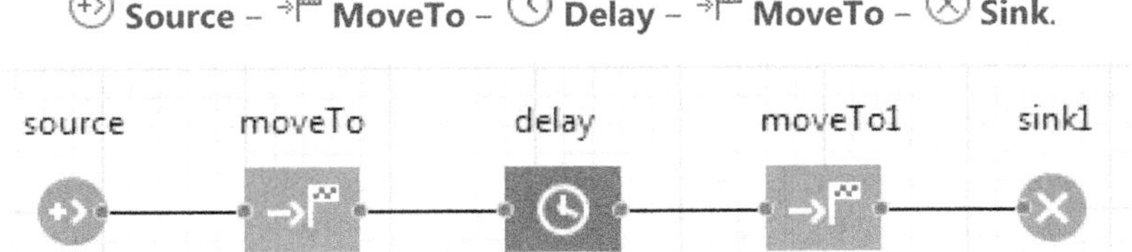

- The **Source** block generates a truck.

- The first **MoveTo** block drives the truck to the job shop entrance.

  MoveTo flowchart blocks move agents to new locations in the network. If resources are attached to the agent, they will move with it.

- The **Delay** block simulates pallet unloading.

- The second **MoveTo** block drives the truck away.

- The **Sink** block removes the truck from the model.

8. Name the **Source** block *sourceDeliveryTrucks*.

9. In the *sourceDeliveryTrucks* block's **Properties** area, do the following to have a new agent of the custom *Truck* type arrive to the driveway entry once per hour at a specific speed:

    a. In the **Arrivals defined by** list, click **Interarrival time**.

   b.   In the **Interarrival time** box, type *1*, and select **hours** from the list on the right.

   c.   In the **New agent** list, click **Truck**.

   d.   In the **Location of arrival** list, click **Network/GIS node**.

   e.   In the **Node** list, click **exitNode**.

   f.   In the **Speed** box, type *40*, and select **kilometers per hour** from the list on the right.

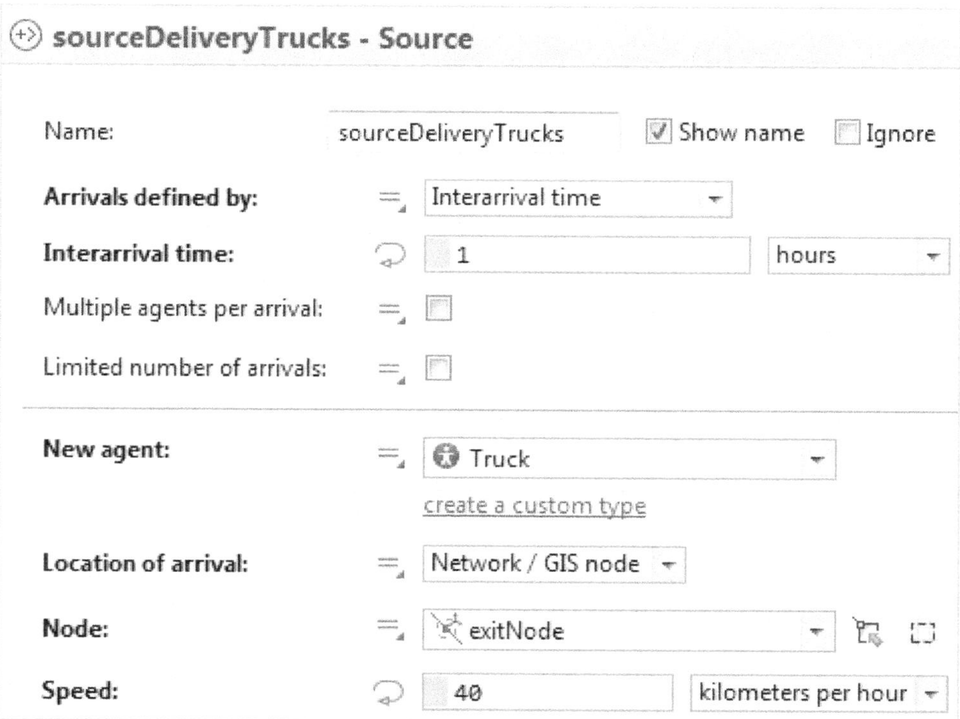

10. Name the first **MoveTo** block *drivingToDock*.

11. In the *drivingToDock* block's **Properties** area, in the **Node** list, click **receivingDock** to set the agent's destination.

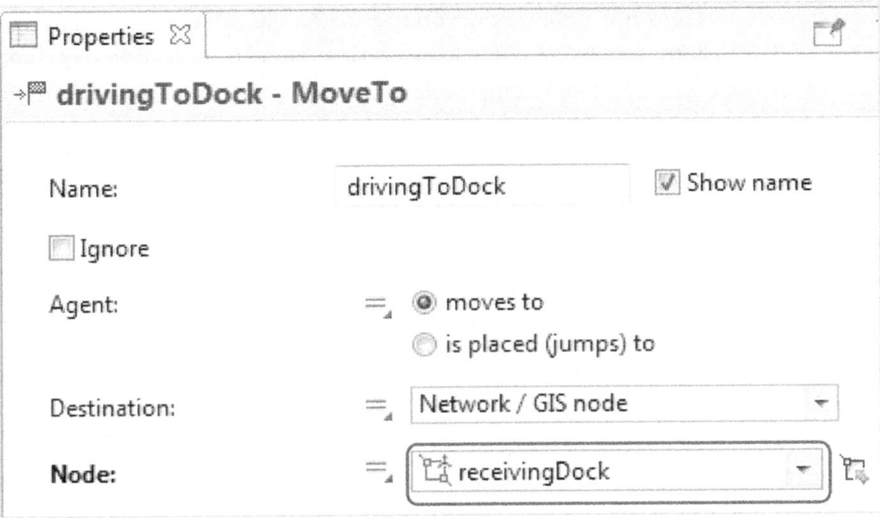

12. Rename the **Delay** block to *unloading*.

13. In the *unloading* block's **Properties** area, do the following:

    a.   In the **Type** area, click **Until stopDelay() is called**.

    b.   In the **Agent location** list, click **receivingDock**.

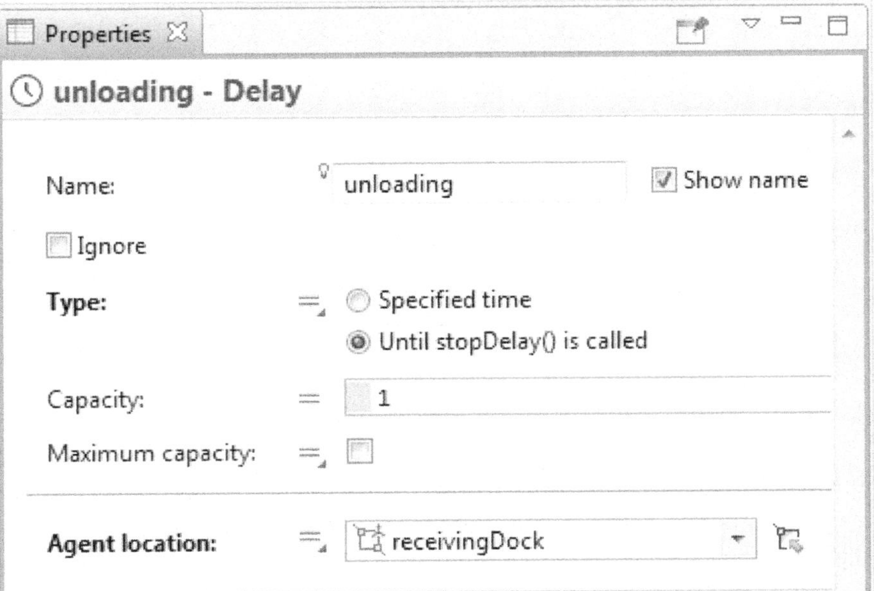

The operation's duration depends on how quickly the pallets are unloaded and removed by forklift trucks. We'll consider this operation complete when the **RackStore** block has finished storing pallets, and we'll model this by changing the **Delay** block's operating mode.

Programmatically controlling the delay time

You'll typically specify a **Delay time** for the **Delay** block's operation. It can be a fixed duration such as five minutes or a stochastic expression that produces a delay time such as *triangular(1, 2, 6)*.

You can also programmatically control the operation's duration and stop the delay when necessary by calling the block's corresponding function. If you need to stop waiting for all agents that are in the **Delay**, call the block's function *stopDelayForAll()*. Another function -- *stopDelay(agent)* -- ends the operation and releases the specified agent.

14. Name the second **MoveTo** block *drivingToExit.*

15. In the *drivingToExit.* block's **Properties** area, in the **Node** list, click **exitNode** to set the destination node.

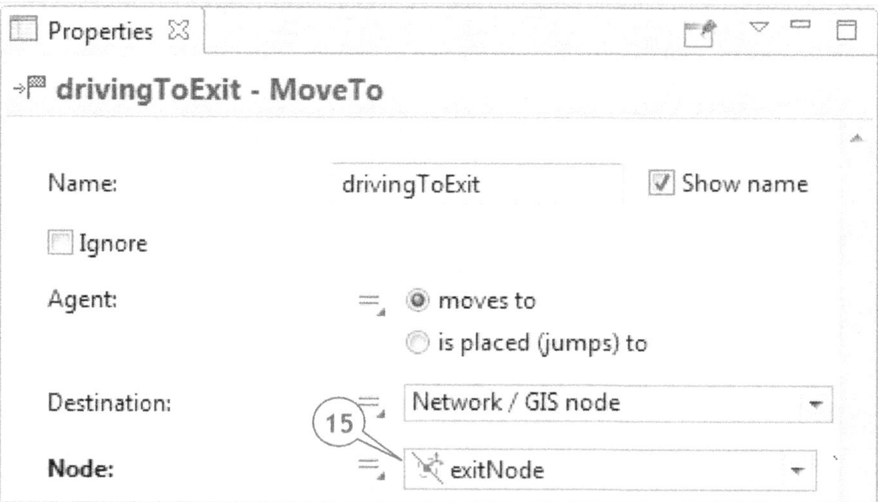

Our model's two **Source** blocks generate two agent types: the trucks that appear each hour and the pallet that is generated every five minutes. Since we want pallets to appear when the truck unloads, we'll change the arrival mode for the **Source** block that generates them.

Controlling agent generation

You can have the **Source** block generate agents at set intervals by setting the block's **Arrivals defined by** parameter to **Calls of inject() function**. You'll be able to control the agent creation at runtime by calling the block's function *inject(int n)*.

This function generates the given number of agents at the time the call occurs. You set the number of agents that the block will generate by using a function argument such as *sourcePalltets.inject(12);*.

16. In the *sourcePallets* block's **Properties** area, in the **Arrivals defined by** list, click **Calls of inject() function**.

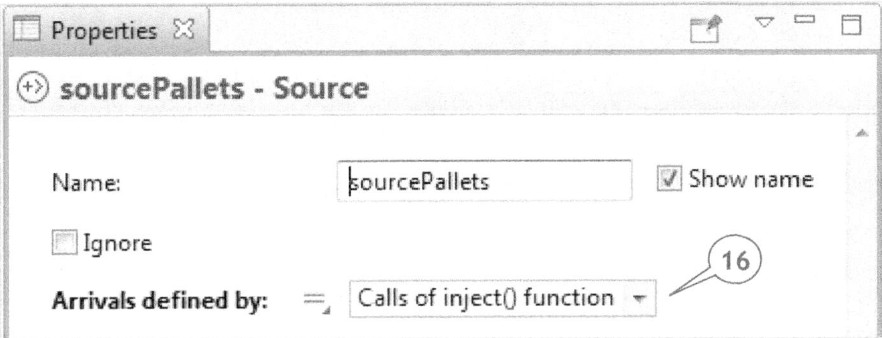

17. Do the following to have the *sourcePallets* block generate pallets when a truck enters the *unloading* block:

   a. In the *unloading* block's **Properties** area, expand the **Actions** section.

   b. In the **On enter** box, type the following:

   sourcePallets.inject(16);

   This Java function will ensure our model generates 16 pallets each time a truck starts to unload.

Now that we've added trucks to our model, let's make the first delivery truck appear on the model startup so we don't have to wait for an hour of model time to elapse.

18. In the *Main* agent type's **Properties** area, expand the **Agent actions** section and then type the following Java function in the **On startup** box:

sourceDeliveryTrucks.inject(1);

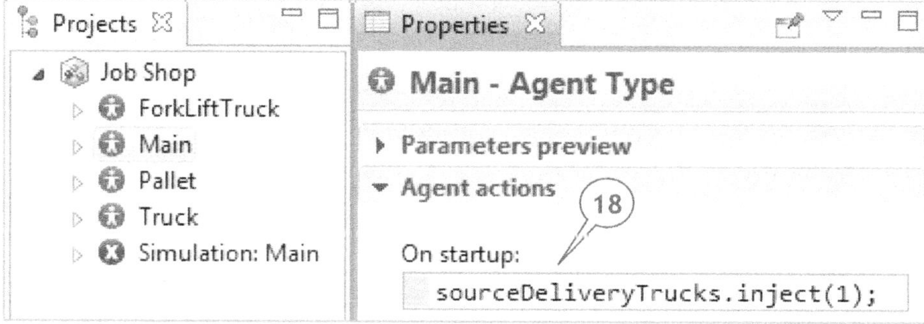

Model startup code

The model's **Startup code** executes at the model initialization's final stage after the model's blocks are constructed, connected, and initialized. This is a place for additional initialization and starting agent activities such as events.

19. In the *storeRawMaterial* block's **Properties** area, expand the **Actions** section, and in the **On exit** box, type the following:

```
if( self.queueSize() == 0 )
unloading.stopDelayForAll();
```

In this example, `self` is a shortcut we use to refer to the block *storeRawMaterial* from its own action.

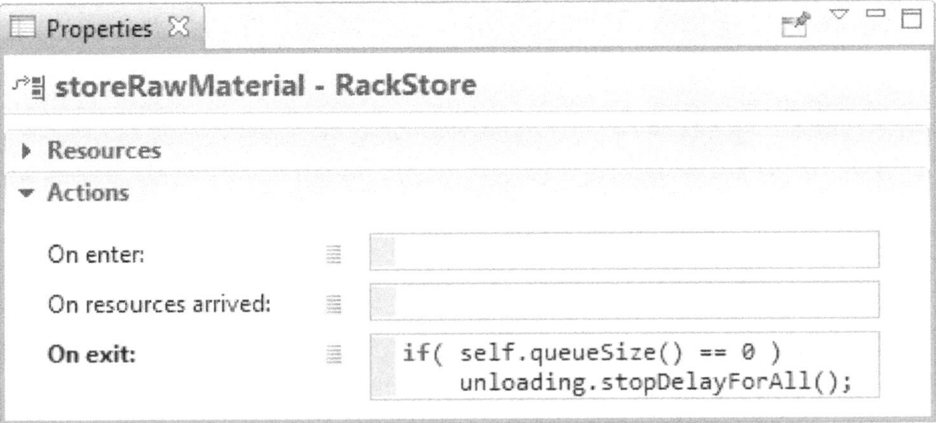

If there are no pallets in the storage queue, the *unloading* block's delay time ends (in other words, *stopDelayForAll()* is called), and the truck leaves the *unloading* block and enters the next flowchart block, *drivingToExit*.

20. Run the model.

21. If the truck is aligned incorrectly as in the figure below, do the following to fix it.

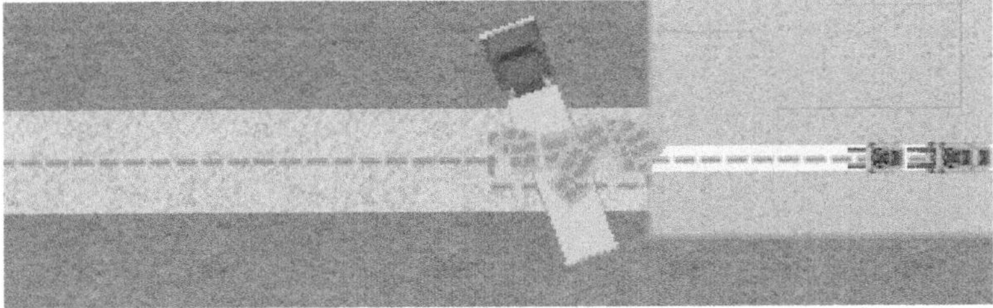

  a. In the **Projects** tree, double-click the **Truck** agent type to open its diagram and view the truck animation figure.

  b. In the graphical editor, select the truck shape and then use the round handle or the **Rotation Z,°** property in the shape's **Position** properties area to rotate the truck to -180 degrees.

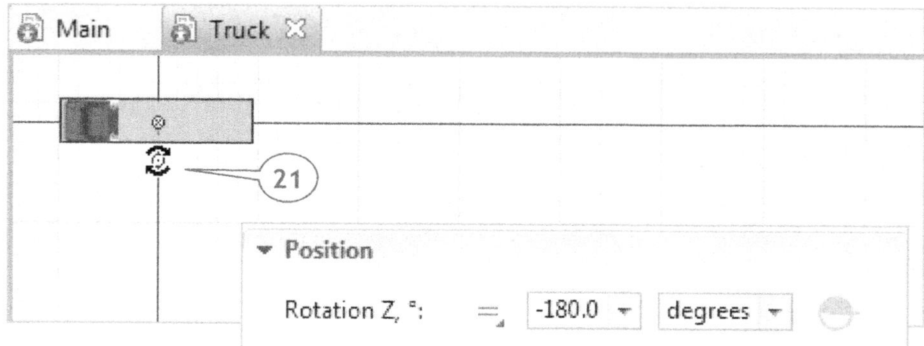

We've changed the truck figure's position, but we'll also need to change AnyLogic's default setting to make sure the program doesn't rotate it a second time.

22. Do the following to change AnyLogic's default setting:

   a.   In the **Projects** area, click **Truck**.

   b.   On the *Truck* agent type's **Properties** area, click the arrow to expand the **Movement** area.

   c.   Clear the **Rotate animation towards movement** check box.

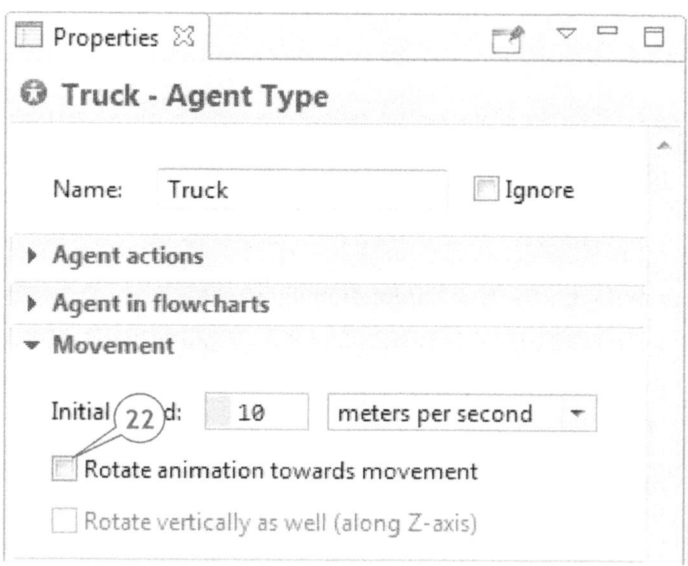

23. Open the *Main* diagram.

24. To ensure the pallets are correctly positioned in the *receivingDock* network node, open the **Space Markup** palette, and drag an **Attractor** ⊕ into *receivingDock*. Let it face the entrance.

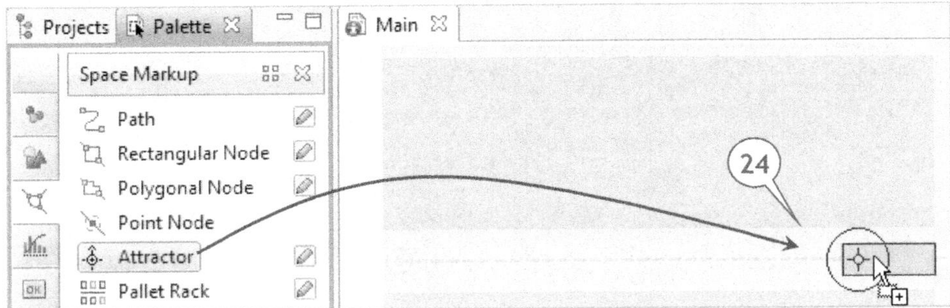

Attractors in nodes

Attractors allow us to control agent location inside a node.

- If the node defines the destination that our agents move toward, attractors define the exact target points inside the node.

- If the node defines the waiting location, attractors define the exact points where agents will wait inside the node.

Attractors also define the agent animation's orientation while the agent waits inside the node. Here we use attractor for this particular purpose.

You can add attractors by dragging them individually on to the *Main* diagram, but if attractors form a regular structure, you should use the special wizard to add several attractors at the same time. The wizard offers several different creation modes as well as the option to clear all attractors, and you can display it by clicking the **Attractors** button in a node's **Properties** area.

25. Run the model to check the truck behavior.

The animation should work as we expect.

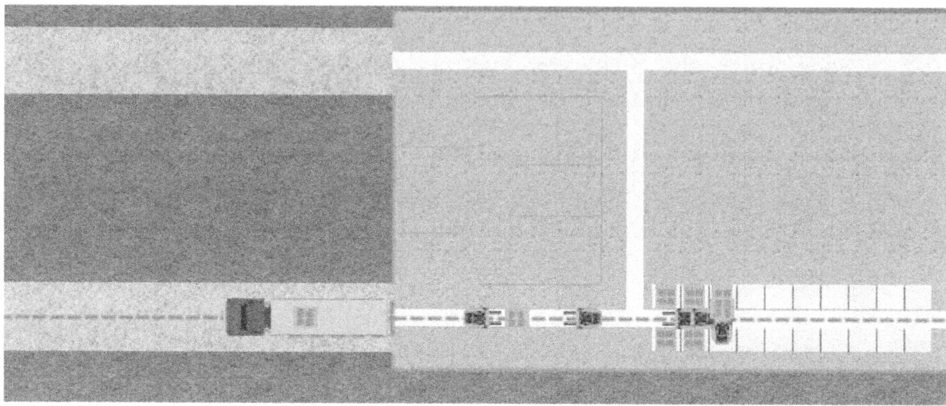

Phase 5. Modeling CNC machines

In this part of our tutorial, we'll simulate the CNC machines that process raw materials. We'll start by marking up the space and using point nodes to define the CNC machine locations.

1. On the **Space Markup** palette, drag the **Point Node** element on to the job shop layout, and name it *nodeCNC1*.

2. Copy this node to mark up the space for the second CNC machine.

   AnyLogic will name the second node *nodeCNC2*.

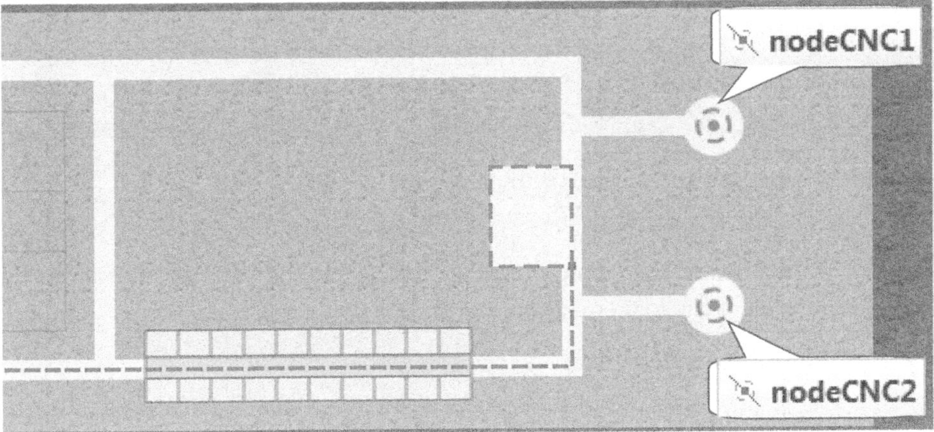

We'll need to create paths to connect both of these nodes to our network. Our model's forklift trucks will need them to reach the CNC machines.

3. On the **Space Markup** palette, click the **Path** element and draw paths as shown in the figure below. To connect a path to a point node, click the point node's center.

   NOTE: Make sure the paths that you draw connect the *nodeCNC1* and *nodeCNC2* to the network. You can test a path's connection by clicking twice to select it. If the path is connected to the network, cyan highlights will appear around its end points.

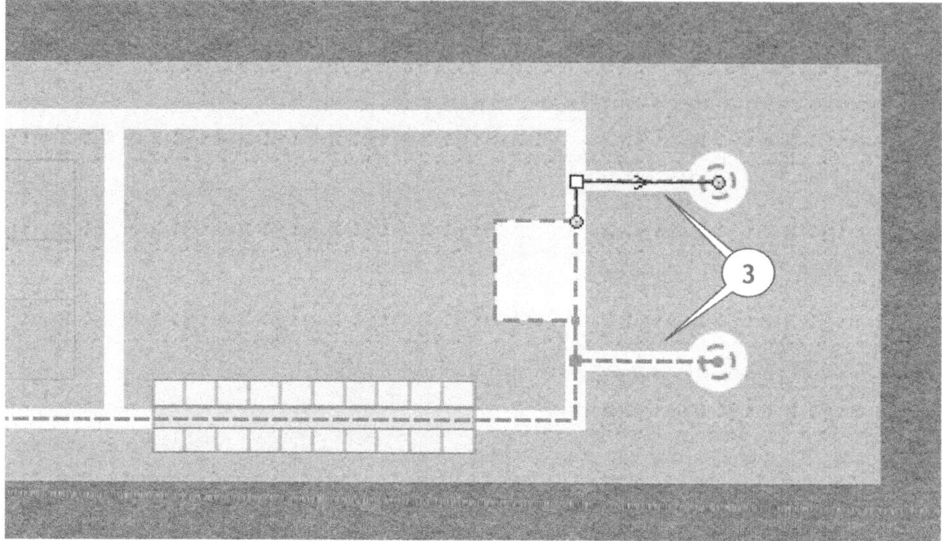

A CNC machine is a resource unit, and we'll add it to our model by creating a resource type and using the **ResourcePool** block to define the resource pool.

4. On the **Process Modeling Library** palette, click and drag the **ResourcePool** block on to the **Main** diagram.

5. In the **ResourcePool** block's **Properties** area, do the following:

    a.   In the **Name** box, type *cnc.*

    b.   In the **Resource type** list, click **Static** to reflect the fact this is a static resource.

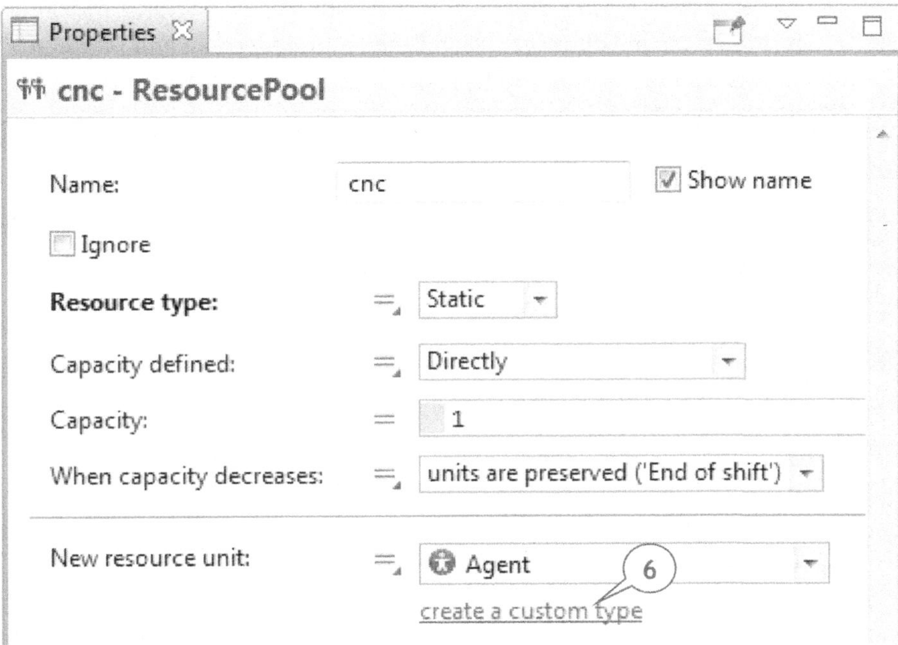

With our resource pool complete, we're ready to create a new resource type.

6. Under the **New resource unit** list, click the **create a custom type** link.

7. In the **New agent** wizard, do the following:

    a.   In the **Agent type name** box, type *CNC*.

    b.   Click **Next**.

    c.   On the next page of the wizard, expand the last section (**CNC Machines**), and select **CNC Vertical Machining Center 2 State 1**.

    d.   Click **Finish**.

8. Close the new *CNC* type's diagram and return to the *Main* diagram.

9. In the *cnc* **ResourcePool** block's **Properties** area, do the following to place our model's two CNC machines at the places defined by our point nodes, *nodeCNC1* and *nodeCNC2*.

    a.   In the **Capacity defined** list, click **By home location**.

       The **By home location** option sets the number of resources equal to the number of home location nodes that you set for this resource pool.

b.   Click the plus button and then add *nodeCNC1* and *nodeCNC2* into the **Home location (nodes)** list.

After you've added the nodes, the list should resemble the figure below.

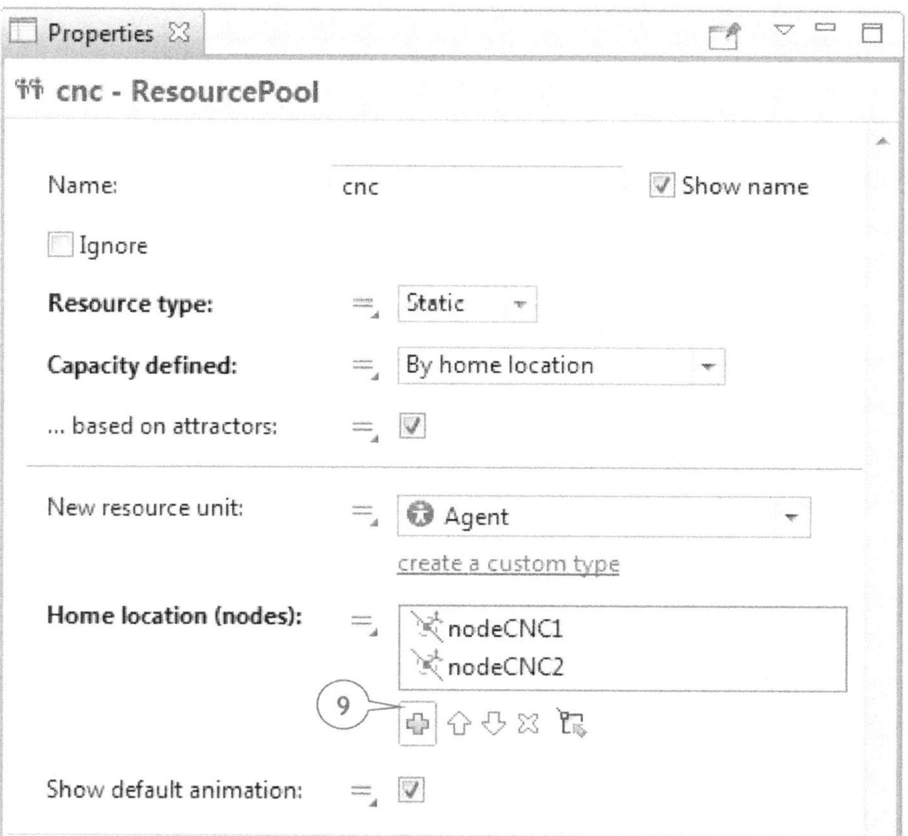

We're ready to modify the flowchart our model uses to define the pallets' behavior by adding a **Seize** block that will seize a CNC machine. Later, a **Delay** block will simulate a CNC machine's processing of raw materials and a **Release** block will release a CNC machine so it can process the next pallet's raw material.

NOTE: Remember that our model's flowchart already has a *pickRawMaterial* block that simulates the moving resource (the forklift trucks) that delivers pallets to the CNC machine.

10. In the flowchart that defines the pallets' behavior, drag the *pickRawMaterial* and *sink* blocks to the right to make space for a new block.

11. On the **Process Modeling Library** palette, drag the **Seize** block, and insert it in the pallets' flowchart after the *rawMaterialinStorage* block.

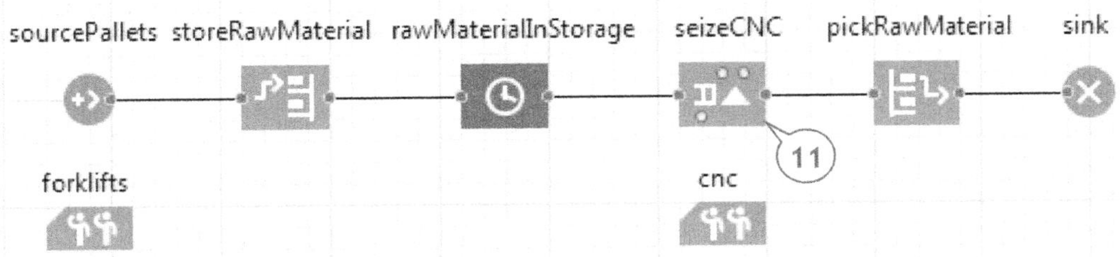

12. In the **Seize** block's **Properties** area, do the following:

    a. In the **Name** box, type *seizeCNC*.

    b. Under the **Resource sets** option, click the plus button , and then click **cnc**.

Completing this step ensures the **Seize** block will seize one resource from the *cnc* resource pool.

13. In the *pickRawMaterial* flowchart block's **Properties** area, do the following:

    a. In the **Destination is** list, click: **Seized resource unit**.

    b. In the **Resource** list, click **cnc**.

This block will simulate how the pallets are transported to the seized CNC machine rather than the forklift trucks' parking zone.

14. Do the following to simulate the CNC machine's processing of raw materials:

    a. Add a **Delay** block, place it immediately after *pickRawMaterial*, and name it *processing*.

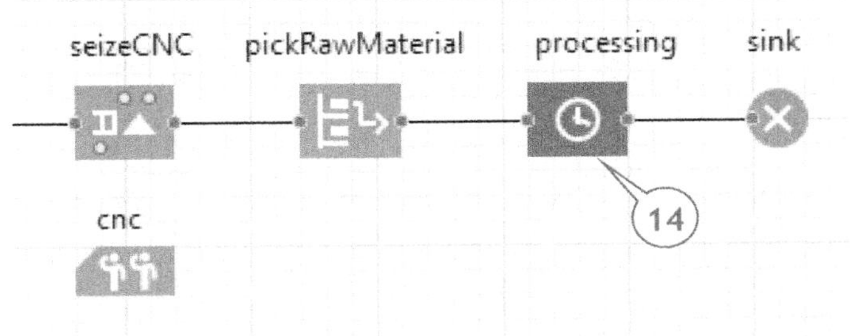

15. In the **Delay** block's **Properties** area, do the following:

a. In the **Delay time** box, type *triangular(2,3,4)* and select **minutes** from the list on the right.

b. Select the **Maximum capacity** check box to allow the machines to process several pallets.

Each agent that arrives to the **Delay** block must have one of our model's two CNC machines.

16. On the **Process Modeling Library** palette, drag the **Release** ▼ block on to the pallets' flowchart and place it after the *processing* block.

17. Name this **Release** block *releaseCNC.*

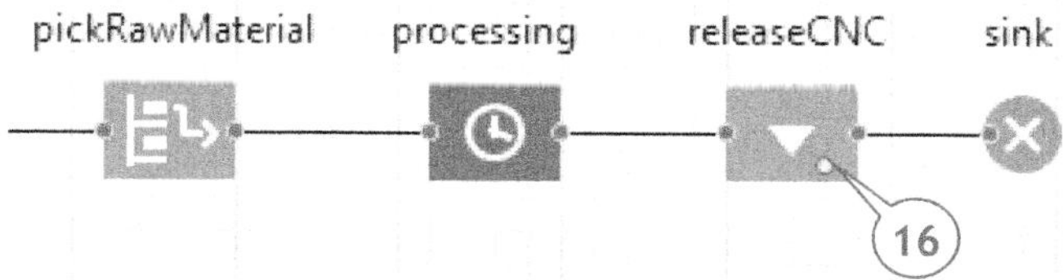

If you run the model, you'll see that while the processes are simulated correctly, the 3D animation draws a pallet in the middle of the CNC machine shape. This occurs when the CNC machine, the pallet it is processing, and the animation location all use the same point node. To resolve the problem, we'll need to shift the CNC machine to the right and rotate it to face the pallet.

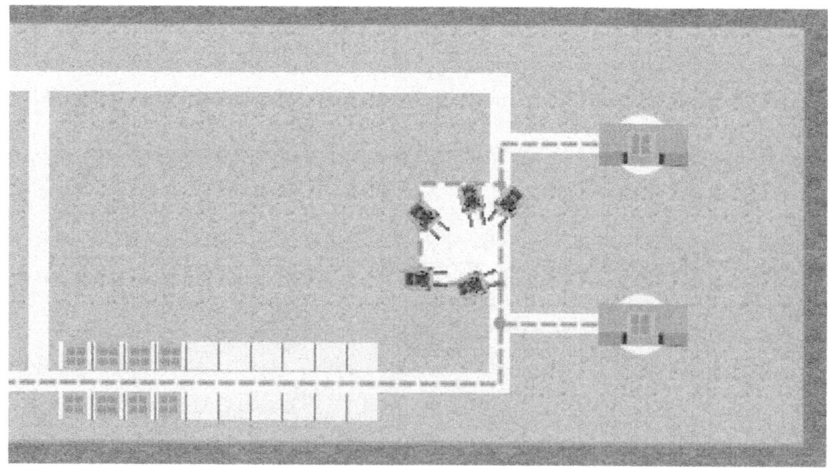

18. In the **Projects** view, double-click the *CNC* agent type to open its diagram.

19. Move the animation to the right, and rotate the CNC machine shape by using the round handle or setting the figure's **Rotation** property to *90* degrees.

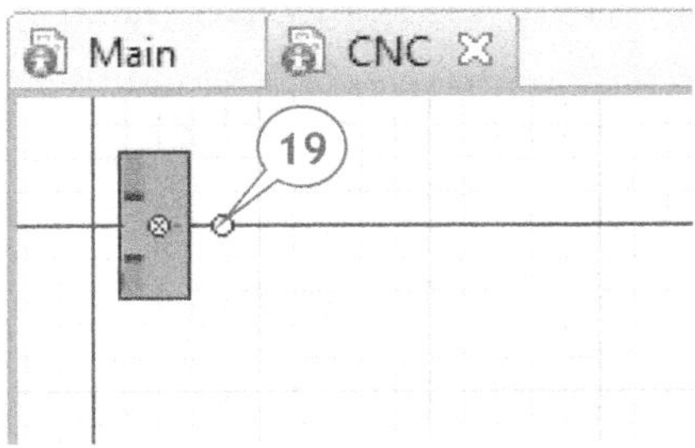

We're ready to use two similar 3D animation shapes to animate the CNC machine: one shape will represent the idle machine and the other will represent the machine as it processes the raw materials. We'll define dynamic values for each shape's **Visible** property that will allow our model to use the CNC machine's state to determine which shape the model will display at runtime.

20. Do the following to change the CNC animation shape's visibility setting:

    a.   Select the CNC animation shape.

    b.   Hover your mouse over the static parameters icon $=$ that displays next to the **Visible** label and click **Dynamic value**.

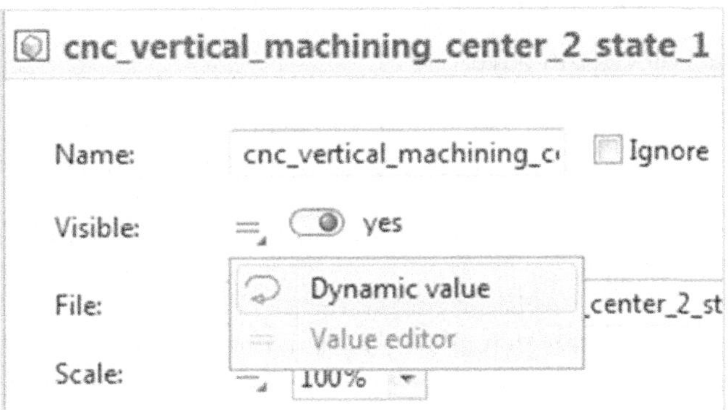

       The icon $=$ changes to a dynamic properties icon and a box where you can define the value's dynamic expression displays. You can use the box to enter Java expression that returns a *true* or *false* value.

    c.   In the box, type *isBusy()*

This standard function for an AnyLogic resource returns *true* when the resource is busy. In our case, the function will make the 3D animation shape display when the CNC machine is processing raw materials.

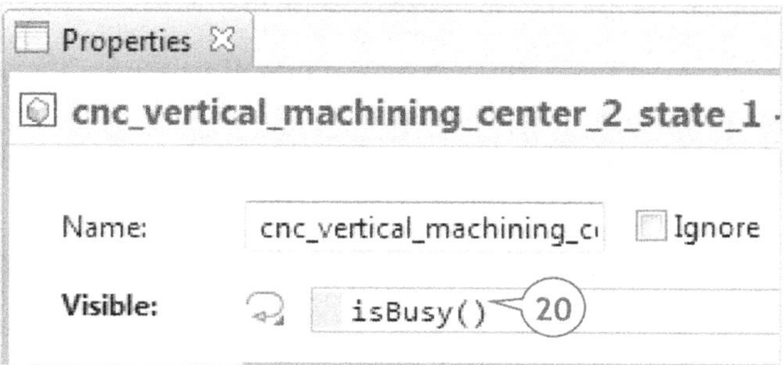

Dynamic properties

When you define an expression for a property's dynamic value, our model will reevaluate the expression on every animation frame during runtime, and then use the resulting value as the property's current value. Providing dynamic values for a shape's position, height, width, or color allows AnyLogic users to animate their models.

If you do not enter a dynamic value, the property retains the default static value throughout the simulation.

- Flowchart blocks can have:

    = **Static parameters** that retain the same value throughout the simulation unless a *set_parameterName(new value)* function changes it.

    ↶ **Dynamic properties** whose value is reevaluated each time a new agent enters the block.

    ≡ **Code parameters** that allow you to define actions that will be executed at a key moment in the flowchart block such as the **On enter** action or **On exit** action. In most cases, you'll find code parameters in a flowchart block's **Properties** area, in the **Actions** section.

- The small triangle at the parameter icon shows that you can click the icon and switch between static value editor and the field where you can enter the value's dynamically reevaluated expression.

21. Do the following to add one more animation shape that will be visible only when the CNC machine is not processing raw materials.

a. Open the **3D Objects** palette that has AnyLogic's ready-to-use 3D objects.

b. Expand the **CNC Machines** area and drag the **CNC Vertical Machining Center 2 State 2** shape on to the *CNC* diagram.

c. Rotate the shape and place it directly on top of the first animation figure.

d. In the **Visible** box, switch to the dynamic value editor, and type *isIdle()* as the dynamic expression for the shape's **Visible** property.

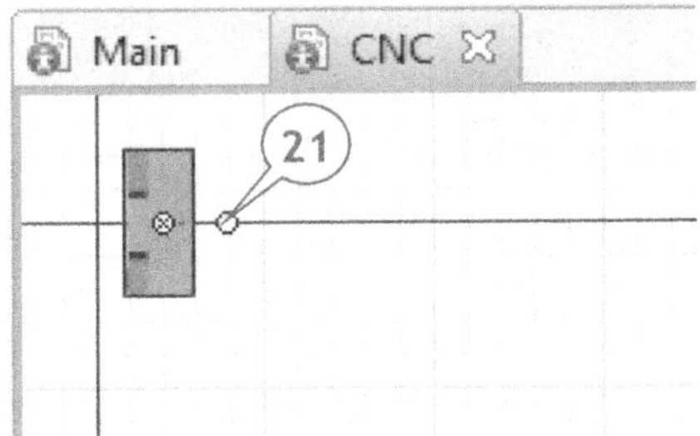

22. Expand the **3D Objects** palette's **People** section and drag the **Worker** shape on to the *CNC* diagram.

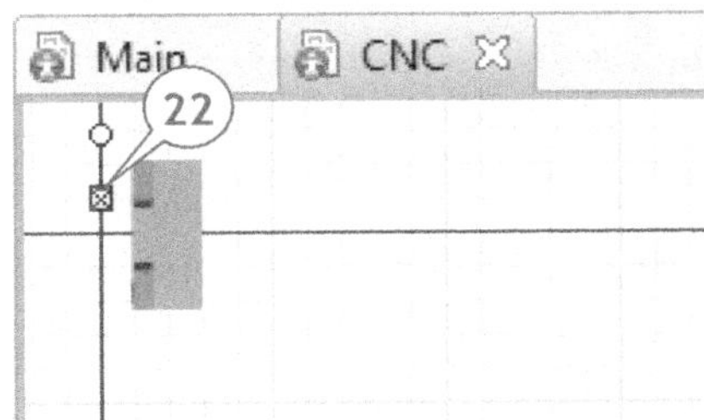

23. Run the model and observe the process.

You'll see how forklift trucks transport pallets to CNC machines for processing. You should also see animated CNC machines, changing 3D shapes depending on their state.

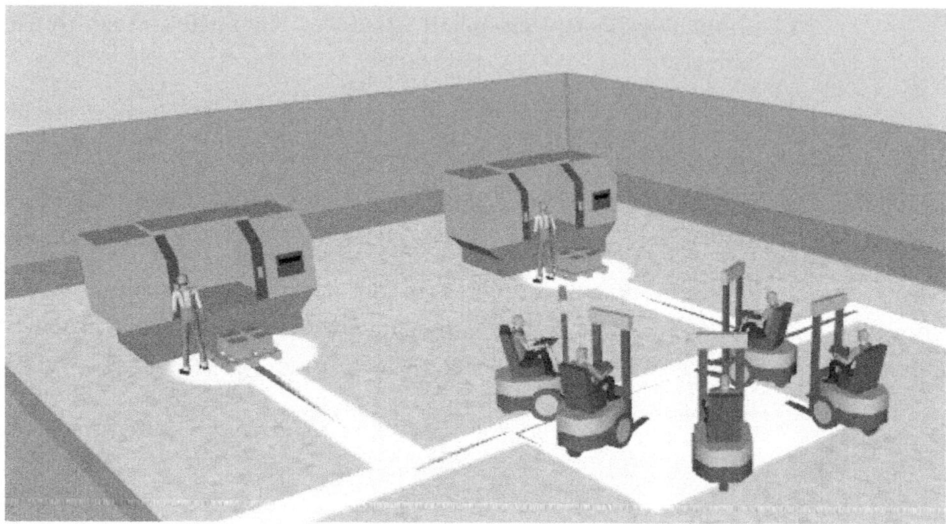

We've finished our simple model that simulates the manufacturing and shipping process in a small job shop. You now have a basic knowledge of AnyLogic resources and how to work with them. You also know how to use a flowchart constructed from **Process Modeling Library** blocks to define process logic.

Your next step might be to model how the pallets with the finished parts are moved to another storage area at the shipping dock where they will stay until they are shipped. You've already used the blocks that you'll need to model this part of the process, so you may want to try adding this logic on your own.

The next exercise will also use a process-centric flowchart, but this time it will be a pedestrian model that we'll discuss in another chapter.

Pedestrian modeling

Pedestrian traffic simulation is an important part of constructing, expanding, or redesigning facilities such as shopping centers, airports, railway stations, and stadiums. These analyses can help architects improve their designs, facilities owners review a potential change to a building, and civil authorities simulate possible evacuation routes. Since pedestrian flows can be complex, they require a full-blown simulation.

Pedestrians follow basic rules that have been determined by detailed theoretical studies; they move at predetermined rates, they avoid physical spaces such as walls as well as other people, and they use information about the crowds that surround them to adjust their distance and speed. The results have been proven many times in field studies and customer applications.

You can create metrics such as the total travel time between specified points and vary your experiments to highlight these metrics during times of peak congestion. Finally, you can import background layouts, floor plans, and maps and create multiple 3D views that will make your pedestrian flow analysis easier to understand.

AnyLogic can help you solve these pedestrian traffic problems:

- *Time and throughput calculation.* Assume you're designing a supermarket, a subway or railway station, or an airport building. If your goal is to create a layout that minimizes travel time and ensures pedestrian flows don't interfere with each other, an AnyLogic simulation can easily test for normal, special, or peak volume conditions.

- *Pedestrian traffic impact analysis.* Managers of high-traffic areas such as theme parks, museums, and sports stadiums can use a simulation to understand how changes such as a new kiosk or a relocated advertising panel will affect their operations, pedestrian travel times, and the customer experience.

- *Evacuation analysis.* The increased frequency of natural and man-made disasters makes it important to assess and optimize evacuation plans. Emergency event modeling can help emergency management agencies develop effective evacuation plans that save lives.

Airport model

Let's build a model that simulates how passengers move within a small airport that hosts two airlines, each with their own gate. Passengers arrive at the airport, check in, pass the security checkpoint and then go to the waiting area. After boarding starts, each airline's representatives check their passengers' tickets before they allow them to board.

We'll use a six-phase approach to develop our model. In the final phase, you'll learn how to read the database's flight data (available in a Microsoft Excel spreadsheet) and configure pedestrians by assigning flight information to them.

Phase 1. Defining the simple pedestrian flow

In our first phase, we'll use AnyLogic's *Pedestrian Library* to create a simple model of an airport where passengers arrive and then move to the gate.

Pedestrian Library

- Traditional modeling methods such as discrete-event and queuing may not work well in areas with high amounts of pedestrian movement.

- AnyLogic's Pedestrian Library simulates pedestrian flows in "physical" environments by allowing you to create models of buildings and areas with large numbers of pedestrians such as subway stations, security checkpoints, and streets.

- Your model's pedestrians move in continuous space while they react to obstacles and one another. This allows you to collect data about a given area's pedestrian density, ensure acceptable performance levels for service points with a hypothetical load, estimate how long pedestrians will stay in specific areas, and detect potential problems that interior changes such as adding or removing obstacles may cause.

In most cases, you'll start to create a pedestrian dynamics model by adding the simulated building's layout and then drawing walls over it.

1. Create a new model and name it *Airport*. Select minutes as the model time units.

2. Drag an **Image** from the **Presentation** palette on to the *Main* diagram.

3. Choose the image file you want to display. In this example, you'll select the *terminal.png* image file from *AnyLogic folder/resources/AnyLogic in 3 days/Airport*.

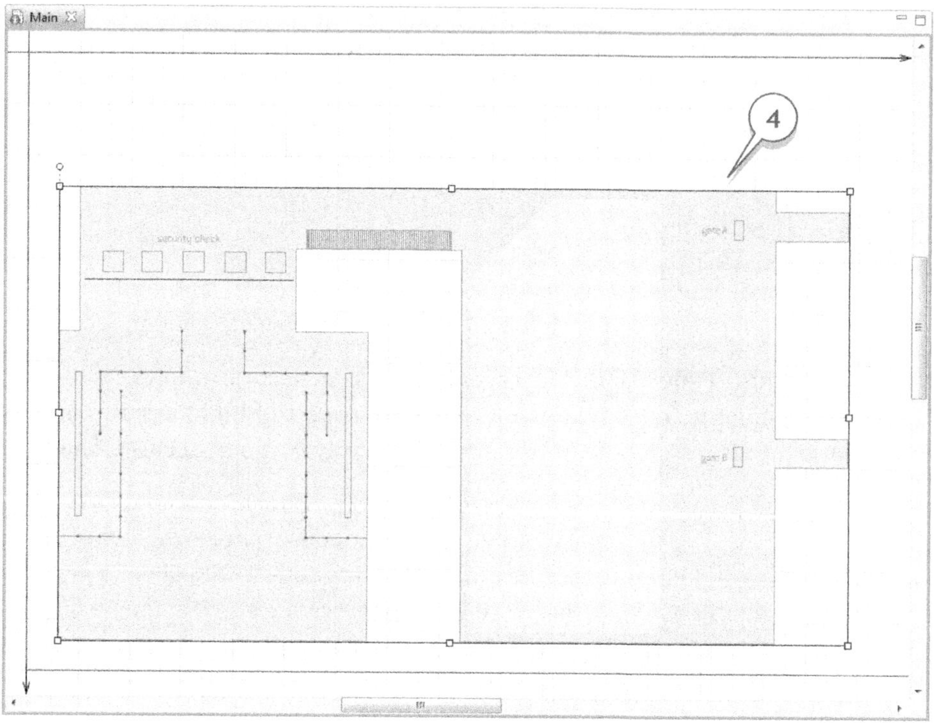

4. On the *Main* diagram, place the image in the blue frame's lower left corner. If the image is distorted, click the **Reset to original size** button and then select the **Lock** checkbox to lock the image shape.

We'll now use a set of space markup shapes from AnyLogic's **Pedestrian Library** palette to define our pedestrian model's space. You can use space markup shapes to draw walls, services (locations such as turnstiles and ticket offices where pedestrians receive services), and waiting areas.

Space markup shapes for pedestrian models

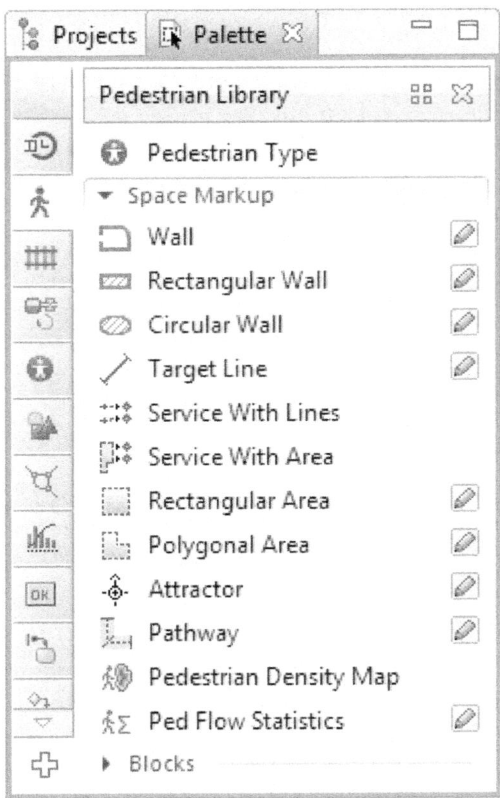

The Pedestrian Library palette's Space Markup section

We'll use walls – objects within our model's simulated space that pedestrians can't cross – to start creating our model. In simple terms, we're about to use the three markup shapes below to place "AnyLogic walls" on top of the walls that appear in our image.

Walls

Wall – Use this shape to draw exterior and interior walls.

Rectangular Wall – Use this shape to draw rectangular areas such as working spaces that aren't accessible by pedestrians.

Circular Wall - Use this shape to draw circular obstacles such as columns, pools, and fountains.

5. Use the **Pedestrian Library** 🚶 palette to draw the airport's walls. Double-click the **Wall** ⬭ element you'll find in the **Pedestrian Library** palette's **Space markup** section and then draw the wall around the airport building's border by clicking your mouse each time you want to add a point. When you're ready to set the wall's final point, double-click your mouse.

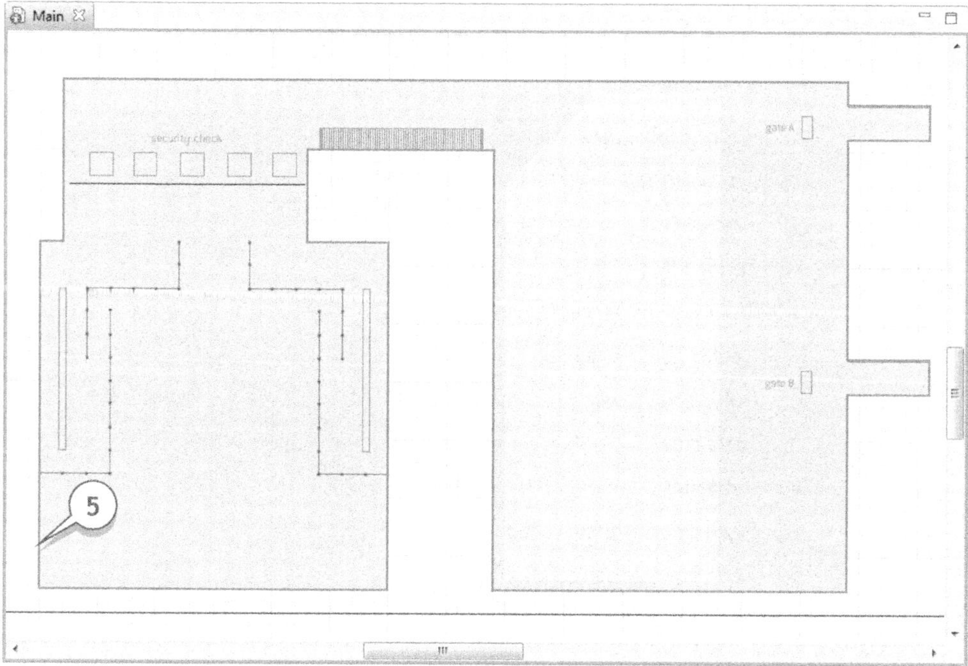

Let's change our wall's appearance by choosing a new color and height.

6. Navigate to the wall's properties and then select the **Color**: *dodgerBlue* in the **Appearance** section.

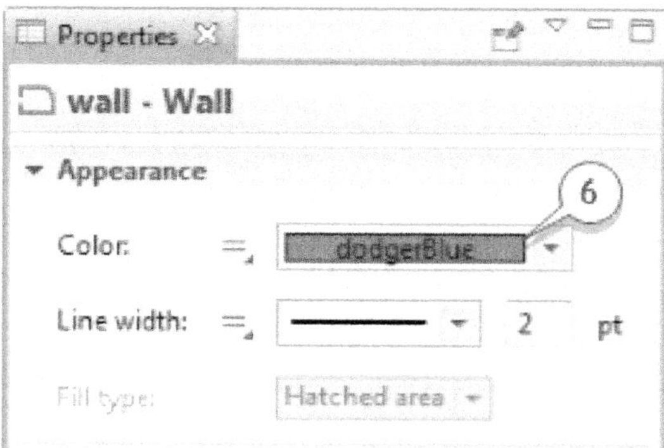

Now that we've defined the building's walls and chosen their color, we'll use the special *Target Line* space markup element to ensure our model's pedestrians appear at the airport entrance and then move toward the gate.

Target line

In a pedestrian dynamics model, the *Target Line* element defines the locations where pedestrians appear in the simulated space, where they wait (though *areas* typically define waiting locations), and their destination.

7. Define the location where your model's passengers appear by dragging the **Target Line** ✓ element from the **Pedestrian Library** palette on to the graphical diagram, as shown in the figure below.

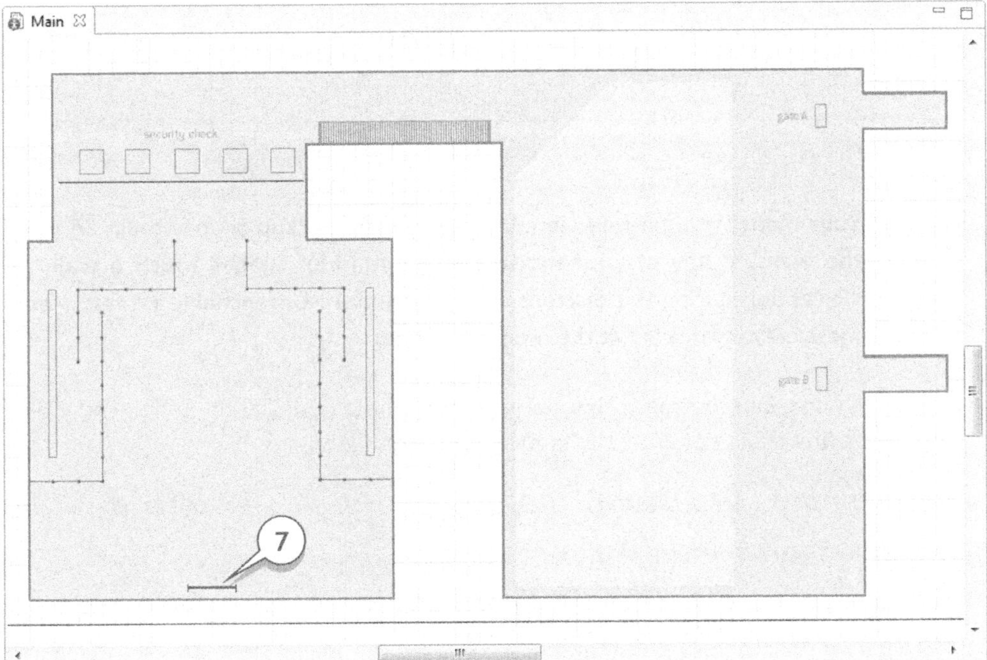

8. Name the target line *arrivalLine*.

9. Define a second target line that passengers will move toward after they enter the airport, place it in the gate area as shown in the figure below, and then name it *gateLine1*.

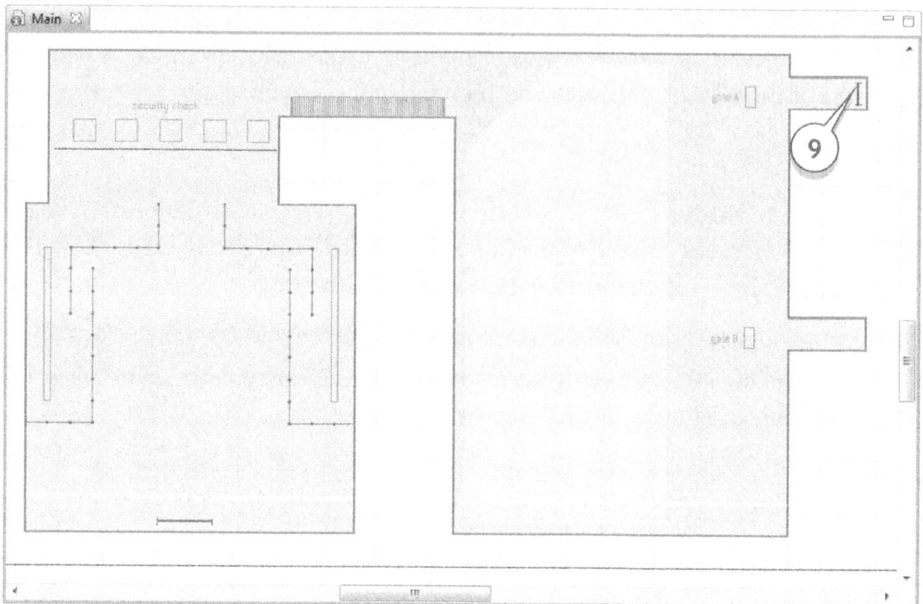

♦ **Your model's target line elements and space markup shapes must lie inside the walls. If any of your model's space markup shapes touch a wall, the "Exception during the discrete event execution: Unreachable target…" error message may display at the model runtime.**

We've marked the space that defines our simple pedestrian model, and we'll now use a flowchart to define the model's process logic.

Defining pedestrian flow logic using Pedestrian Library flowchart blocks

You'll use a flowchart to define the processes that take place in your pedestrian dynamics models. Your model's pedestrians pass through a flowchart and perform the operations defined by the blocks.

The most important **Pedestrian Library** blocks are:

PedSource – This block generates pedestrians much like **Source** generates agents in a regular Process Modeling Library flowchart. You'll typically use this block as your pedestrian flow's starting point.

PedGoTo – This block makes pedestrians go to a specified target.

PedService – This block simulates how pedestrians receive services at service points.

PedWait – This block causes pedestrians to wait for a given time in a specified location.

PedSelectOutput – This block uses specified conditions to route incoming pedestrians to several routes or processes.

PedSink – This block disposes pedestrians and is usually the pedestrian flow's end point.

10. Start by dragging the **PedSource** block from the **Pedestrian Library** palette on to our *Main* diagram.

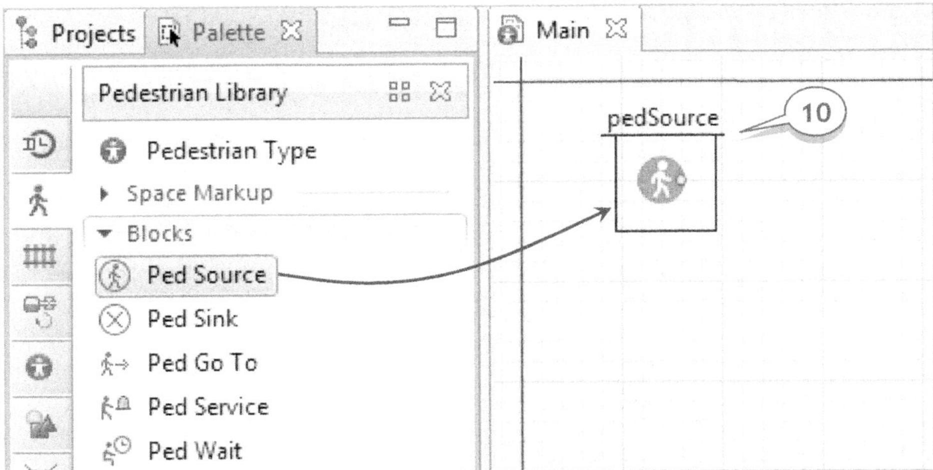

11. Since we want passengers to arrive randomly at an average rate of 100 passengers per hour, go to the *pedSource* block properties and then type *100* in the **Arrival rate** box.

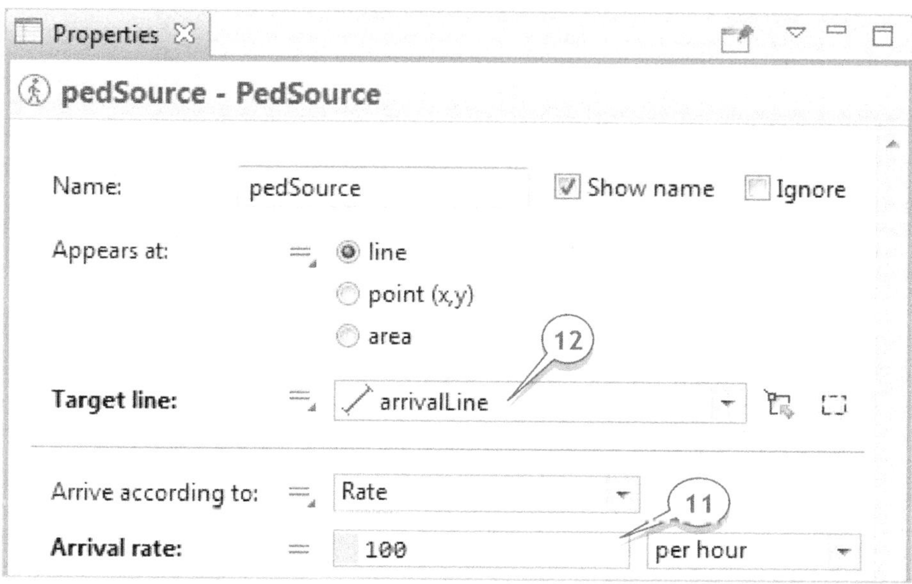

12. Specify the location where the passengers appear in the simulated system by clicking *arrivalLine* in the **Target line** list.

13. Add a **PedGoTo** ⵏ block to simulate pedestrian movement to the specified location and then connect it to *pedSource*. Since we want our passengers to go to the gate, name the object *goToGate1*.

To connect the blocks, add a new block from the palette on to the graphical diagram and place it near another block.

14. Specify the movement destination by selecting *gateLine1* from the **Target line** combo box.

15. Add a **PedSink** ⊗ block to discard incoming pedestrians. Pedestrian flowcharts typically start with a **PedSource** block and end with a **PedSink** block.

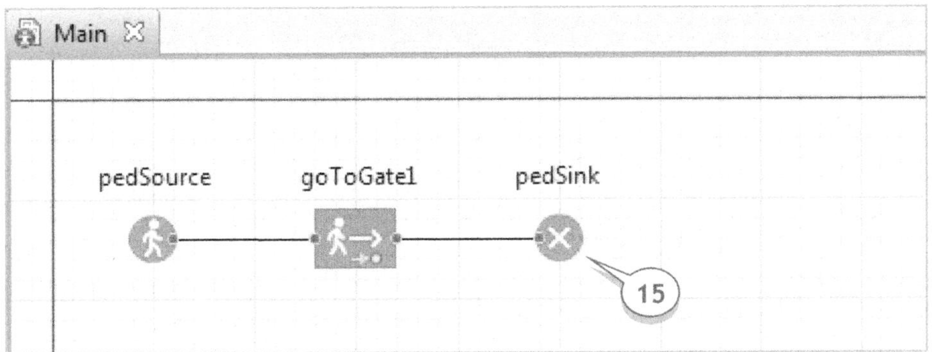

Your flowchart should resemble the figure above.

16. Run the model. In the 2D animation, you'll see the pedestrians move from the airport entrance to the gate.

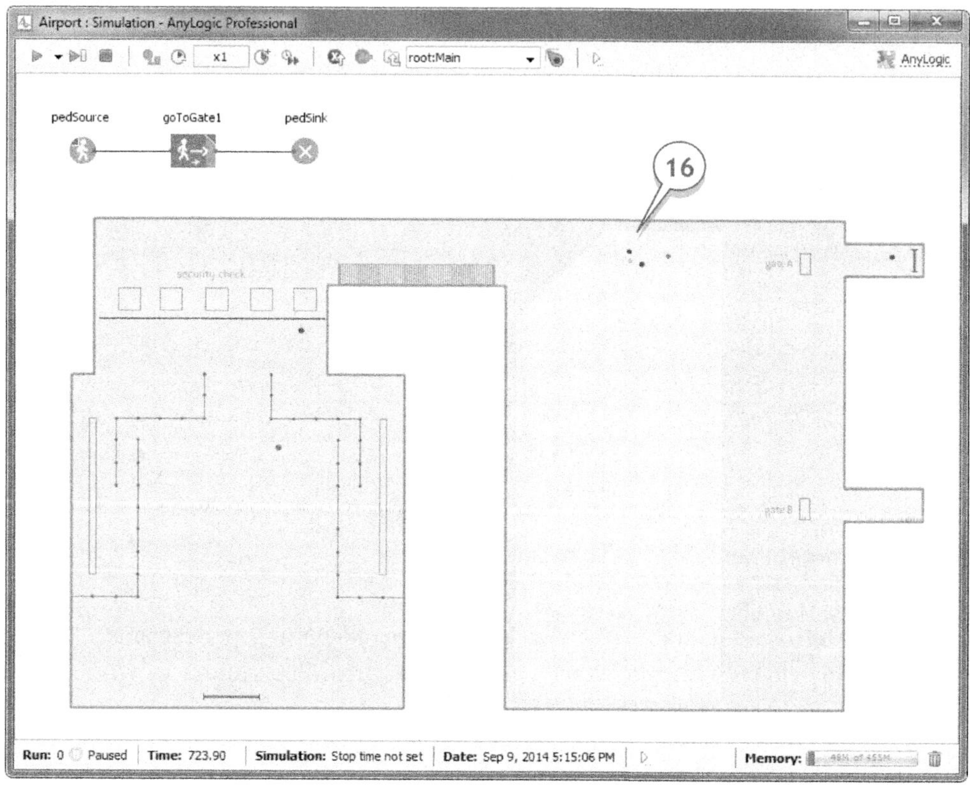

Airport : Simulation - AnyLogic Professional
x1
root:Main
AnyLogic
pedSource
goToGate1
pedSink
16
security check
gate A
gate B
Run: 0   Paused   Time: 723.90   Simulation: Stop time not set   Date: Sep 9, 2014 5:15:06 PM   Memory:

Phase 2. Drawing 3D animation

Let's add 3D animation to our model by adding 3D-specific elements (3D window, camera) and a 3D model of a passenger. We'll start by assigning a custom 3D animation shape to the passenger, a decision which means we need to create a custom **Pedestrian type**.

> ⬥ **If you want to add 3D animation, custom attributes, or collect statistics for pedestrians, you must create a custom pedestrian type.**

1. From the **Pedestrian Library** palette, drag the **Pedestrian Type** ⊕ element on to the *Main* diagram.

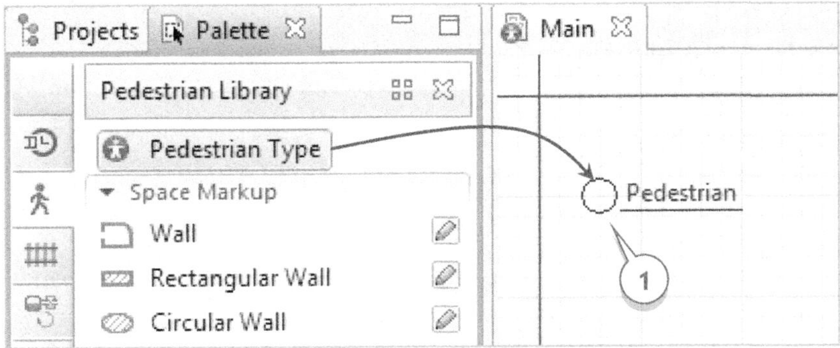

2. In the **New agent** wizard, enter the new pedestrian type's name – *Passenger* – and then click **Next**.

3. On the **Agent animation** page, select the **General** list's first item: **Person**, and click **Finish**.

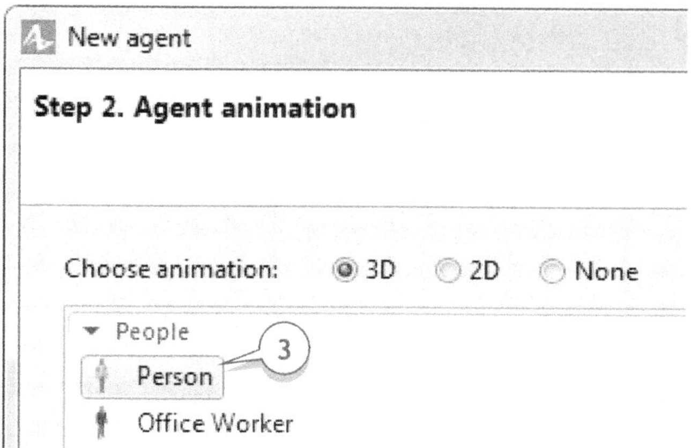

4. After the *Passenger* diagram opens, return to the *Main* diagram.

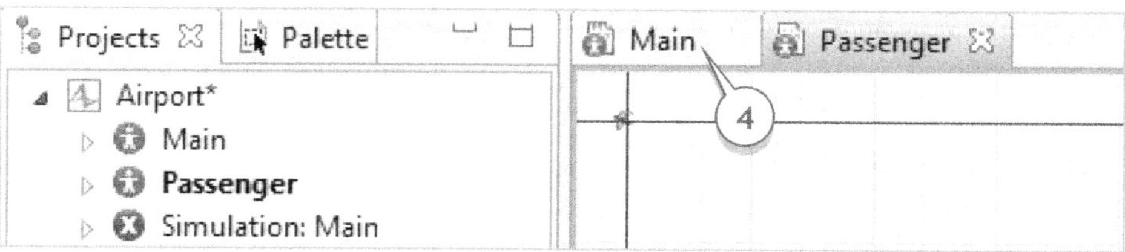

5. From the **Presentation** palette, drag the **Camera** on to the *Main* diagram
   and place it so it faces the terminal.

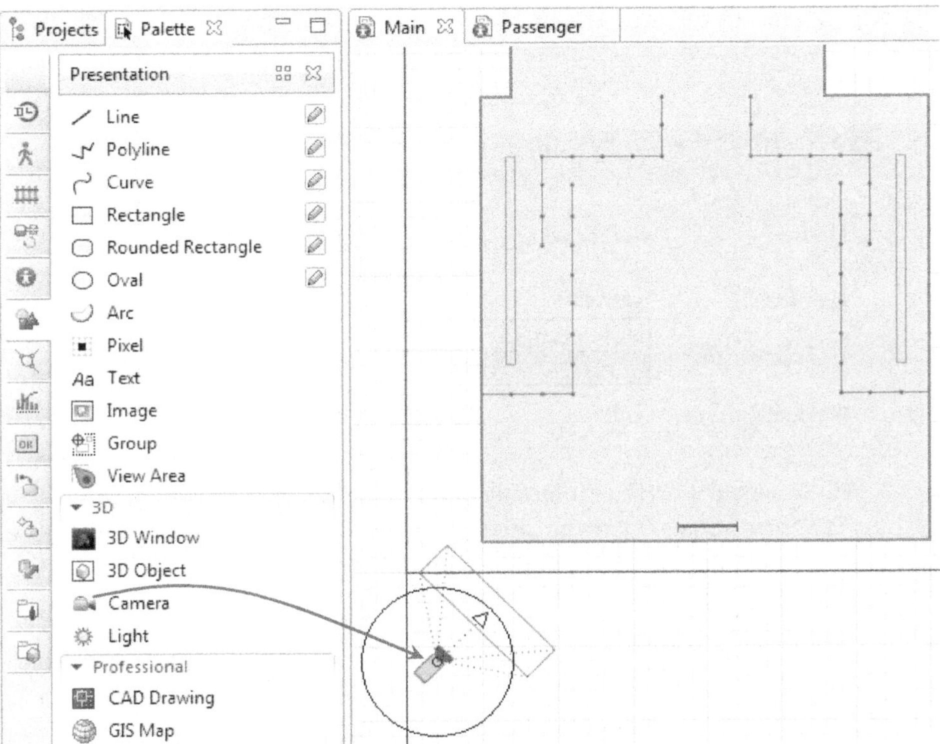

6. Drag the **3D Window** 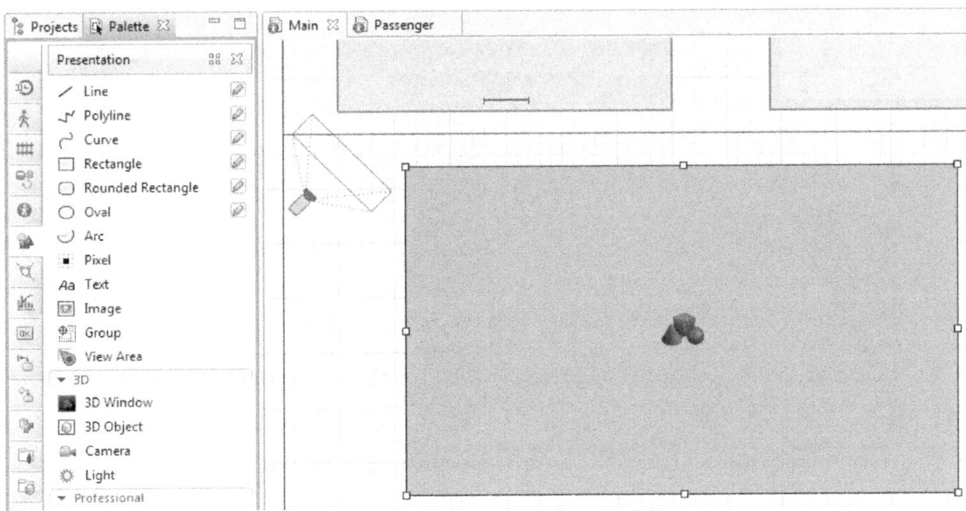 on to the *Main* diagram and place it below the terminal layout image.

7. Open the **3D Window** properties, and then select *camera* from the **Camera** list.

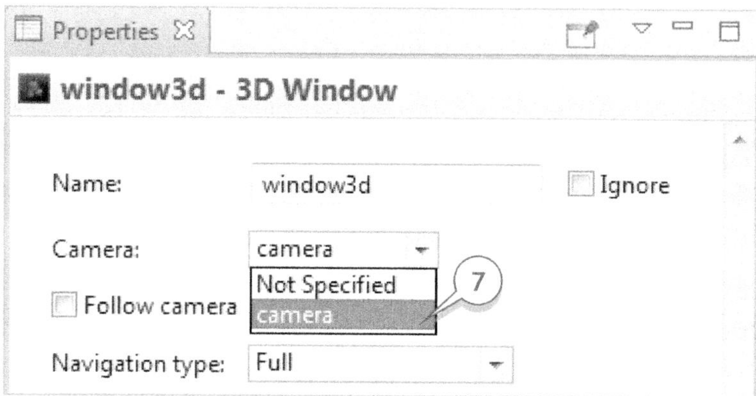

8. We want our flowchart block *pedSource* to create pedestrians of our custom *Passenger* type. Open the *pedSource* properties, and then select *Passenger* from the **New pedestrian** box in the **Pedestrian** section.

9. Run the model, and you'll see pedestrians move from the entry to the gate inside the building. You can switch to a 3D view by clicking the toolbar's Navigate to view area... button and then selecting **[window3d]** from the list.

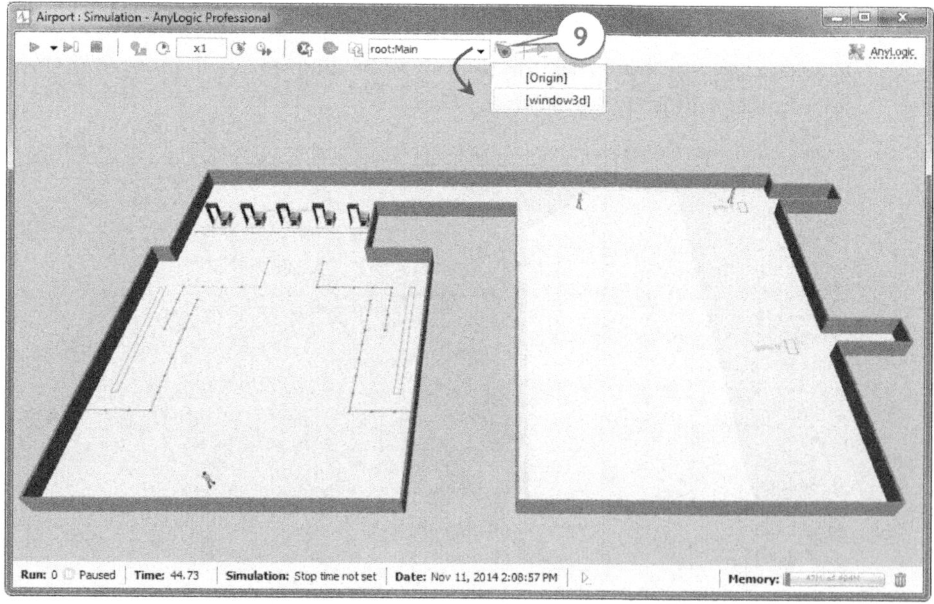

You can use your computer mouse to navigate in 3D at runtime.

Navigation in 3D scene

- **Move the camera, left, right, forward or backward** by dragging the mouse in the selected direction.

- **Move the camera closer or further from the scene's center** by rotating the mouse's wheel.

- **Rotate the scene relative to the camera** by dragging the mouse while the ALT key and the left mouse button are being pressed.

10. Navigate the scene to get the best view, right-click (Mac OS: CTRL+click) inside the 3D scene, and then click **Copy the camera's location**.

11. Close the model's window, open the camera's properties, and then apply the optimal camera you selected during the previous step by clicking **Paste coordinates from clipboard**.

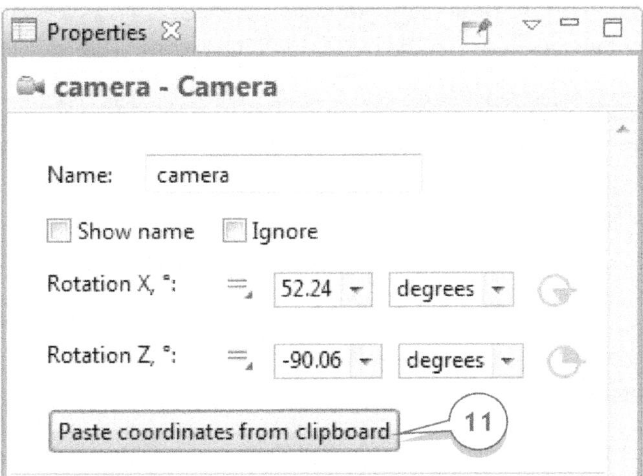

If you can't locate the camera, use the **Projects** tree to locate it. You'll find it under the **Presentation** branch of the airport's *Main* agent.

12. Run the model a second time and view the 3D view that the new camera position provides.

Phase 3. Adding security checkpoints

In this third phase, we'll start modeling the processes that take place inside the airport by adding security checkpoints. All of the security checkpoints are service points.

Services in pedestrian models

In pedestrian flow simulations, services are the objects – such as turnstiles, cash desks, ticket windows, and ticket machines – where pedestrians receive services. If a service is in use, the other pedestrians will wait in line until it is available.

You'll need to complete a two-step process to define the services your model's pedestrians will use. The first of these two steps is to use the **Service with Lines** and **Service with Area** markup shapes to draw your pedestrian model's services.

- **Service with Lines** – This markup shape defines a service such as a turnstile or a checkout area where pedestrians wait in a line until the service is available.

- **Service with Area** – This markup shape defines a service such as a ticket office or a bank office with an electronic queue where pedestrians wait in a neighboring office area until the service is available.

After you've drawn your model's services, you'll define the pedestrian flow logic by adding the Pedestrian Library's **PedService** block to the flowchart.

We'll add five security checkpoints, which means we'll add five services and five individual queues for each service point.

1. Drag the **Service with Lines** element from the **Pedestrian Library** palette on to the terminal layout. By default, a service will have two service points and two queue lines that lead to the service points.

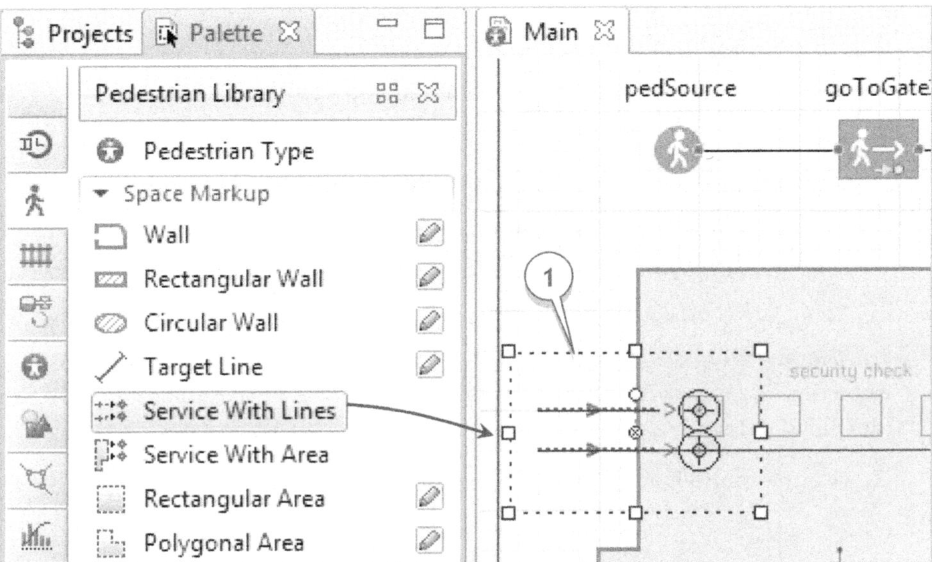

2. Open the **Service With Lines** properties area, use the **Name** box to name the shape *scpServices* - in this case, "scp" stands for security checkpoints - and then change the **Type of service** to *Linear*.

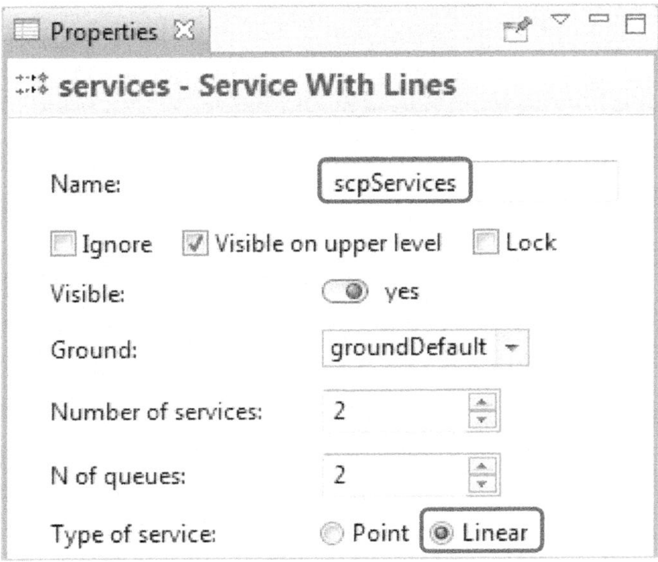

After you change the service type from a point service to a linear service, the service shapes will change from points to lines.

Linear and point services in pedestrian models

A pedestrian service can be a linear service or a point service.

- In a *linear service* like a turnstile, pedestrians continually move from the line's starting point to the line's ending point.

- In a *point service* like a ticket window, the pedestrian services occur at a specific point where pedestrians wait for the given delay time.

We're using a linear service to ensure our model's passengers walk along the service line and pass through the security check's metal detector. Now, we'll make sure the linear service point vertically crosses the space holder that represents the metal detector.

3. Use the round handle above the shape's center to rotate the service.

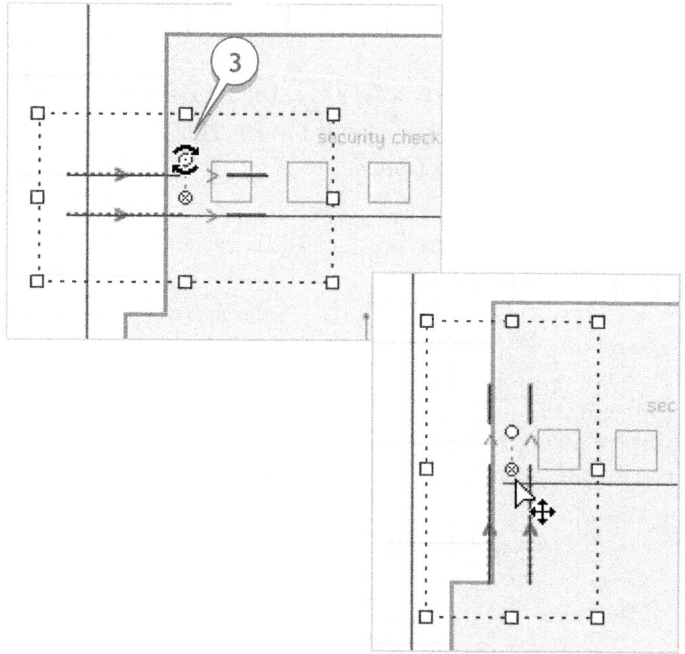

4. Move the service in a way that ensures the first linear service crosses the rectangle that represents the metal detector frame.

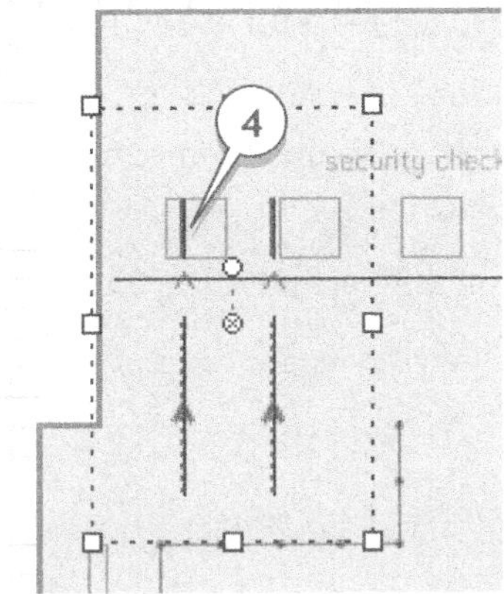

How to move elements ignoring the grid

If you want to move an element without automatically aligning the element to the grid, press and hold down ALT as you move the element or use the toolbar's **Enable/Disable Grid** button to disable the grid.

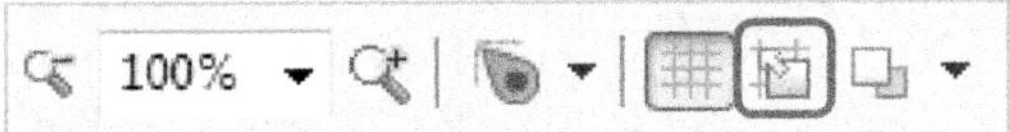

5. Select the next service line.

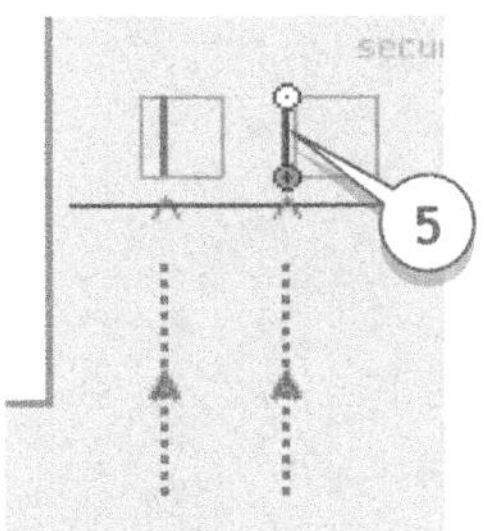

Complex space markup shapes

Complex space markup shapes are made up of several component shapes. For example, the **Service with Lines** shape is made up of **Service** and **Queue Line** space markup shapes, while the **Service with Area** shape is made up of the **Service** shape(s) and the **Polygonal Area**.

You'll need to pay close attention to these rules as you work with complex space markup shapes:

- Your first click will select the full complex space markup shape (**Service with Lines**).

- After you select the complex space markup shape, you can click any component shape to select it (**Service** or **Queue Line**).

6. Accurately place the service line on top of the second security checkpoint placeholder and then adjust the queue location.

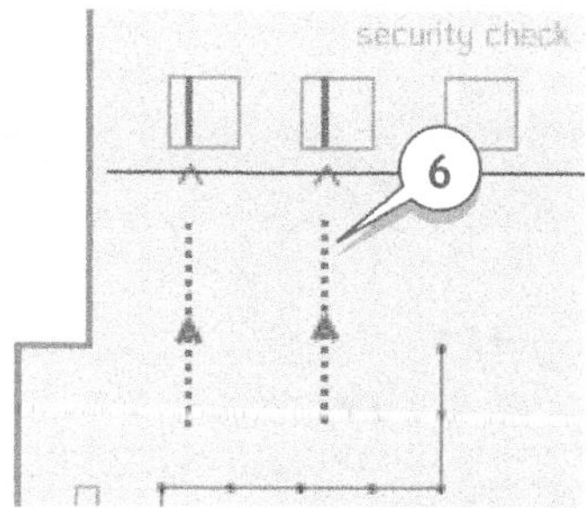

7. Navigate to the **Service with Lines** shape's properties and then change both the **Number of services** and **Number of lines** to *5*.

8. If necessary, adjust the new service and queue lines. After you've completed this step, the service shapes should look like those in the figure below.

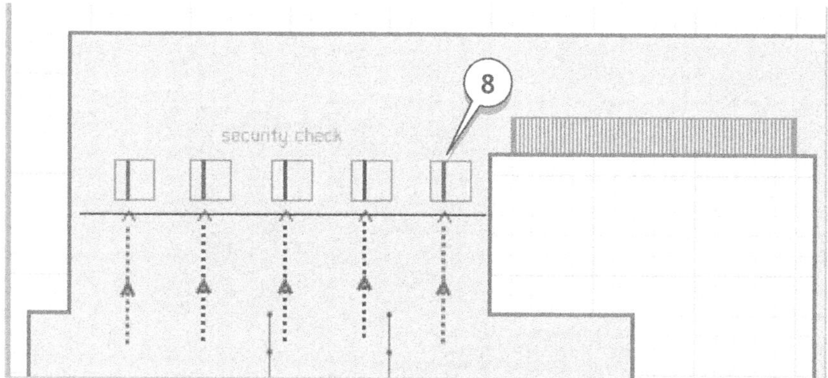

Now that we've drawn the services, we'll add them to our model's logic. We'll use a special **Pedestrian Library** block named **PedService** to simulate how passengers move through our security checkpoint services.

9. Add the **PedService** block on to the flowchart between the **PedSource** and **PedGoTo** blocks to make pedestrians pass through the service we defined

using the referenced Service with Lines shape, and then name it *securityCheck*.

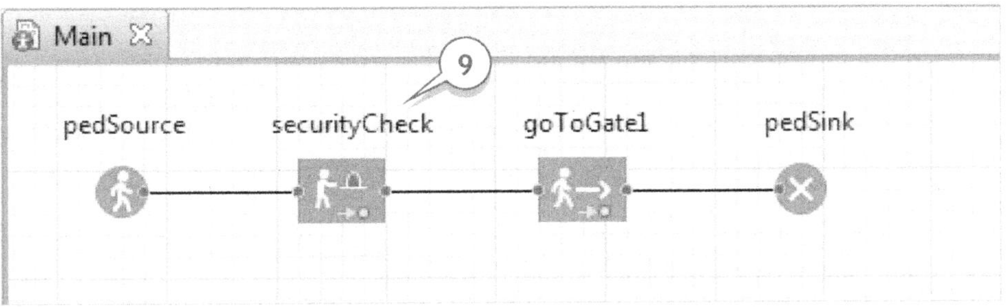

10. Go to the *securityCheck* block's properties. Select the services *scpServices* as **Services**.

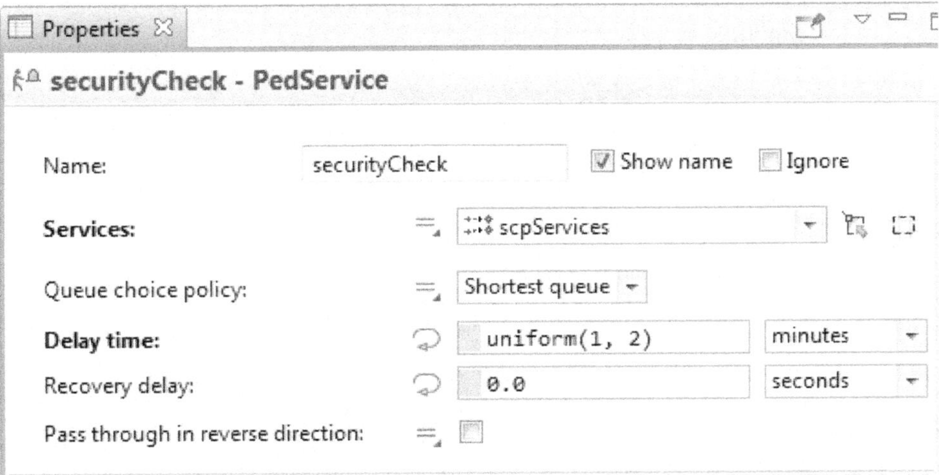

11. Since we assume it takes between 1 to 2 minutes to pass through the security checkpoint, type *uniform(1, 2)* **minutes** as the **Delay time**.

12. Now let's add 3D models of the security checkpoints. Using the **3D Objects** palette, **Airport** section's *Metal Detector* and *XRay Scanner* elements, draw five security checkpoints. You will see the message box, prompting you to change the scale of 3D object. Select the option **Do not ask me again** and click **OK**.

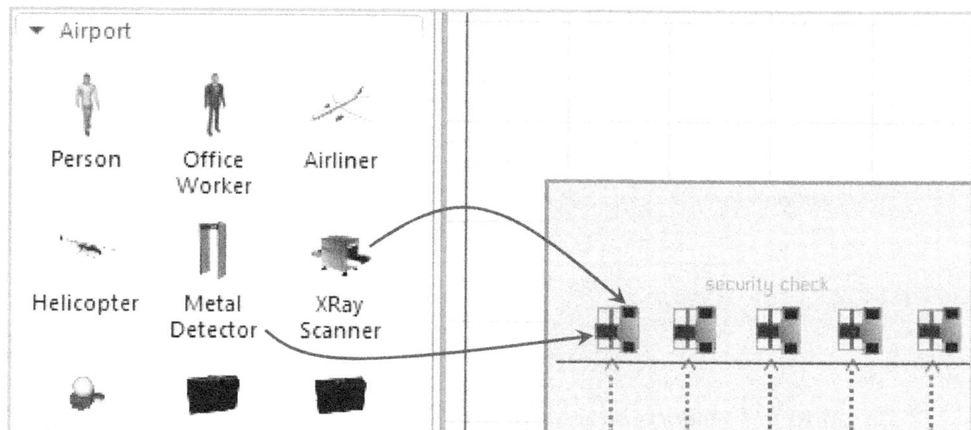

13. Run the model. You'll see that passengers are now scanned at the security checkpoints.

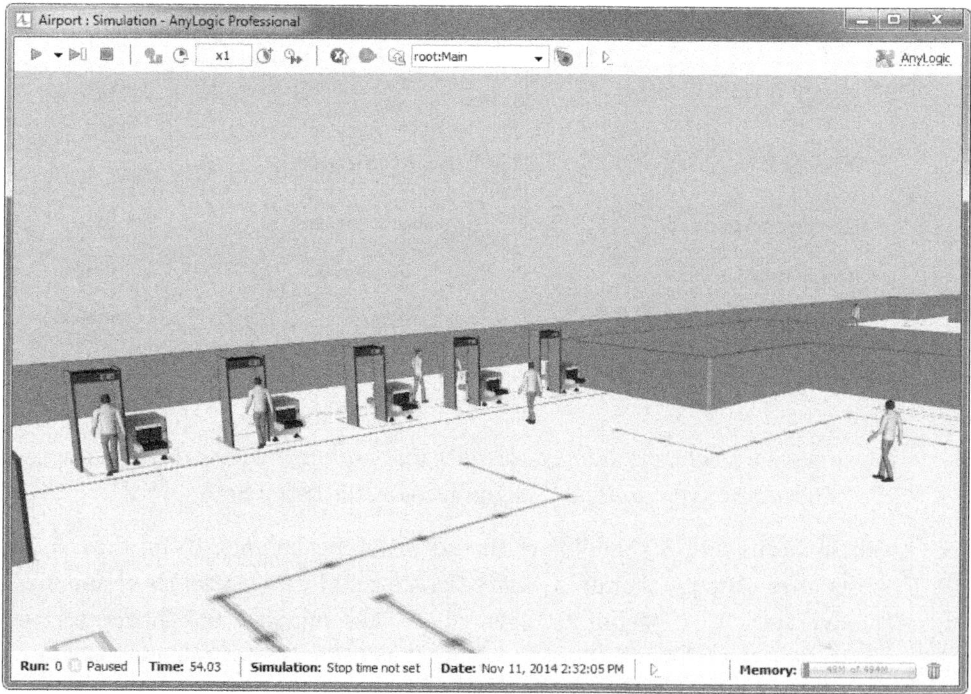

Phase 4. Adding check-in facilities

We're ready to simulate the airport's check-in facilities in a way that represents
the several ways passengers can check in for their flight.

1. Draw check-in locations with another **Service with Lines** shape. This time
   we'll need four service points, and one "serpentine" queue (the one with belt
   barriers that is common in areas where passengers check in for their flights).

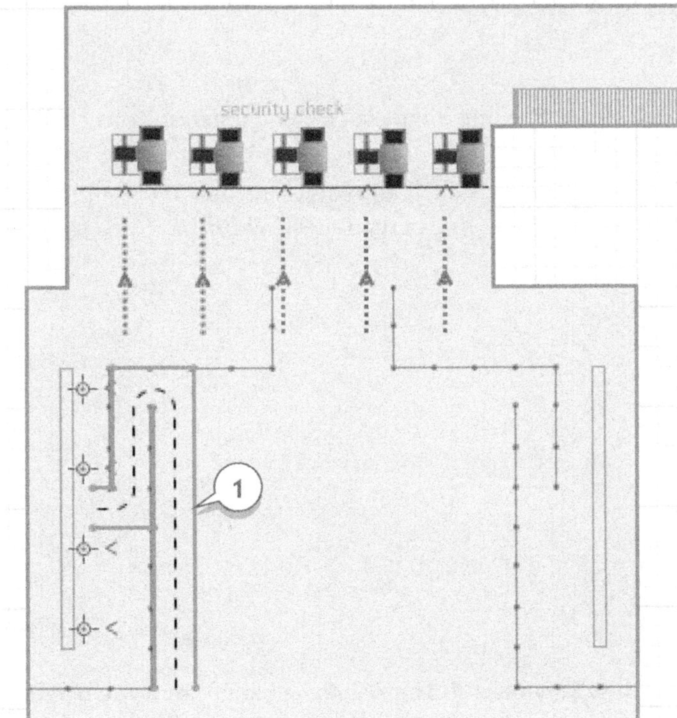

2. Name the services *checkInServices*. Place the shape in the location shown in
   the figure below. To make the line look like what you see on the figure, move
   the line to the required location, and then place the end point where the line
   starts turning.

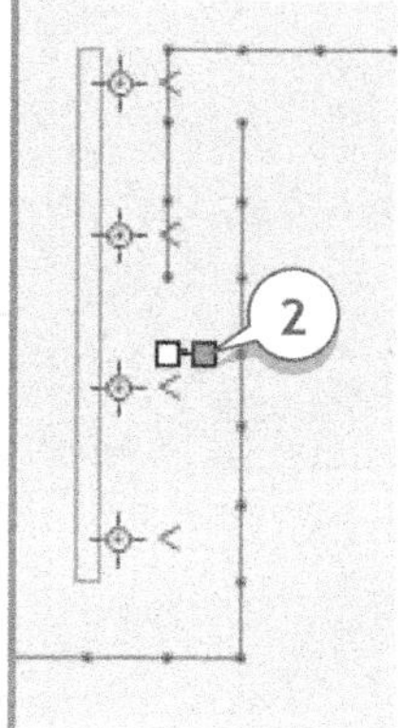

3. Add more salient points to the line. Right-click the queue line and choose **Add points** from the pop-up menu. Add more points by clicking where you want to place the line's salient points. Finish drawing the line by double-clicking. Finally you should get the queue line of the following form:

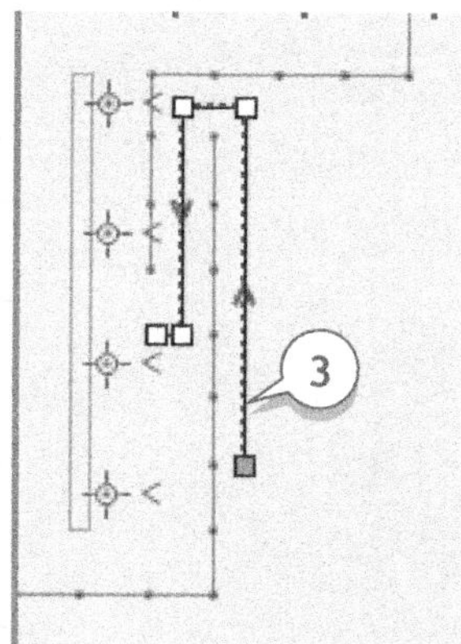

4. In the properties of this **Service with Lines** shape, change the **Type of queue** to **Serpentine**. Use this option to simulate serpentine (also named "zigzag") queues. You will see that the queue has borders now. In 3D animation they will appear as belt barriers.

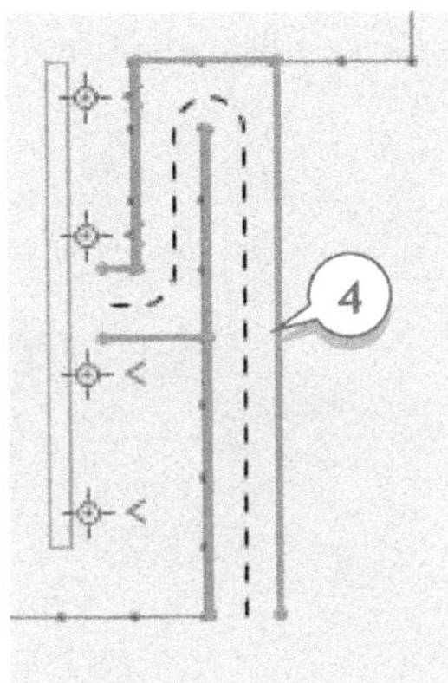

5. Add another **PedService** block and name it *checkInAtCounter*.

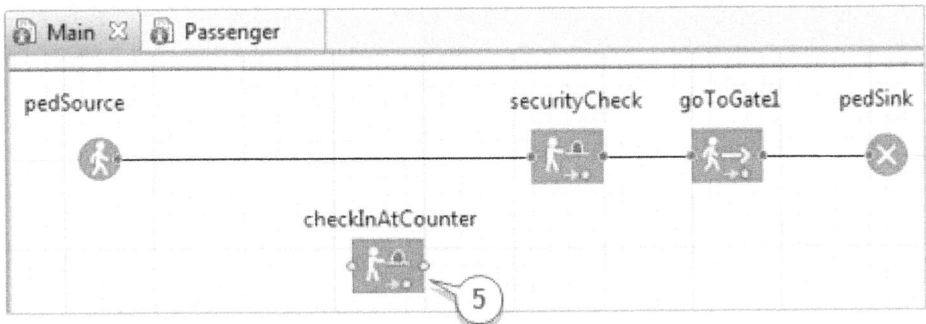

6. In the block's properties, select the space markup shape *checkInServices* as **Services**.

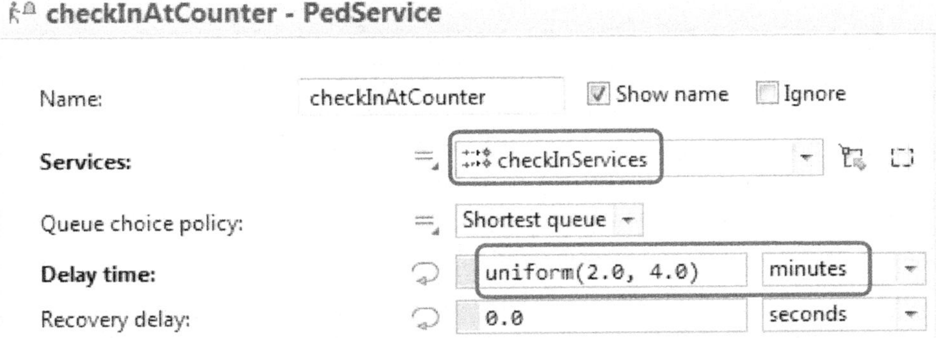

7. Since we assume it takes between 2 to 4 minutes to check in, type *uniform(2, 4)* **minutes** as the **Delay time**.

8. Add the **PedSelectOutput** ⊛ block to route passengers to different flowchart branches.

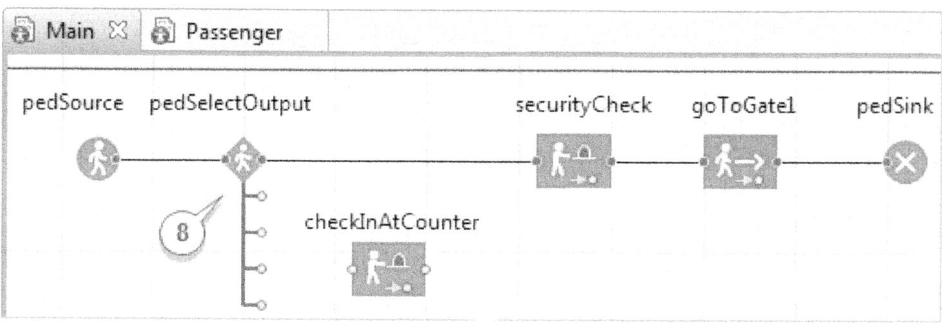

9. Connect the *checkInAtCounter* block to the existing flowchart blocks as shown in the figure below.

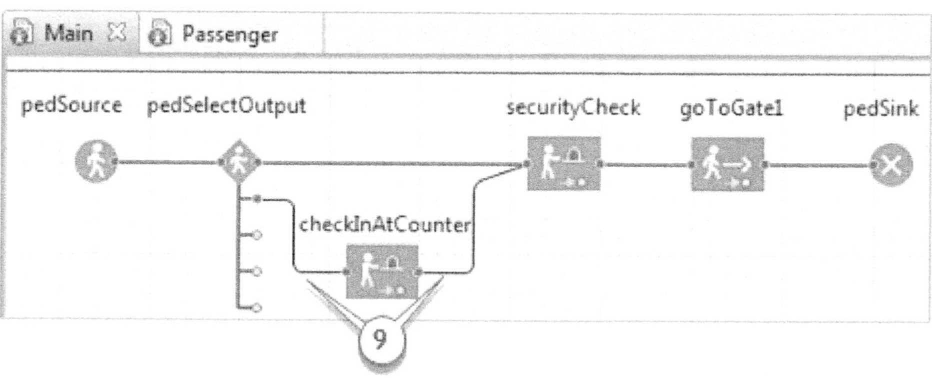

How to draw connectors

Your model's flowchart blocks will automatically connect when you place them near one another, but you can also use a connector to manually connect blocks. To draw a connector, double-click the first block's port and then click in another block's port. If you need to add an angle in the connecting line, add it with a click. After you draw the connector, you can add turning points by double-clicking the connector and dragging the points that appear. To remove a turning point, double-click it.

10. Since we're assuming 30 percent of our passengers will check in online and 70 percent will check in at the counter, we'll model this behavior by setting *pedSelectOutput*'s **Probability 1**: to *0.3* and **Probability 2**: to *0.7*. This action will route 30 percent of the passengers to the upper flowchart branch and 70

percent of the passengers to the lower branch. You must set **Probability 3**, **Probability 4**, and **Probability 5** to *0* to prevent AnyLogic from routing passengers to the block's lower three output ports.

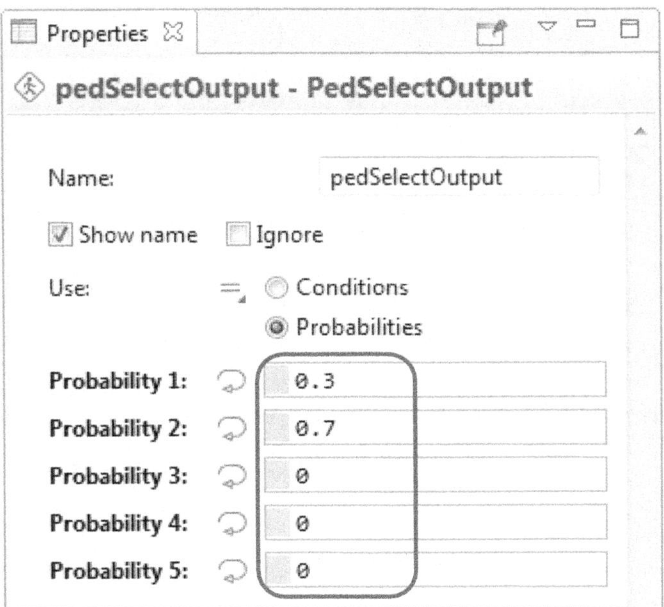

11. Let's add ready-to-use 3D models to the airport's check-in area. On the Palette's **3D Objects** tab, expand the **People** section, and then add two copies of both *Office Worker* and *Woman 2.* to the diagram.

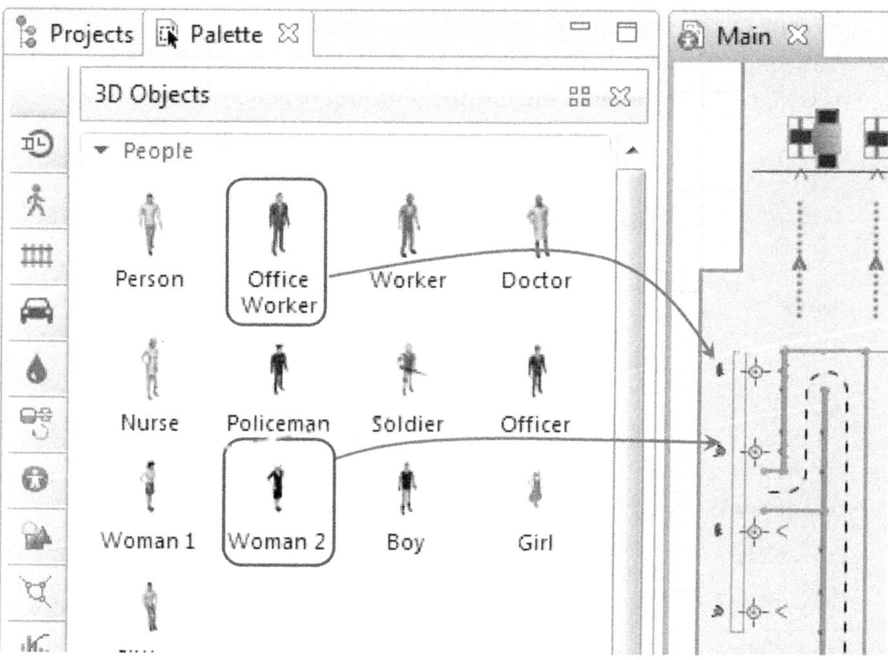

12. Define the area that is not accessible by passengers. Add the **Rectangular Wall** element from the **Space markup** section of the **Pedestrian Library** palette and place it as shown in the figure below. In the wall's properties, set **Visible** to **no** to make this wall invisible at the model runtime.

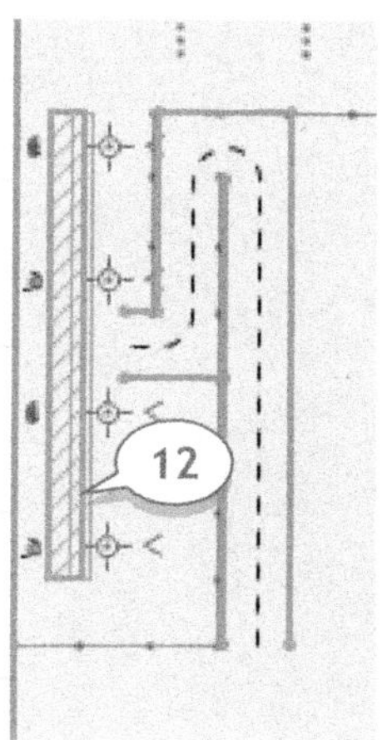

13. On the Palette's **3D Objects** tab, select the **Office** section, and then drag four copies of the **Table** object on to the diagram. Since the tables aren't facing the correct direction, use their **Properties** section's **Position** area to set **Rotation, Z**: *90 degrees.*

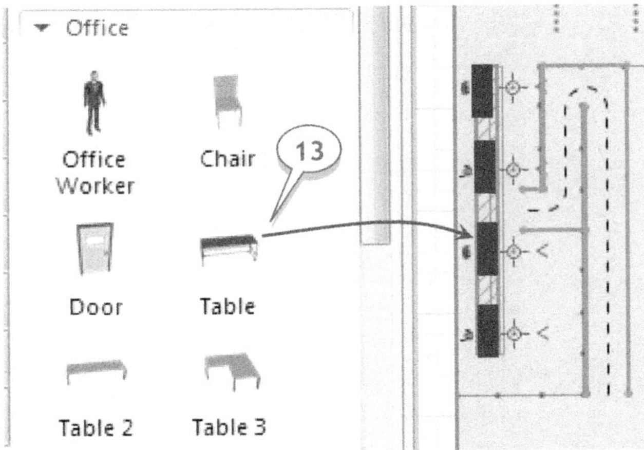

14. Run the model. You'll see some passengers check in and then go through the metal detector.

We want the passengers to wait before they go to the gate. To do this, we need to draw the waiting area where the passengers will wait and then add a flowchart block (**PedWait**) to simulate the waiting.

15. Draw the waiting area before the gates using the **Polygonal Area** element from the **Space Markup** section of the **Pedestrian Library** palette. Switch to the drawing mode and draw the area as shown in the figure below by clicking your mouse each time you want to add a point. When you're finished, double-click your mouse.

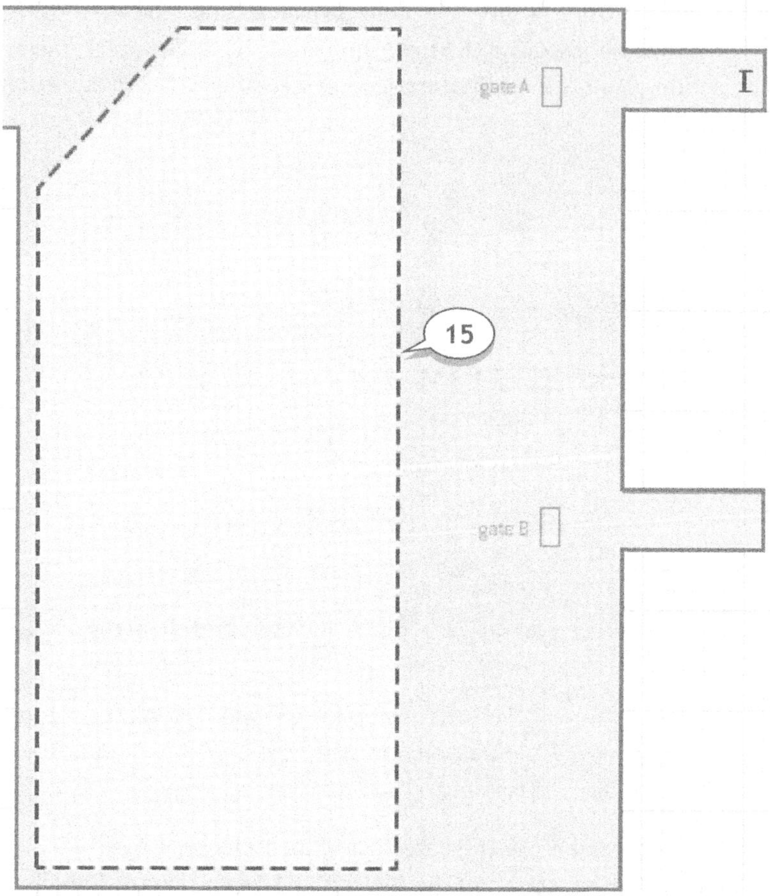

16. Add the **PedWait** ⏱ block on to the flowchart between **PedService** and **PedGoTo**.

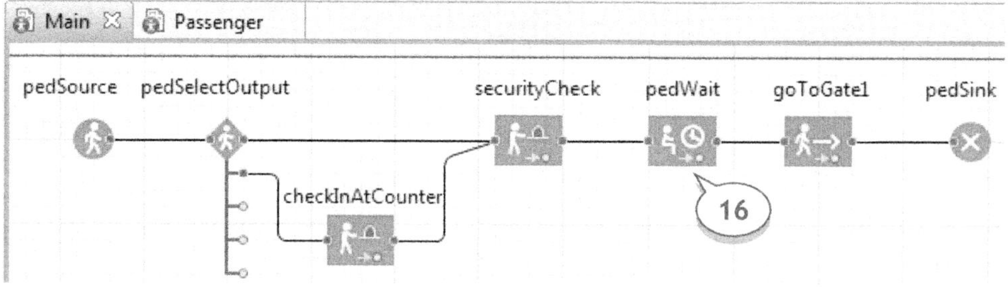

17. Modify the block's properties by selecting the area from the **Area** list, and then setting the **Delay time** to *uniform(15, 45)* **minutes**.

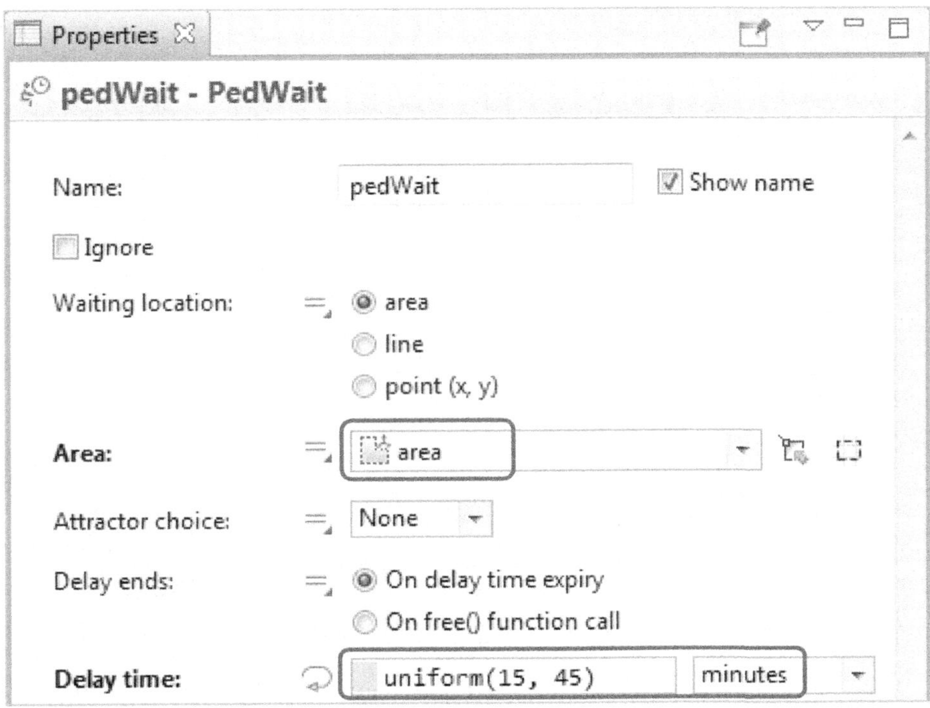

18. Run the model again, and you'll see the passengers now wait in the waiting area before they proceed to the gate.

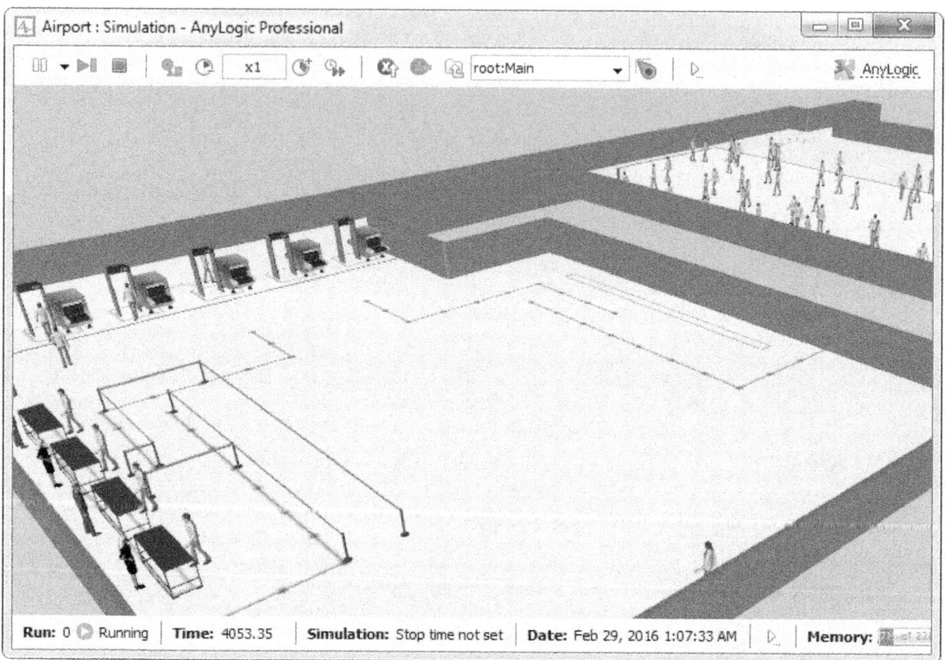

You can add more check-in facilities on the right and configure the **PedSelectOutput** to separate the pedestrian flow to more branches.

? How to simulate automatic check-in machines?

Phase 5. Defining the boarding logic

In this phase, we'll simulate the processes that take place at our airport's gate. The ticket checkpoint that each passenger must pass before they board their plane has one line for business class passengers – who are serviced first – and another for economy passengers. We'll add custom information to pedestrians to distinguish business class passengers from economy class passengers.

1. In the **Projects** tree, open the *Passenger* agent type diagram by double-clicking the *Passenger* item.

2. Add a **Parameter** ⌕ from the **Agent** ⊕ palette to define the passenger's class. Name it *business*, and set **Type**: *Boolean*. If the parameter is equal to *true*, this is a business class passenger, otherwise (if the parameter is *false*), this is an economy class passenger.

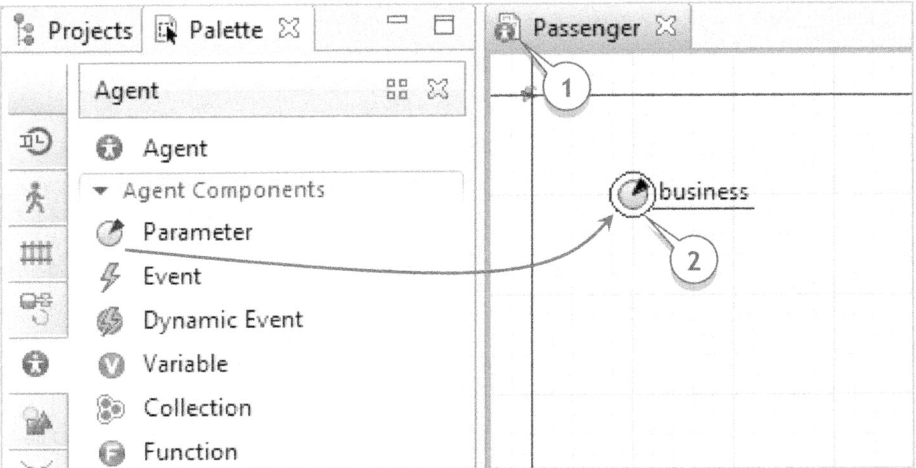

We want to distinguish passengers in 3D animation, namely animate business class and economy passengers with different 3D models. To do this, we'll use the existing *Person* 3D object to represent economy passengers and add another 3D shape to represent business class passengers.

3. Add the 3D object **Office worker** to animate a business class passenger and then place the figure on the axis origin point (0,0), right on the *Person* shape.

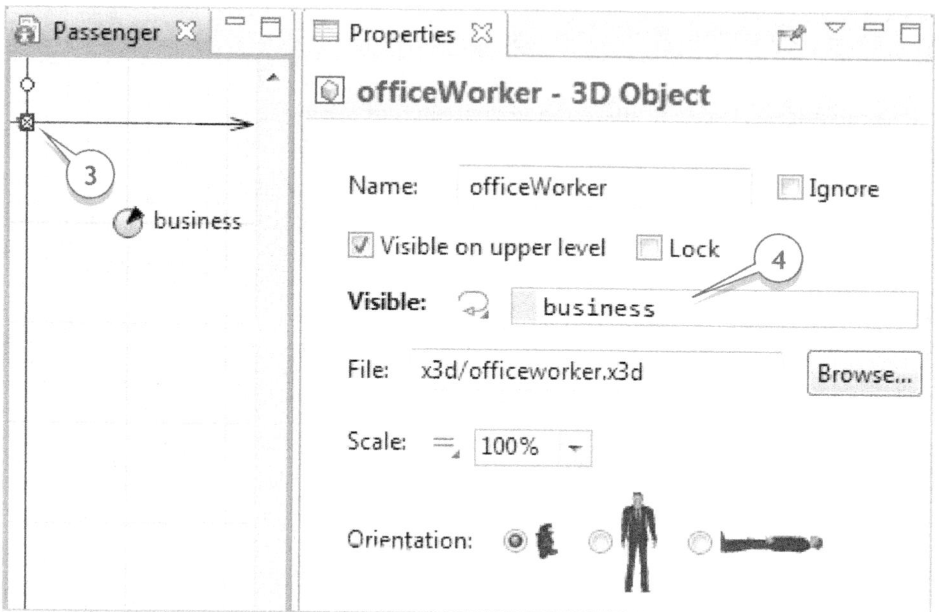

4. Change the visibility of these objects. First, click the *Office worker* shape. We want this shape to be visible only when this is a business class passenger, that is, when its *business* parameter is *true*. Switch to the **Visible** property's dynamic value editor by clicking the icon to the right of the **Visible** label, and then type *business* in the box. By doing this, we're making this 3D shape visible only when pedestrian's *business* parameter is *true*.

5. Now select the *person* 3D object (you can do this from **Projects** tree), and set **Visible**: *! business* . This shape will be visible only if the passenger is an economy passenger.

The symbol ! is the boolean operand NOT. The expression *!business* returns *true* when the business is NOT true – when the passenger is not a business class passenger but is an economy passenger.

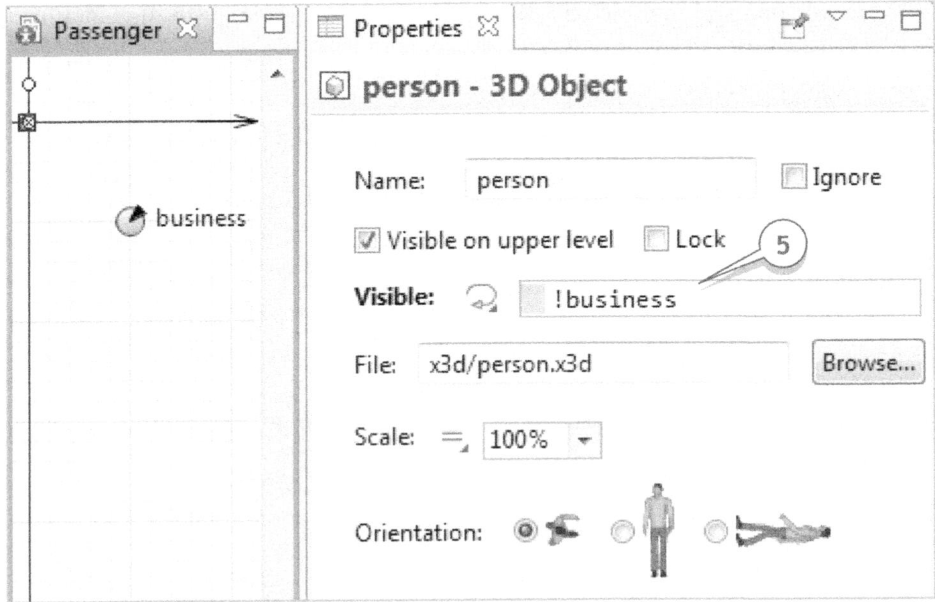

We want to set up the passengers' class when they arrive to the airport terminal.

6. Return to the *Main* diagram and add a **Function** ⓕ from the **Agent** palette. Name it *setupPassenger*.

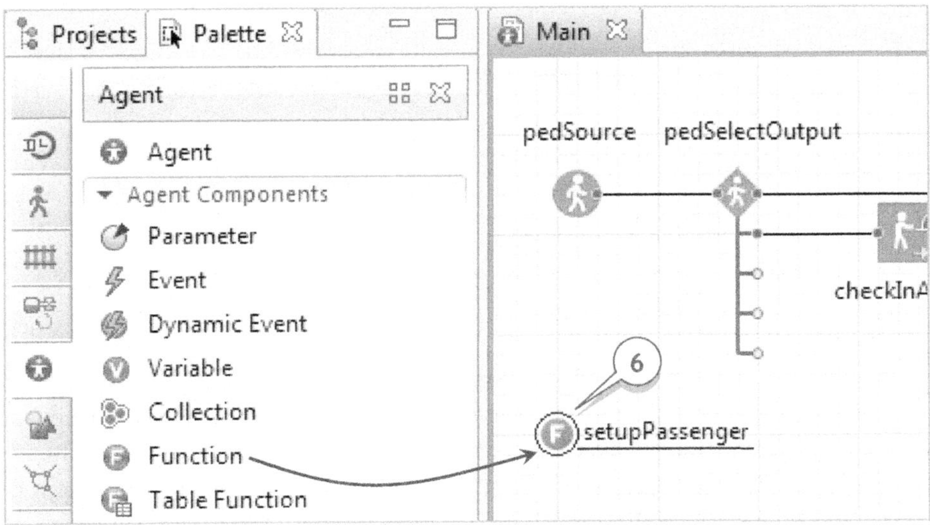

7. Configure the function as follows:

- Create one argument to pass the newly-created passenger to the function:
  Name: *ped*
  Type: *Passenger*

- The function's code defines the frequency with which the business class passengers appear in the model:
  ped.business = randomTrue(0.15);

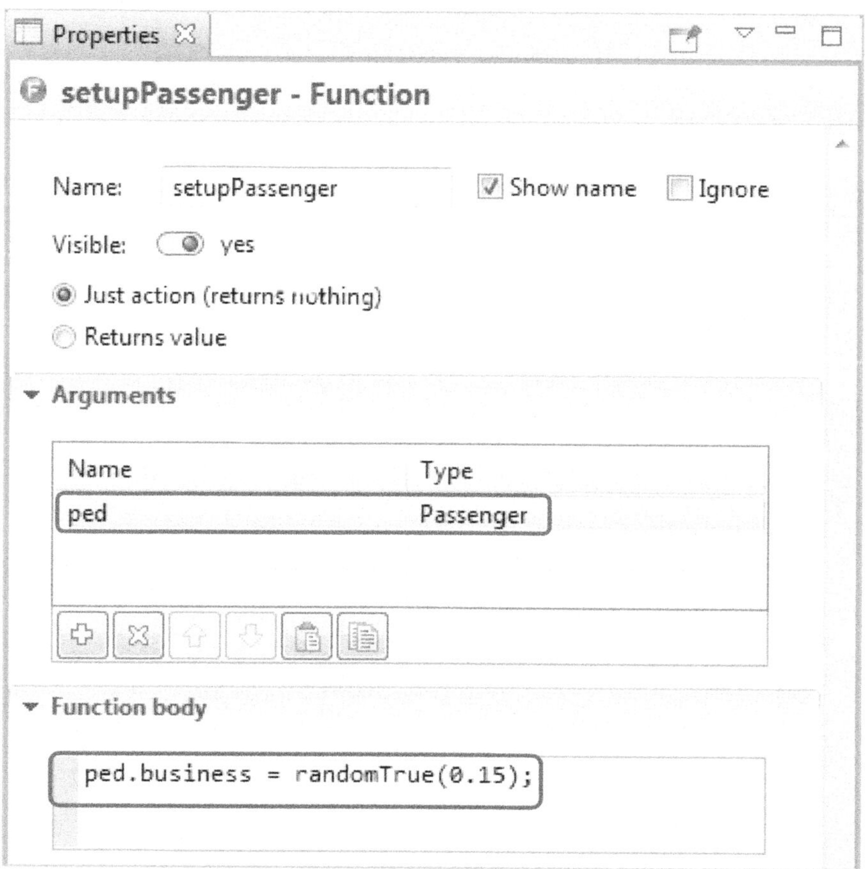

In this case, *ped* is the function's argument, of type *Passenger*. Having set up the *Passenger* as the argument type, we can directly access the custom pedestrian field *business* simply as *ped.business*. The function *randomTrue(0.15)* returns *true* in an average of 15 percent of cases, which means an average of 15 percent of our model's passengers will travel in business class.

8. Call this function when a new pedestrian is created by the *pedSource* block. In the *pedSource* properties area, click the arrow to expand the **Actions** section, and then enter the following code in the **On exit** box: *setupPassenger(ped);*

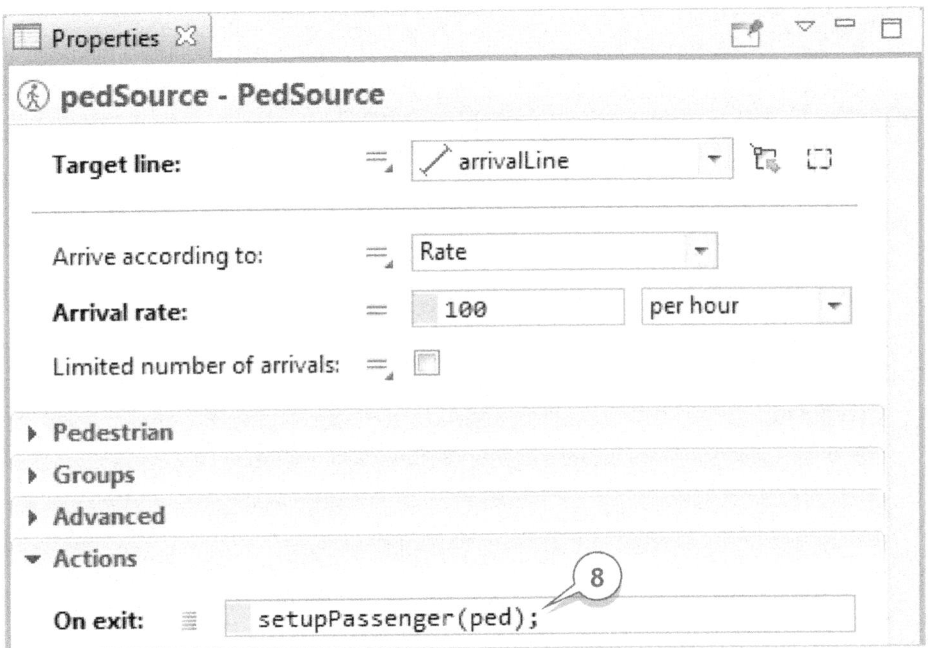

Here we call our function *setupPassenger* for the newly-created pedestrian. This pedestrian is passed to the function via its argument.

Draw two services with lines for the upper gate, one for business class and one for economy passengers.

9. Draw a Service with Line, defining the priority line (point service, 1 service, 1 line). Name this service *business1*.

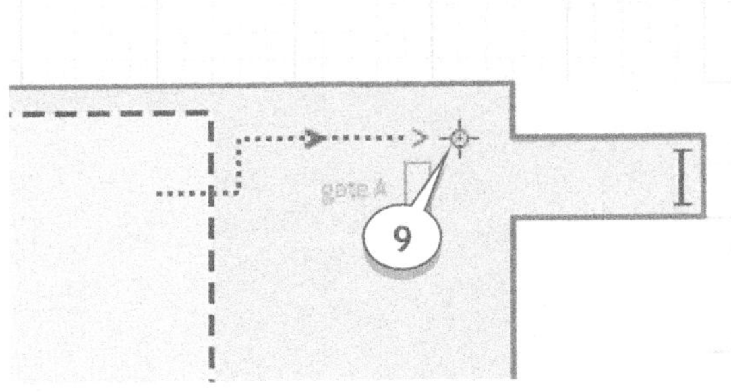

10. Add one more Service with Line, and name it *economy1*.

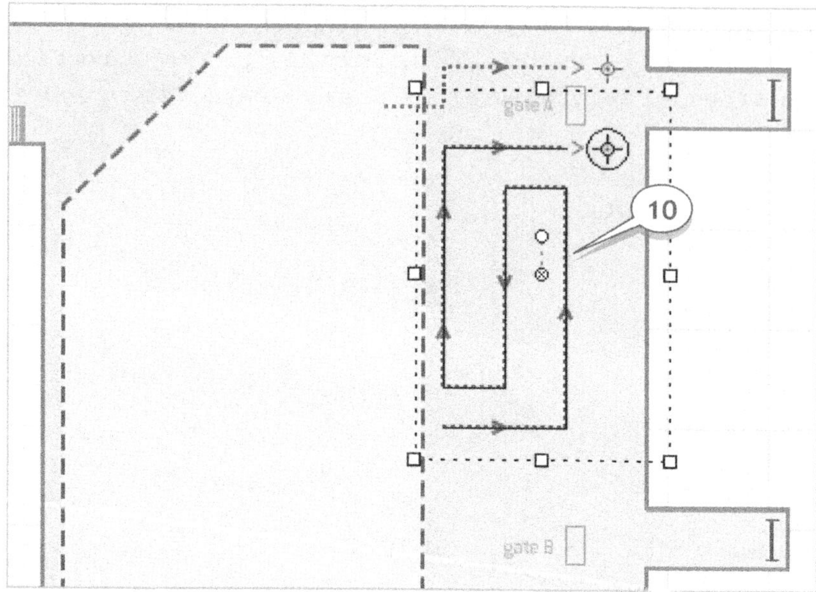

11. Draw an area at the gate with the **Rectangular Wall** element, and then add a table and two 3D woman models at the table. In the wall's properties, set **Visible** to **no** to make this wall invisible at the model runtime.

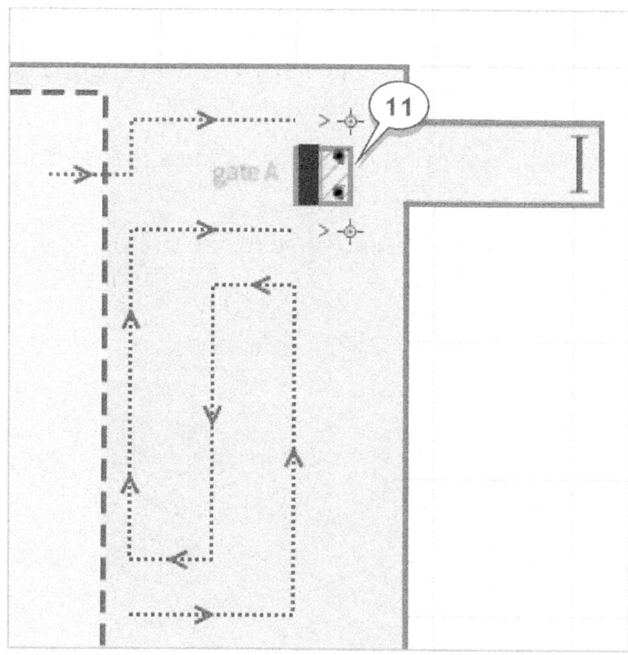

Insert the blocks into the flowchart between the *pedWait* and *goToGate1* objects.

12. Add **PedSelectOutput** to route business class and economy passengers to different lines.

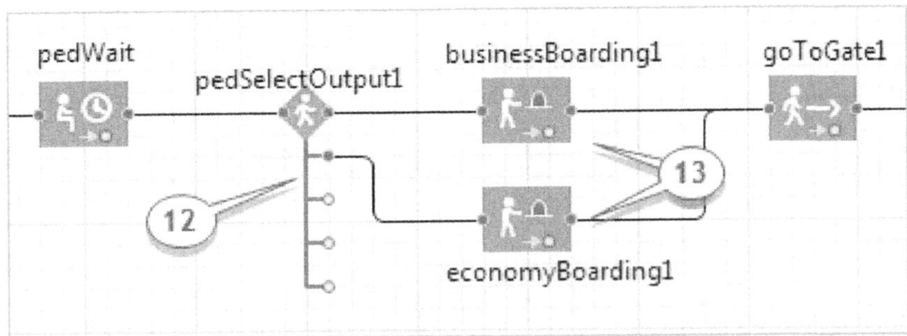

13. Add two **PedService** blocks: *businessBoarding1* and *economyBoarding1* to simulate the process of checking passengers' tickets at the gate.

14. Since the **PedSelectOutput** block routes business class and economy passengers to different lines, select **Use: Conditions**, and then type *ped.business* in the **Condition 1** box. This expression will return *true* for all business class passengers, which means they will follow the upper flowchart branch and join the priority line. After you set up the conditions for the block's next output ports (*true*, *false*, *false*), the model will direct all other passengers to the second output port.

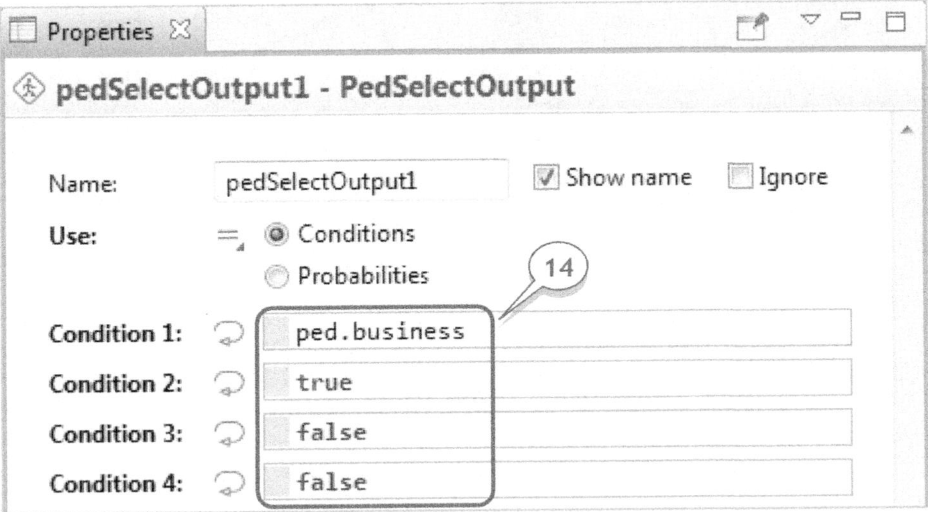

15. For the **PedService** block *businessBoarding1*, choose *business1* as **Services**. Since it takes between two to five seconds to check a passenger's ticket, you can slightly change the **Delay time**.

16. For *economyBoarding1*, set **Services**: *economy1*, adjust the **Delay time**.

17. Run the model. You'll see passengers pass the checkpoint, and a small number of them will take the priority line.

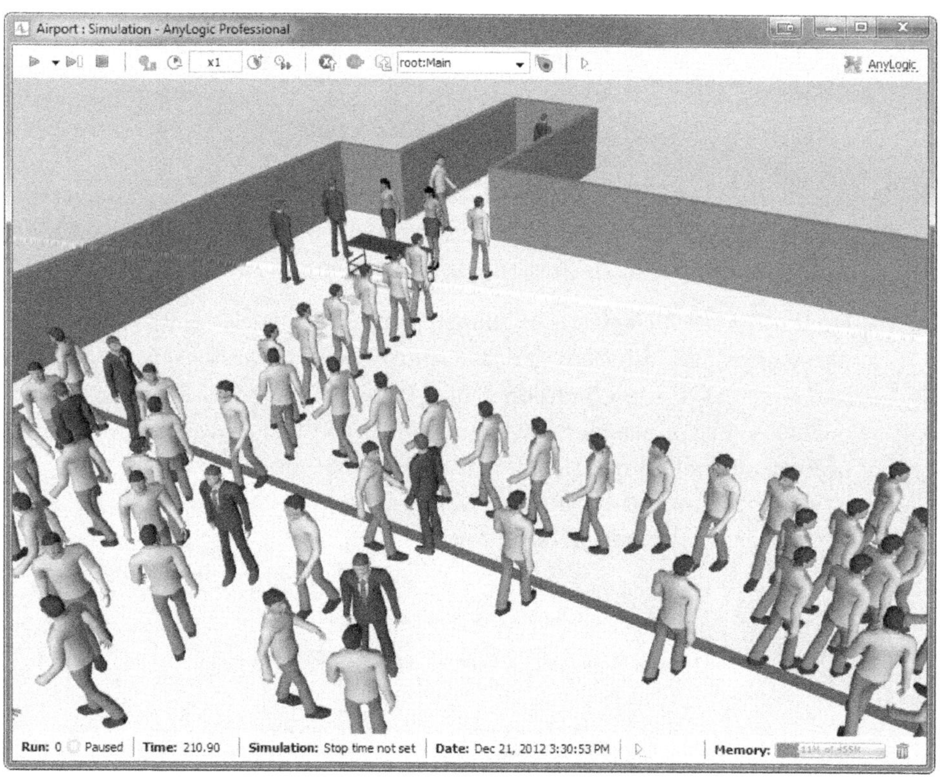

Phase 6. Setting up flights from MS Excel spreadsheet

In this phase, we'll model how airplanes take off at specific times according to a timetable stored in an Excel file.

AnyLogic database

Each AnyLogic model now has a built-in fully integrated database to read input data and write simulation output.

```
▲ 🔢 Airport
    ▷ 👤 Main
    ▷ 👤 Passenger
    ▷ ✖ Simulation: Main
      🛢 Database
```

With the database, you can:

- Read parameter values and configure models

- Create parameterized agent populations

- Generate agent arrivals in the process models

- Log flowchart activities, events, statechart transitions, and so on

- View resource utilization, waiting, processing and travel times

- Store and export statistics, datasets, and custom logs

- Export data to MS Excel spreadsheet.

You can easily import the database into your AnyLogic project from external database or spreadsheet. Alternatively, you can create empty database tables and enter data manually.

We will show how to import data from the database.

1. In the **Projects** view, right-click the **Database** 🛢 and select **Import database tables...** from the pop-up menu.

2. You will see the **Import database tables** dialog box. Select the database you want to import into your project. Click **Browse...** to specify the *Flights.xlsx* file.

You'll select the file from *AnyLogic folder/resources/AnyLogic in 3 days/Airport.*

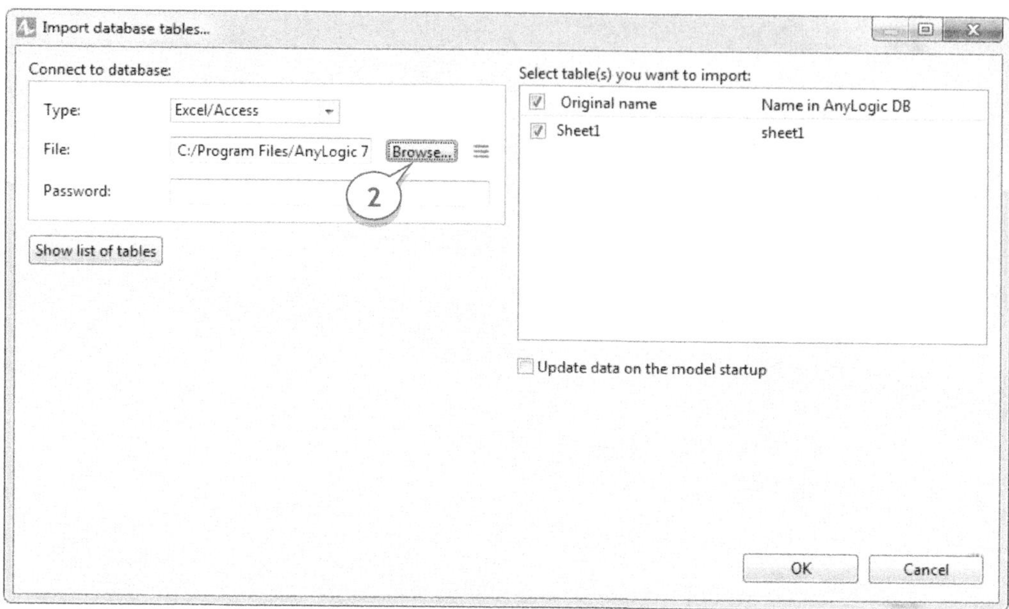

3. You will see *Sheet1* table added into the **Select table(s) you wish to import** list on the right. Click **OK** to import data from the selected database table into your model.

4. In the **Projects** view, you will see *sheet1* item added under the **Database** item. Double-click it, and you will see the data stored in this table displayed in the table editor. The table contains three columns storing information on the flight's destination, departure time and gate number.

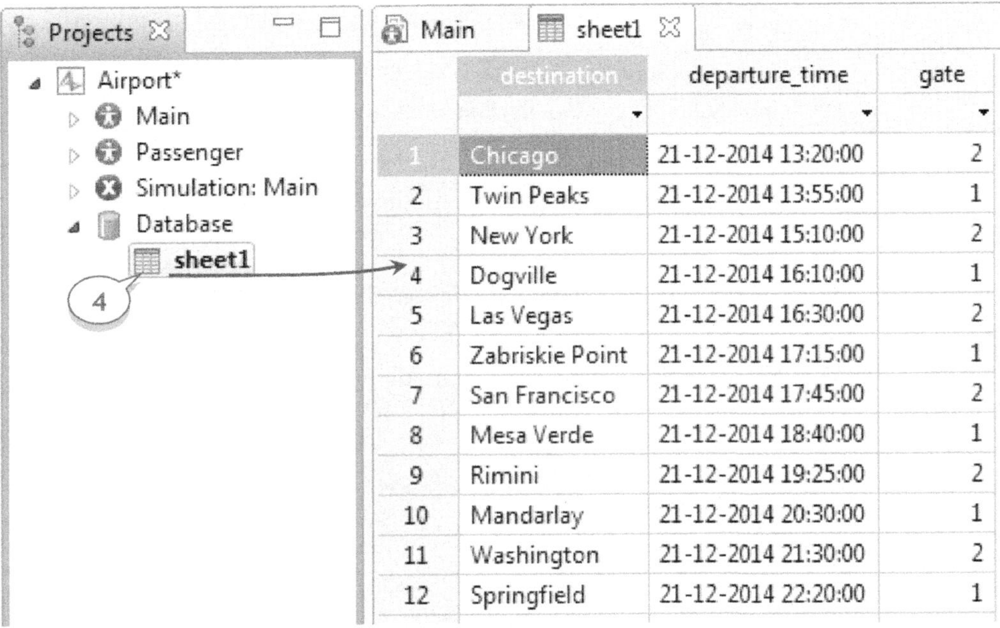

Now we will create a new agent type: *Flight*.

5. Add an empty agent population of the new *Flight* agent type by dragging the **Agent** element from the **Agent** palette on to the *Main* diagram.

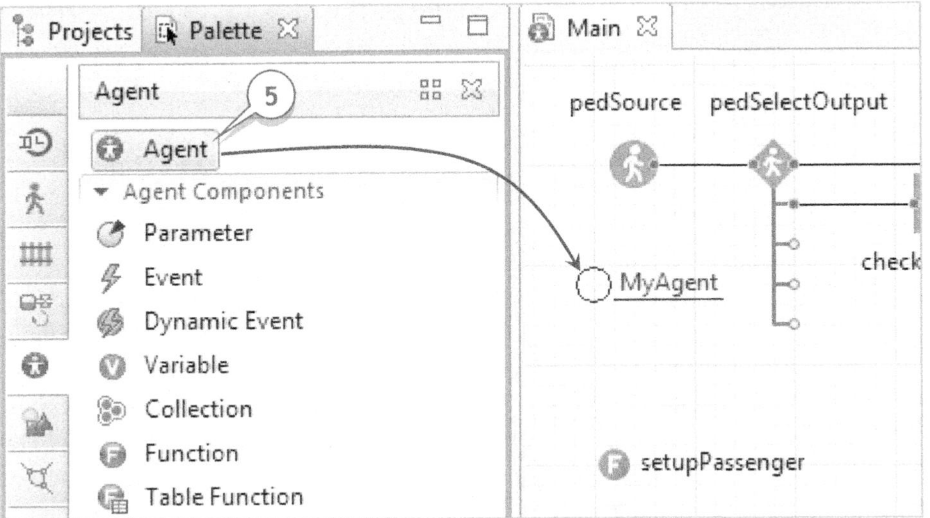

6. In the **New agent** wizard, do the following:

a. Select **Population of agents**.

b.   Select the option **I want to create a new agent type**. Click **Next**.

c.   Specify **Agent type name**: *Flight*. The population name will prefill as *flights*. Select the **Use database table** option and click **Next**.

d.   On the next page of the wizard leave the default settings (we will use data from *sheet1* table of the model's built-in database). Click **Next**.

e.   The next page proposes to create parameters *destination*, *departureTime* and *gate* for every agent of the type *Flight*. That is exactly what we need. Click **Next** to continue.

f.   Since we won't need to animate flights, select **None** for the animation.

g.   Click **Finish**.

7. In the **Projects** view, double-click *Flight* to open its diagram. On the *Flight* diagram, you will see three different parameters:

- *destination*, **Type**: *String*.

- *departureTime*. **Type**: *Date*.

- *gate*, **Type**: *int*.

These parameters store the flight's departure time, destination, and gate number.

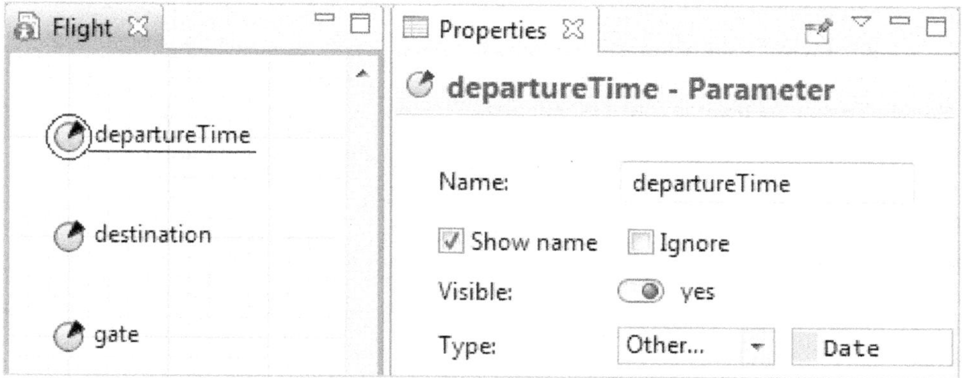

8. Add a **Collection** from the **Agent** palette on to the *Flight* diagram, name it *passengers*, and then set the **Collection class** to *LinkedList*, and the **Elements class** to *Passenger*. This collection will store the list of passengers that have bought tickets for the flight.

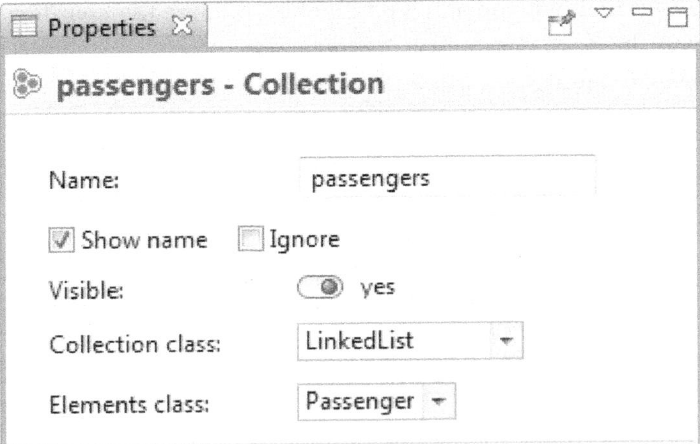

Collections

Collections define data objects that group multiple elements into a single unit to store, retrieve and manipulate aggregated data. They typically represent data items that form a natural group.

9. Now that we've created the *Flight* agent type, we'll add a *flight* parameter to the *Passenger* diagram and set the parameter's **Type** to *Flight*. This parameter will store the passenger's flight.

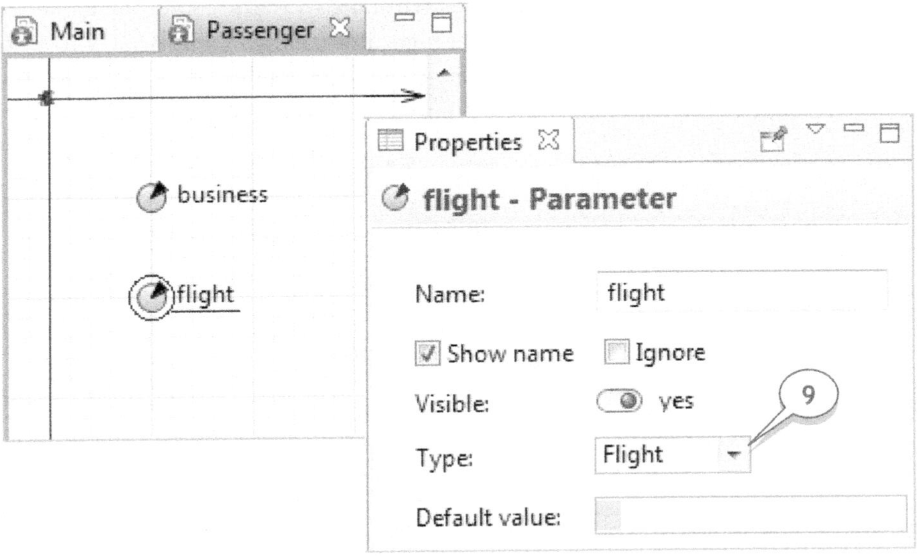

10. Return to the *Main* diagram and add a parameter to define the boarding time duration. Name the new parameter *boardingTime*, and then choose **Type: Time, Unit: minutes**, and **Default value:** *40.*

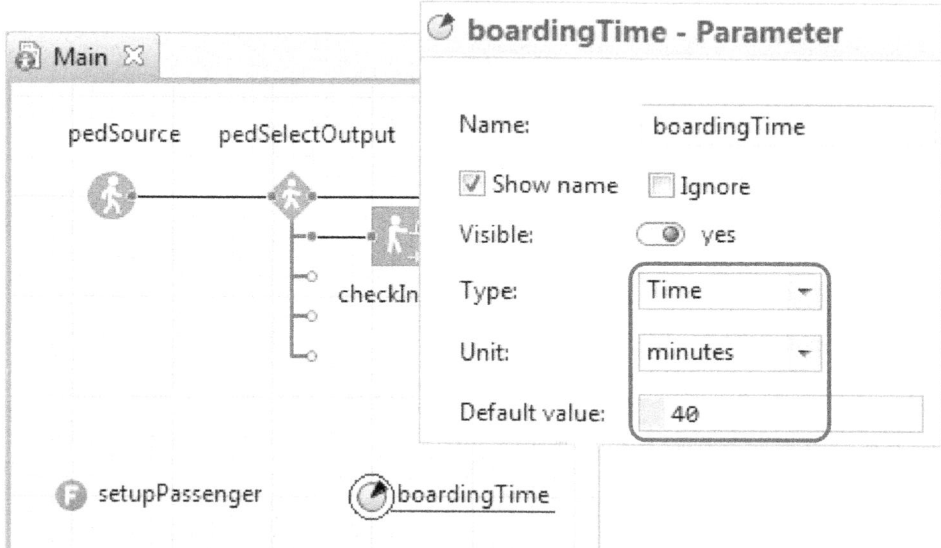

11. Select the function *setupPassenger* that we created earlier to complete our setup process. The function now uses the *random()* function to randomly select the flight that the passenger will take from the list of available flights. The flight is stored in a passenger's parameter *flight*, and AnyLogic adds the passenger to a collection of passengers who are taking the same flight. Modify the code in the **Function body** section:

```
ped.business = randomTrue(0.15);
Flight f;

do
{  f = flights.random(); }
while (dateToTime(f.departureTime) - boardingTime < time() );

ped.flight = f;
f.passengers.add(ped);
```

The function *dateToTime()* converts the given date to model time with respect to the start date, and model time unit settings. The function *add()* adds an element to the collection.

Working with collection contents

You can use the following functions to manage the collection's contents:

- *int size()* - Returns the number of elements in the collection.

- *boolean isEmpty()* - Returns *true* if the collection has no elements, *false* otherwise.

- *add(element)* - Appends the specified element to the end of this collection.

- *clear()* - Removes all the collection's elements.

- *get(int index)* - Returns the element at the specified position in the collection.

- *boolean remove(element)* - Removes the specified element from the collection if it is present. Returns *true* if the list contained the specified element.

- *boolean contains(element)* - Returns *true* if this collection contains the specified element.

12. Define the second gate:

- Add two **Service with lines** elements: *business2* and *economy2*.

- Draw the rectangular wall, table and women figures.

- Draw the **Target line** *gateLine2*.

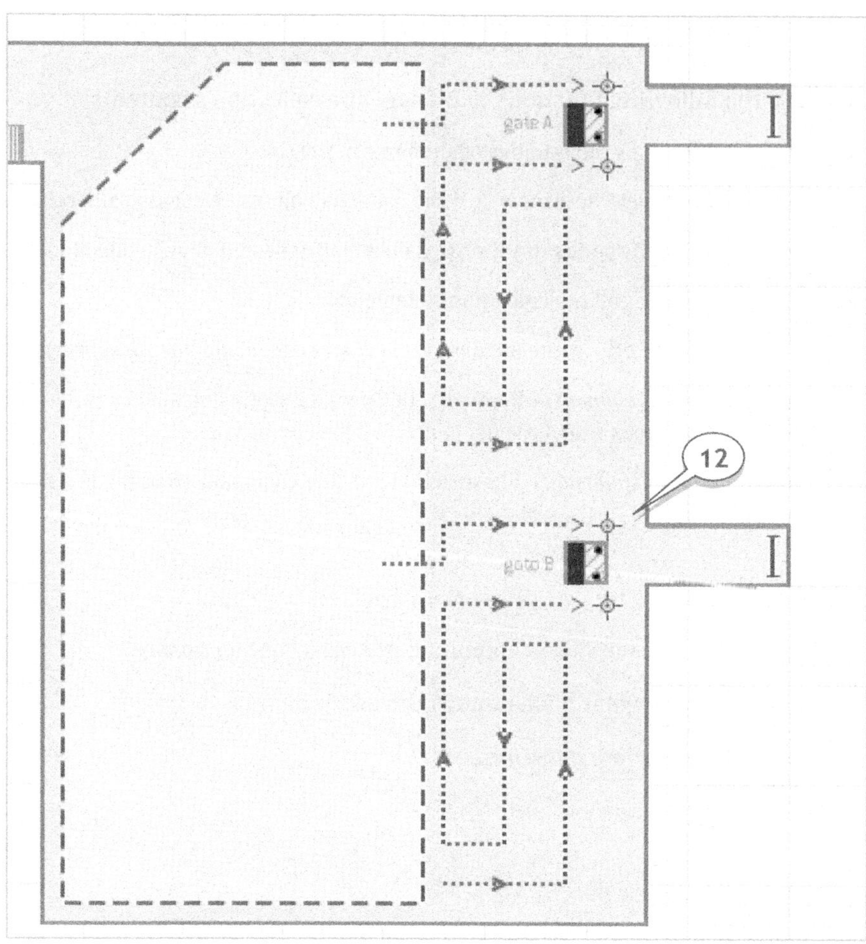

13. Add two more **PedService** blocks, *businessBoarding2* and *economyBoarding2*, that go out of **PedSelectOutput** and go into **PedGoTo**. Let **PedSelectOutput** directs passengers to four different ports.

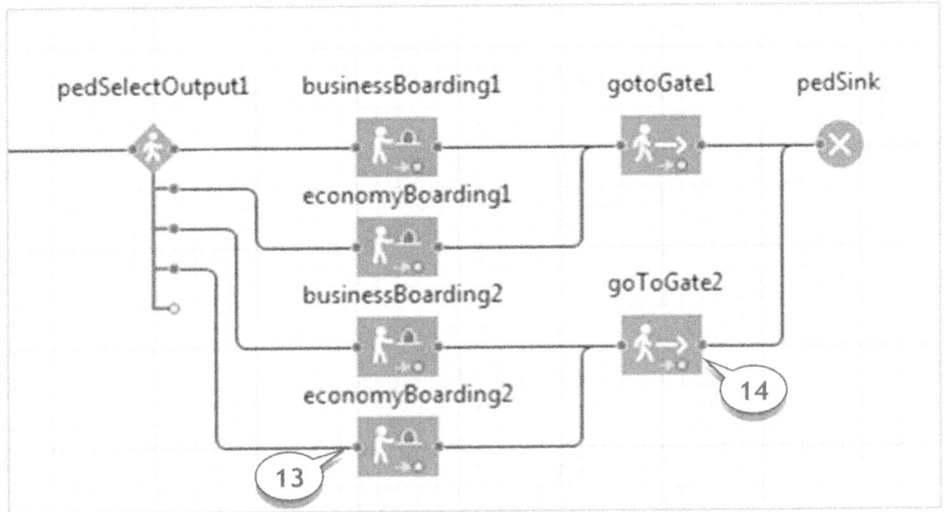

14. Add another **PedGoTo** ↑→ block to model how passengers move to the second gate. Select *gateLine2* as the block's **Target line**.

15. For *businessBoarding2*, set **Services**: *business2*. For *economyBoarding2*, set **Services**: *economy2*. For both, set **Service time**: *uniform(2, 5)* seconds.

16. With our flights set up, we can change the *pedSelectOutput1* conditions that define which gate our passengers select.

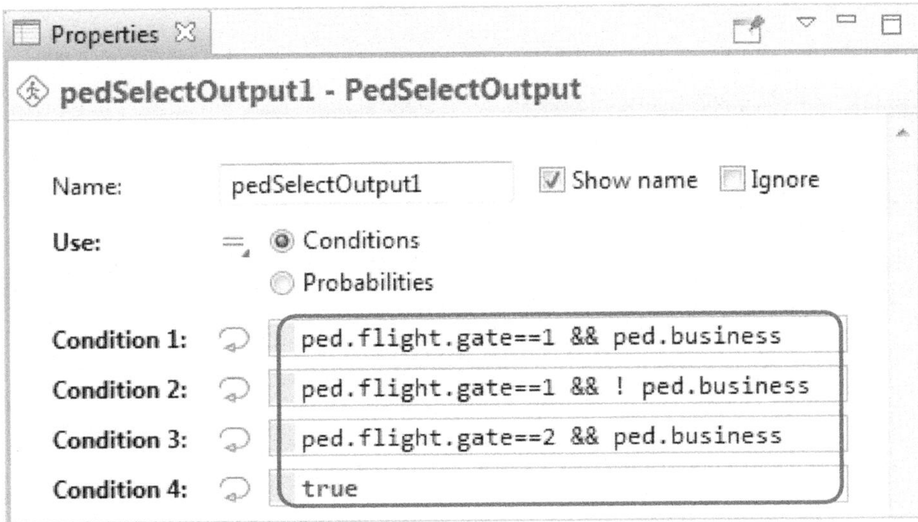

Dynamic events

We'll now use dynamic events that schedule a model's user-defined actions to schedule departure and boarding actions. A model can have several instances of the same dynamic event scheduled concurrently, and they can be initialized by data that are stored in the event's parameters.

You should use dynamic events in your model:

- When you expect several events, performing similar actions, to be scheduled at the same time.

- When your dynamic event's action depends on specific information.

> ◆ **NOTE: Since AnyLogic represents a dynamic event as a Java class, your dynamic event's name should start with an uppercase letter.**

17. Add two **Dynamic Event** ⚡ elements from the **Agent** ✪ palette on to the *Main* diagram.

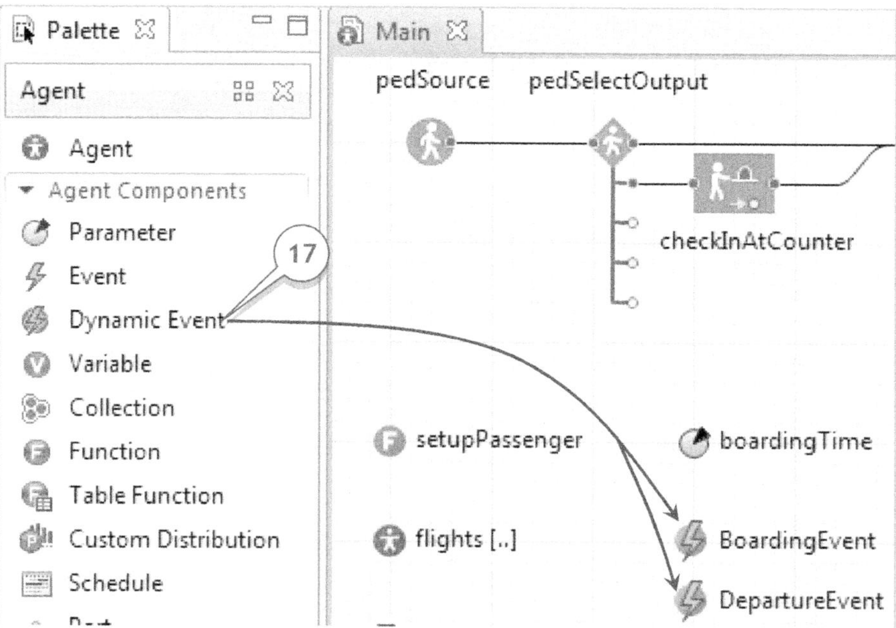

18. The dynamic event *DepartureEvent* schedules a plane's departure by removing the flight from the agent population that contains upcoming flights. Use the figure below to help you set up the event.

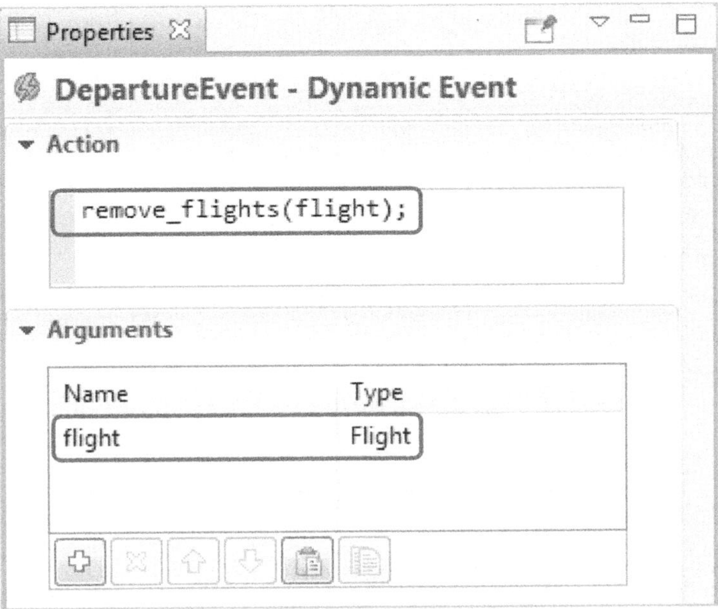

19. A second dynamic event, *BoardingEvent*, schedules the plane's boarding and then creates an instance of the dynamic event *DepartureEvent* that schedules the flight to depart in 40 minutes.

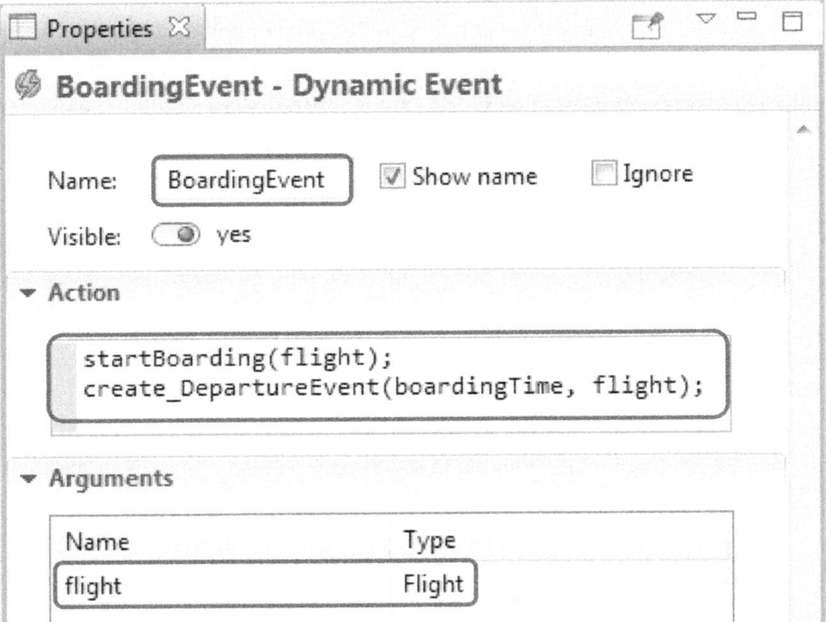

You create an instance of a dynamic event by calling the method *create_ <DynamicEventName>*. In our case, we're using the *create_DepartureEvent()* function to create an instance of a dynamic event that we've named *DepartureEvent*.

20. Change the *pedWait* block's **Delay ends** parameter from **On delay time expiry** to **On free() function call** to ensure passengers who need to wait to board their plane will wait for the announcement in the waiting area.

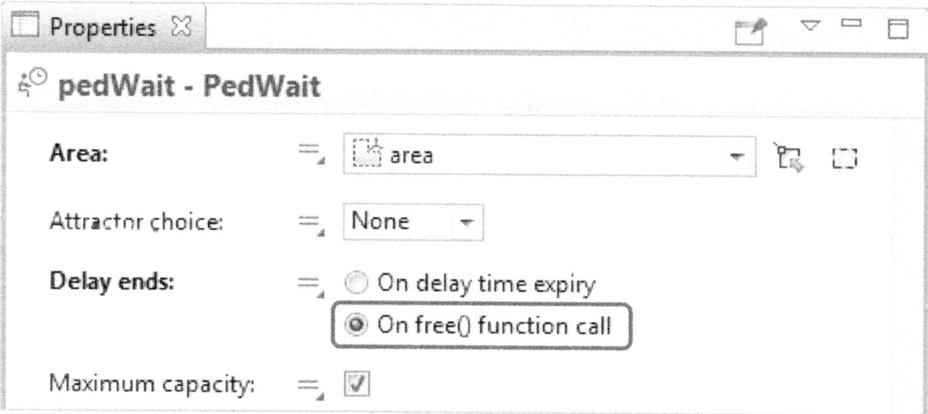

21. Define a **Function** ⓕ *startBoarding* to model the start of the plane's boarding process. This function iterates through the passengers who are waiting to board for the given flight and allows them to board by ending their delay in the block *pedWait* with the call of the block's function *free()*.

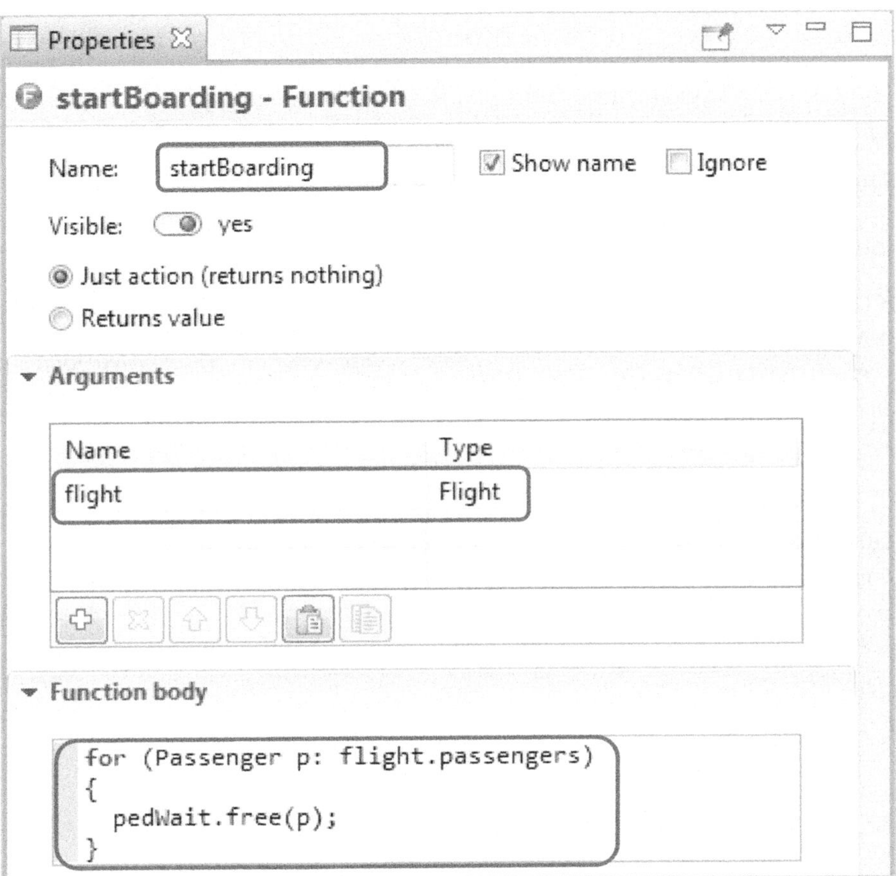

In this example, we're using a **For Loop** to go through the *passengers* collection defined inside the *flight*. The passengers who are boarding the plane have to leave the waiting area.

Iterating through a population of agents using "for" loop

The "for" loop's two forms are the simplest way to have AnyLogic iterate through a population's agents:

Syntax	Example

Index-based:
 	
for(<initialization>; <continue condition>; <increment>) {
  <statements executed for each element>
}
	for(int i=0; i<group.size(); i++) {
	  Object obj = group.get(i);
	  if(obj instanceof ShapeOval) {
	    ShapeOval ov = (ShapeOval)obj;
	    ov.setFillColor(red);
	  }
	}

Collection iterator:
for(<element type> <name> : <collection>) {
  <statements executed for each element>
}
	for(Product p : products) {
	  if(p.getEstimatedROI() < minROI)
	    p.kill();
	}

22. Define a *planBoardings* function to schedule boarding for all registered flights. The function iterates through the agent population *flights* in the For Loop. It allows flights that are set to take off before their boarding time has elapsed to immediately start boarding. Flights that do not meet this condition will start their boarding process 40 minutes before their departure time as we defined in the *boardingTime* parameter.

```
▼ Function body

    for (Flight f : flights)  {
      double timeBeforeBoarding =
        dateToTime(f.departureTime) - boardingTime;
      if ( timeBeforeBoarding >= 0 )
        create_BoardingEvent(timeBeforeBoarding, f);
      else {
        create_DepartureEvent(dateToTime(f.departureTime), f);
        startBoarding(f);
      }
    }
```

The *if* operator checks the specified condition. If the selected flight's boarding is taking place, we schedule the departure, and allow boarding by calling the *startBoarding* function (passing the reference to this flight as the function argument value). Otherwise, we schedule *BoardingEvent*.

23. In *Main*'s **Agent actions** area, in the **On startup** box, add the call of the *planBoardings()* function.

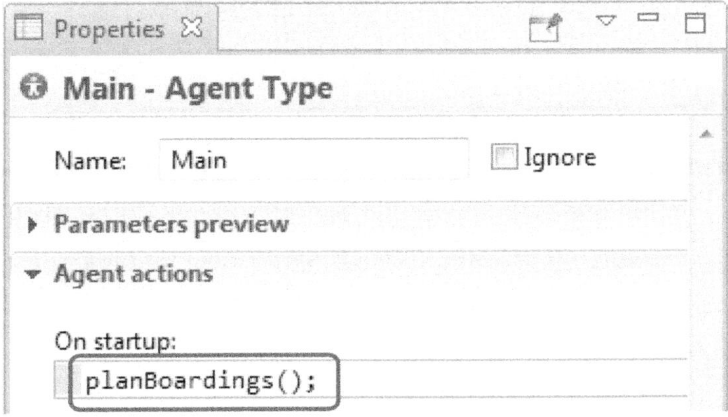

We need to tie the simulation's starting point to a specific date within the Excel file that defines the departure time.

24. In the **Projects**, select *Simulation*. In the **Model time** section of the experiment properties, set the database's flight date as the start date. Set the **Start date** to *21/12/2014, 12:00:00*. On the **Stop** list, click **Stop at specified date** and then set the **Stop date** to *21/12/2014, 22:00:00*.

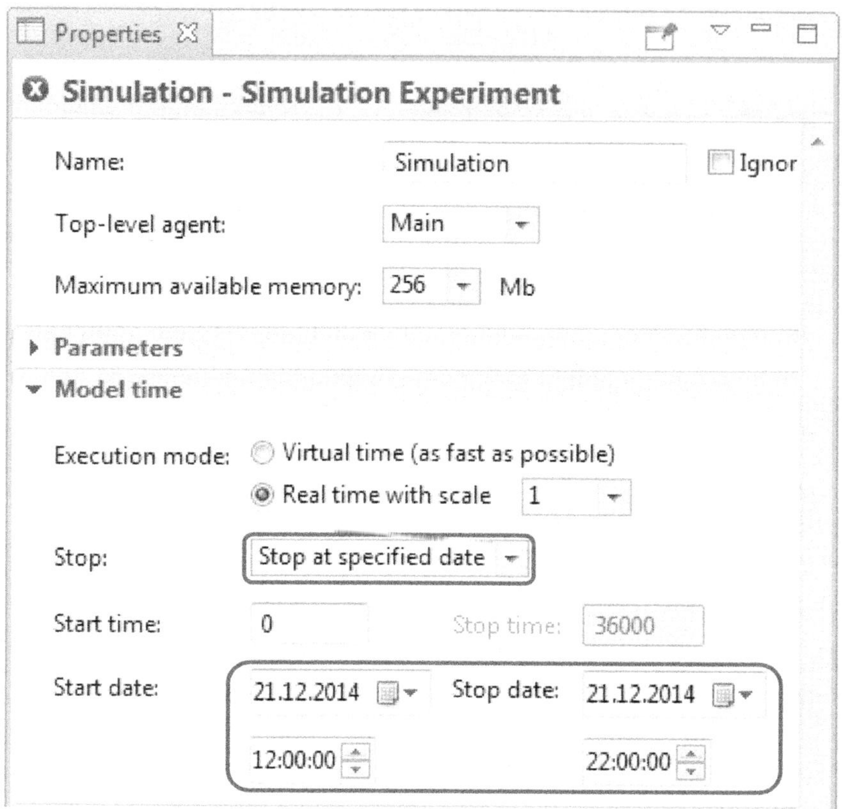

25. Use the **Pictures** palette to add a **Clock** element that will display the model date.

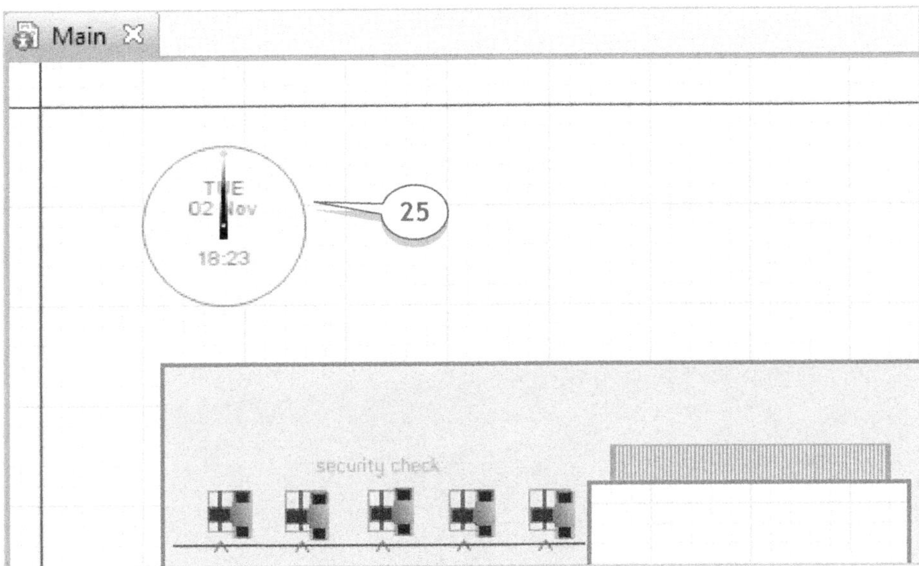

26. Run the model. You'll see passengers wait for the boarding announcement in the waiting area and then go to their gate.

You may find this model more complex than those we covered earlier, especially since we've shown how to use AnyLogic to define custom logic that draws on events, functions, and action charts.

To take the next step in developing your own simulation projects, we encourage you to use AnyLogic's Help feature as well as the sample models that each demonstrate a specific modeling technique. As you evaluate AnyLogic, you can use the **Get Support** button to contact our support team. They're happy to answer your questions about AnyLogic and help you address any problems that might occur as you develop your models.

References

Borshchev, A. (2013). *The Big Book of Simulation Modeling. Multimethod modeling with AnyLogic 6.* AnyLogic North America.

Compartmental models in epidemiology. (n.d.). Retrieved June 1, 2014 from the Wiki: http://en.wikipedia.org/wiki/Compartmental_models_in_epidemiology

Conway's Game of Life. (n.d.). Retrieved May 15, 2014 from the Wiki: http://en.wikipedia.org/wiki/Conway's_Game_of_Life

Geer Mountain Software Corporation (2002) *Stat::Fit* (Version 2) [Software]. Geer Mountain Software Corporation. Available from: http://www.geerms.com

Oracle. (2011). *Java™ Platform, Standard Edition 6. API Specification.* [Online]. Available from: http://docs.oracle.com/javase/6/docs/api/ [Accessed 23rd May 2013]

Random number generator. (n.d.). Retrieved June 29, 2014 from the Wiki: http://en.wikipedia.org/wiki/Random_number_generator

Sterman,J. (2000). *Business dynamics : Systems thinking and modeling for a complex world.* New York: McGraw.

Sun Microsystems, Inc. (1999). *Code Conventions for the Java TM Programming Language.* [Online]. Available from: http://www.oracle.com/technetwork/java/javase/documentation/codeconvtoc-136057.html [Accessed 23rd May 2014]

System Dynamics Society, Inc. (2014). System Dynamics Society [Online]. Available from: www.systemdynamics.org [Accessed 23rd May 2014]

The AnyLogic Company. (2014). *AnyLogic Help.* [Online]. Available from: http://www.anylogic.com/anylogic/help/

The Game of Life. (n.d.). Retrieved June 15, 2014 from the Wiki: http://en.wikipedia.org/wiki/The_Game_of_Life

UML state machine. (n.d.). Retrieved June 15, 2014 from the Wiki: http://en.wikipedia.org/wiki/UML_state_machine

Index

3D animation, 159

  navigation, 161
3D window, 159

Agent, 22

Agent-based modeling, 21

Arrival triggered transition, 51

Attractor, 179

Build, 39

Camera, 159

Chart

  time axis format, 64
  time window, 61
Charts, 57

Circular wall, 195

Clock, 248

Code completion assistant, 47

Condition triggered transition, 51

Controls, 87

Ctrl+space, 47

Database, 28, 233

Entity, 135

Environment, 37

Evacuation analysis, 191

exponential(), 83

Function, 227

Get Support, 249

Graphical editor, 27

Guard, 70

Internal transition, 68

Locking shapes, 139

Message triggered transition, 51

Model execution modes, 53

Model time, 52

Model time units, 52

Model window, 40

  status bar, 41
Moving resource, 151

New Model wizard, 25

normal(), 84

Palette view, 27

Path, 140

Pause, 42

Pedestrian Library, 193

Pedestrian service

  linear, 210
  point, 210
Pedestrian traffic simulation, 191

Pedestrian Type, 203

PedGoTo, 198

PedSelectOutput, 199

PedService, 199

PedSink, 199, 201

PedSource, 198, 199

PedWait, 199

Plot, 58

Portable resource, 151

Presentation window, 40

   status bar, 41

Problems view, 74

Projects view, 27, 28

Properties view, 27, 38

Queue Line, 211

RackPick, 149

RackStore, 146

Rate, 50

Rate triggered transition, 50

Real time mode, 53

Rectangular Node, 140

Rectangular Wall, 220

Reset perspective, 27

Resource

   moving, 151
   portable, 151
   static, 151

Run, 39

Run from the current state, 42

Running a model, 150

Running the model, 40

Serpentine queue, 215

Service, 211

   linear, 210

   point, 210
Service with lines, 208

Simulation speed, 53

Sink, 149

Slider, 88

State, 43

Statechart, 43

Statechart entry point, 44

Static resource, 151

Status bar

   model window, 41

Step, 42

Support, 249

Table function, 129

Target line, 197

Terminate execution, 42

Time axis format, 64

Time units, 52

Time window, 61

Timeout triggered transition, 50

Transition

   condition triggered, 51
   guard, 70
   internal, 68
   rate triggered, 50
   timeout triggered, 50

triangular(), 83

uniform(), 83

uniform_discr(), 84

Virtual time mode, 53

Wall, 196

Welcome page, 24

Z-height, 163

Zigzag queue, 215

Made in United States
North Haven, CT
31 December 2021

13926252R00141